Presidential Leadership
in Political Time

Presidential Leadership in Political Time

REPRISE AND REAPPRAISAL

Second Edition, Revised and Expanded

Stephen Skowronek

 University Press of Kansas

Published by the University Press of Kansas (Lawrence, Kansas 66045),
which was organized by the Kansas Board of Regents and is operated
and funded by Emporia State University, Fort Hays State University,
Kansas State University, Pittsburg State University, the University of
Kansas, and Wichita State University

Library of Congress Cataloging-in-Publication Data

Skowronek, Stephen.
Presidential leadership in political time : reprise and reappraisal /
Stephen Skowronek. — 2nd ed., rev. and expanded.
    p. cm.
Includes bibliographical references and index.
ISBN 978-0-7006-1783-8 (cloth : alk. paper)
ISBN 978-0-7006-1762-3 (pbk. : alk. paper)
1. Presidents—United States. 2. Presidents—United States—History.
3. Political leadership—United States. 4. Political leadership—United
States—History. 5. Bush, George W. (George Walker), 1946–
6. United States—Politics and government—2001–2009. I. Title.
JK516.S56 2011
352.23'60973—dc22

                                                    2010044912

British Library Cataloguing-in-Publication Data is available.

Printed in the United States of America

10 9 8 7 6 5 4

The paper used in this publication is acid-free and contains 30 percent
postconsumer waste. It meets the minimum requirements of the
American National Standard for Permanence of Paper for Printed
Library Materials z39.48-1992.

To Michael and Sam

Contents

Preface to the Second Edition

The themes that thread their way through the essays in this collection first appeared in book form nearly twenty years ago.[1] The Clinton presidency was taking shape just at the time I was finishing that work, and I recall feeling a bit uneasy at the thought that readers might be more interested in the final comment I was dashing off about this new man on the scene than in anything I had said in the prior four hundred pages about the politics of leadership from John Adams to George H. W. Bush. It was easy enough for me to describe Bill Clinton's leadership in the terms set out in the book, for in his rise to power, he fit to a T one of the historical types I had distinguished. Taking the Democrats to their first national victory since the Reagan Revolution, submerging his party's liberalism in the promise of a "third way," winning the presidency in a three-way race with about 40 percent of the popular vote, Clinton epitomized what I had called "preemptive" leadership. But therein lay the source of my unease. I had observed in the book that preemptive leaders were prone to spark constitutional showdowns, even impeachment proceedings, and I was loath to close out my long labors with outlandish predictions. Who would have thought that a mechanical extrapolation of the most extreme implications of my thesis would have been right on the money and that scholarly prudence would prove the lesser part of wisdom?

Readers of that earlier book would not have had any difficulty identifying Clinton's successor either. Bringing the party of Ronald Reagan back to power, George W. Bush promised to complete the work the conservative insurgency had started, to adapt its agenda to a new day, and to demonstrate the enduring vitality of its governing commitments. He exemplified what I had called the president as "orthodox innovator." Like everyone else, however, I thought that the events of 11 September 2001 would change everything, presidential leadership first and foremost. This was exactly the kind of contingency that scholars have in mind when they caution against projecting historical patterns lockstep into the future. One of the things I had observed about orthodox inno-vators was that they were prone to engage in little wars of dubious provocation, muscle-flexing adventures driven more by ideology and political management than by necessity. This president, in contrast, was being called on to respond to a concerted and destructive attack on the homeland; there was nothing in his avowed determination to eradicate al Qaeda and its sponsors in Afghanistan to support the designation my analysis would have assigned him. Then came the turn to Iraq, with its shaky presuppositions, headstrong assertions, and political bluster, and things did not seem quite so different after all.

Clinton and Bush turned out to be such eerily vivid exemplars of leadership types and political patterns I had identified in *The Politics Presidents Make* that I thought it might be worth putting together a short collection of essays that would revisit the themes presented in that book and draw them forward. This is the second edition of these essays, which now include an early assessment of Barack Obama as well. The essay format has several advantages: It makes the political time thesis more readily accessible; it offers a flexible structure for updating the thesis; and it preserves the integrity of the original presentation by pre-venting the earlier book from becoming overrun by a succession of postscripts and addendums. Each of the essays in this collection is a suf-ficiently self-contained elaboration of the thesis to be read indepen-dently or in any combination with the others. Anyone who cares to read them all in the order presented should get a pretty good idea of the de-velopment and analytic reach of the argument.

As I indicate in the opening of each chapter, these essays were all prepared for other occasions and written at different junctures in con-temporary American political history. All have been edited for this vol-ume to bring them into better alignment with one another, and some have been revised quite thoroughly. I have, however, resisted the temp-tation to integrate them completely, for that would have meant elimi-nating the sense of the moment in which each essay was written, and it would have suggested a more definitive reformulation of the thesis than

I intend. Preserving the spirit of each assessment as it was ventured at the time better conveys my attitude toward the thesis, which is one of open-ended and continual reappraisal in light of late-breaking developments. I think a thesis like this one—which identifies broad historical patterns in presidential leadership and explains the political dynamics at work behind them—is most interesting in pointing up contemporary expressions of difference and potentially significant deviations from the rule. As the essays collected here indicate, I am less inclined to insist that these patterns never change than to figure out how they might.

Presidential leadership in political time is a window on the institution of the presidency and the workings of the American political system as a whole. The approach calls attention to the often-stark variations we observe in leadership performances from one president to the next, but it resists the temptation to reduce these differences to matters of personality and style or to cull from them some ideal formula for successful leadership in contemporary America. Rather than dwelling on what one incumbent seemed to do right or where another fell short, the perspective of political time refers us back to the politics of leadership in earlier periods, to prior sequences of change in which presidents took on similar challenges in leadership and wrestled them to similar political effect. The recurrent patterns revealed in this way indicate the historical range of political possibilities for presidential leadership in the American system. At issue here is not what we might want presidential leadership to be, but what its capacities are and how it has operated in political circumstances variously configured. The perspective captures the typical political problems the American system throws up to its leaders and the likely political effects of their efforts to resolve them.

While I believe that this perspective reaches deep into the politics of leadership and brings to light essential features of American politics overall, new implications and subtle changes in meaning are continually reflected back through unfolding events. By itself, the discovery that the presidencies of Bill Clinton and George W. Bush exhibited patterns in the politics of leadership that have been with us since the beginning of our constitutional history may be little more than a curiosity. If that finding compels attention, it is, in part, because these patterns reflect basic characteristics of the presidency as a position of national political leadership and, in part, because the circumstances in which these characteristics are now displayed could hardly be more different from the conditions at the start. How leadership syndromes that are, historically speaking, typical come to bear on a modern democracy, on a national government whose stewardship responsibilities dwarf those of earlier times, on the comportment of an international superpower—these, I think, are matters for careful and sustained reflection.

The Obama presidency presents these issues in particularly stark form. Coming to office on the promise of "fundamentally transforming the United States of America,"[2] Obama seemed to go out of his way to signal a classic reconstructive moment. The course of his presidency to date thus provides ample material for reflection on what leadership of this sort has entailed in the past, on whether it was really in the cards in this instance, and on whether it is ever likely to recur.

Twenty years ago, I was fully expecting the historical patterns I had observed in the politics of leadership to be overtaken by developments on other fronts. I thought their significance would gradually wash out in the face of contemporary government's investment in responsible management and effective problem solving. I wrote of the "waning of political time,"[3] teased out evidence of waning in the leadership performances of late-twentieth-century presidents, and speculated about what might be gained and lost in that process of dissipation. These expectations were thrown into doubt by the appearance of such vivid exemplars of the old types as Clinton and Bush. But now, as we approach midterm in the Obama presidency, the question of how robust the old patterns are has been posed anew. President Obama seems to have embraced responsible management and enlightened problem solving as a formula for political transformation. It remains to be seen whether that alone will suffice to reconstruct American government and reset political time.

New Haven
September 2010

Acknowledgments

I would like to thank Fred Woodward of the University Press of Kansas for his keen understanding of the nature of this project and his astute advice on how it might be put together. Richard Ellis of Willamette University, Daniel Galvin of Northwestern University, Bruce Miroff of SUNY–Albany, and Karen Orren of UCLA provided critical readings and offered invaluable comments. At Yale, Stephen Engel and Meredith Levine were inexhaustible aides and consultants. The book benefited also from the able production team of Susan Schott, Susan McRory, and Kathy Delfosse. I have dedicated this collection to my sons, Michael and Sam. My wife, Susan, is, as always, the anchor of my life and work.

I am grateful to Congressional Quarterly Press for permission to reprint "Presidential Leadership in Political Time" from Michael Nelson's *The Presidency and the Political System* and to use substantial portions of "The Setting: Continuity and Change in the Politics of Leadership" from Michael Nelson's *Elections 2000* in chapter 3. Other parts of chapter 3 were drawn from "Notes on the Presidency in the Political Order," first published in *Studies in American Political Development*. "Leadership by Definition: First-Term Reflections on George W. Bush's Political Stance" is revised and reprinted from *Perspectives on Politics*. "The Presidency in American Political Development: A Third Look" first appeared as part of a symposium in *Presidential Studies Quarterly*. Full citations to the original versions can be found at the opening of each chapter.

Presidential Leadership
in Political Time

1. The Presidency in American Political Development: A Third Look

This essay presents the political time thesis as a different way of thinking about presidential history and presidential politics. The piece takes its title and its structure from a review essay published in 2002 in which I considered the developmental perspectives implicit in recent presidential scholarship.[1] The literature review element remains in this version, but the essay has been thoroughly recast from its original form and adapted for this volume to serve as an introduction to my own perspective. Whereas the other essays in this collection speak more directly to the leadership of particular presidents, this one is more concerned with issues of analysis. It is, as I say below, a retooling exercise. By calling attention to the political concerns, historical assumptions, and organizing constructs that have shaped presidential studies over the years, it points to important questions that have been skirted by the field and outlines an alternative approach designed to address them.

Around the turn of the twentieth century, advocates of "progressive democracy" began pressing for a new, more vigorous form of leadership at the national level. They argued that the development of American government and politics had confounded the intentions of the government's original designers and that a different conception of constitutional relationships was needed to meet the demands of the future. Surveying nineteenth-century politics, they charged that Congress, which had been designed to operate as the people's branch and which had been endowed with great power for that purpose, had been overrun by special interests and exposed as an "incurably deficient and inferior organ" for the expression of the popular will. At the same time, they pointed out that the presidency, which had originally been designed as a conservative counterweight to the democratic impulsiveness of the legislature, had shown strong instincts to respond to the demands of the day and overcome obstacles set in its path. Progressive history eyed a people gravitating toward the presidency "as the only organ sufficient for the exercise of their sovereignty," and it encouraged those seeking to build a more robust democracy and a more effective national government to strengthen the institution that had proven itself best suited to the people's purposes.[2]

Much of what has been written about the presidency in American political development has been commentary on this reform vision, and even today its hold over our collective aspirations remains strong. One has only to listen to the rhetoric of an American presidential campaign to hear the contemporary resonance of the Progressives' developmental perspective and appreciate the enduring appeal of their governmental vision. No less impressive is the energy that the Progressives put into advancing their view of political development programmatically. For much of the twentieth century, presidential empowerment served as the intellectuals' catchall solution to the problems of governing in modern America. The breakthrough moment came during the New Deal, when the scholarly advisers on Franklin D. Roosevelt's Committee on Administrative Management proposed a presidency-centered reorganization of the entire federal establishment and Congress relented sufficiently to give their vision a foothold in the structure of American government.[3] As late as 1960, with the federal government taking on additional responsibilities and with presidents beginning to face even more intractable problems, Progressive intellectuals were still steadfast in their faith and ready with new ways to promote their thesis. The single most influential analysis of the office, Richard Neustadt's *Presidential Power,* offered incumbents strategic advice, indicating how they might best husband their political resources to deliver on all that the nation demanded of them.[4]

It was not until the Vietnam War and the Watergate investigations that scholars began to take a serious second look at the presidency in the political development of the nation, and what they saw in the aftermath of those events turned the received wisdom on its head. In the midst of widespread disillusionment with the affairs of state, the Progressives' catchall solution was recast as the centerpiece of the nation's problems. Critics bemoaned the costly distortions of constitutional principle that had gone into the formation and practice of "the modern presidency," they questioned the soundness of the democratic theory behind it, and they exposed an office infected by false pretense and overblown expectations. New histories rendered the Progressive vision as naive and the rise of presidency-centered government as misguided; they broke old linkages between presidential power and good government and replaced them with far less flattering associations—warmongering, demagoguery, wanton disregard for the rule of law. In 1973, Arthur Schlesinger, Jr., dean of the Progressive historians, gave voice to his generation's newfound unease by portraying the development of the office as the rise of the "imperial presidency."[5] In 1985, Theodore Lowi delivered summary judgment on the twentieth century's great experiment in reconfiguring American government and politics around the chief executive: "power invested, promise unfulfilled."[6]

These late-century critics pointed to a doubtful and dangerous future, and the practical response from within the government did little to assuage the concerns they raised. To the extent that hopes were pinned on congressional reforms that might rein in the executive, the results seemed only to underscore the difficulty of reversing course; to the extent that the democratic defense of presidential power had fallen flat, justifications with a harder edge were brought to the fore.[7] Not surprisingly, then, this critique of the development of the presidency has shown few signs of exhausting its relevance. Its insights reach through more recent decades of our history to connect an ever-lengthening chain of disappointments and deceptions, blunders and breakdowns. Cultural aspirations die hard, and this ongoing dissonance sharpens the collective sense of betrayal. No doubt the administration of George W. Bush, with its headstrong self-confidence, its unilateral assertions of power, and its wartime bungling, will infuse the analysis offered by the Vietnam generation with new currency.

Why, then, go back for a third look?

The chief reason is that, like blind faith, disillusionment has its limits. The institution of the presidency may no longer warrant our confidence, but its incumbents continue to alter our polity, shortfalls and dysfunctions notwithstanding. The patina of progress may have been stripped away, but the past thirty years have brought political changes as dramatic as any in American history, and all along the way, those changes have highlighted the pivotal position of the presidency in high-stakes contests over basic commitments of ideology and interest. Progressive advocates of presidential power left an indelible mark on the operations of American government, and the critique of the Progressives' handiwork abides, but we have been carried by our own experience to ask different sorts of questions about the presidency in American political development, questions more closely attuned to the political impact of individual performances, to the sequential reactions of successors to predecessors, and to the formative political effects of presidential action over time.

Consider the presidency of Ronald Reagan. His administration provided ample evidence of the problems that critics of the modern presidency had identified in the operations of American government. Indeed, for many observers the challenge to constitutional government presented by the Iran-Contra affair rivaled that of Watergate.[8] In other equally significant ways, however, Reagan's leadership was a surprise. Not only did he confound the gloomy prognostications of the 1970s, but he also repudiated the priorities of fifty years of liberal government, reset the national agenda, and became the touchstone of legitimacy for a new politics that would revolve around conservative priorities through ensuing decades.[9] Politically speaking, America is still working its way through the Reagan era. George W. Bush came to power in 2000 determined to complete and secure the "Reagan Revolution"; he enters his final year in office amid charges that he betrayed it and shattered the political foundations of conservative governance.[10] Each of Reagan's successors has been subject to political expectations that he set; every one has tested and manipulated standards that he established.

Neither the early proponents of presidential power nor their latter-day critics offered a candid assessment of how this institution works to foment political change and reframe political possibilities. Nor is it clear whether these workings are any different today than they were before the institution took on its modern accouterments. A third look at the presidency in American political development takes aim at an office that has been persistent in driving political change since the beginning of our constitutional history. It attends to the peculiar ways in which the presidency operates politically, to the different sorts of political contests it sets up over time, and to their typical political effects. It offers thereby some insight into the sequence of political change unfolding in our time.

Looking at the presidency in this way, it quickly becomes apparent that the two histories already on the table are not as different from one another as we might have first thought. Reacting against the Progressives' normative and programmatic offensive on behalf of presidency-centered government, the critics did not offer an alternative history of the office so much as an alternative evaluation of the same history. In one view, the rise of the presidency was good for democracy; in the other, it was damaging; in one, presidential empowerment was the solution; in the other, it was the problem; in one, the prospects were bright; in the other, they were grim. Whatever judgment we ultimately bring to bear on our century-long investment in presidential power, it must be said that reckoning with the political development of the American presidency is not the same thing as reckoning with the presidency in the development of American politics. Commentaries aimed at capturing the essential character of the institution as an instrument of modern government are actually quite limited when it comes to characterizing the institution as an engine of political change. These commentaries tend to downplay exactly what needs to be brought into focus—the variations from one incumbent to the next in leadership claims ventured and the political impact of following through.

For the most part, accounting for the different leadership performances we encounter in history and assessing their transformative political effects remains the province of presidential biographers, and by their nature, the biographers' explanations are idiosyncratic, locked in the interplay of a particular personality with a particular set of circumstances. In this way, Reagan's political magnetism and George W. Bush's fearsome obstinacy each opens onto a unique story about the man and his times. The outstanding question for our third look is whether these stories fit larger patterns in the politics of leadership, whether it is possible to observe across the broad history of leadership efforts something more systemic about the political impact of presidential action *in* time and *over* time. Certainly it is not hard to conjure material for thinking about larger patterns: Reagan's magnetic political performance was widely heralded at the time as unexampled since the days of FDR, and no one has missed the parallel between George W. Bush's plunge into Iraq and Lyndon B. Johnson's plunge into Vietnam. But these are just impressions. Some serious conceptual retooling is needed if we are to entertain the suggestion that parallels between Reagan and Roosevelt or Bush and Johnson are indicative of overarching dynamics characteristic of the operations of the presidency in the American political system as a whole. To that end, this essay revisits three closely interlocked issues of presidential politics and American political history: the issue of political agency, the issue of periodization, and the issue of constitutionalism.

POLITICAL AGENCY: RETHINKING THE EFFECTIVENESS OF PRESIDENTIAL ACTION

Assessments of the problem of political agency, or effective political action, in the American presidency have changed a lot over the years, but they have not strayed far from a few basic concerns that the Progressives' vision put at issue: Is the power of the office adequate to the demands placed upon it? How much can we expect a president to get done? How important are the personal qualities of the incumbent to making the system work? For the Progressives themselves, answers to each of these questions could be found in the presidency of Franklin Roosevelt.[11] They saw in Roosevelt's political skill and reform vigor a model for political leadership in modern America, and they distilled from his example the personal attributes likely to prove most valuable to incumbents in negotiating the governing challenges of the future.[12] At the same time, the Progressives knew that the early achievements of the New Deal were the product of some very unusual circumstances, and they worried that the office of the presidency might not otherwise be up to the new tasks at hand. As Roosevelt's Committee on Administrative Management put it in the middle of the New Deal, "The president needs help."[13]

In the decades immediately following the New Deal, it was thought that bolstering the office of the presidency with a more extensive institutional apparatus might make it more continuously effective as a position of national political leadership and neutralize the risks posed by natural variation in the talents and skills of incumbents. Innovations like the National Security Council and the Council of Economic Advisers were designed by reformers who were skeptical of Harry S. Truman's personal capabilities and determined to surround him with the best advice available, whether he liked it or not.[14] By midcentury, however, confidence in institutional solutions to the agency problem had begun to fade. In *Presidential Power,* the last of the great Progressive tracts, Richard Neustadt argued that constitutional impediments to a presidency-centered government remained imposing, that they were unlikely to be overcome by additional reorganization, and that the only thing incumbents could really rely on in meeting their enhanced responsibilities and overcoming the great obstacles in their path was their own political skill. Prescribing "self-help" for presidents, Neustadt pointed to the personal attributes of the incumbent as the factor most critical to making the system work.

Two phases may be discerned in post-Progressive assessments of presidential agency as well. As the mood grew more critical and anxious in the 1970s and 1980s, the Progressives' sense of possibility gave way to perceptions of an even more profound incongruity between power and responsibility, and faith in the individual talents of leaders gave way to fear of their individual psychoses.[15] Duties had been piled on the presidency and expectations had been heightened, but since the basic constitutional structure had not changed, modern American government appeared to have placed incumbents in difficult straits. System incentives virtually compelled them to try to aggrandize power for themselves at others' expense or, worse, to try to deceive those who stood in their way.[16] The view in more recent years, though no more rosy, has been somewhat different. As scholars began to take stock of the success of presidents in acting unilaterally along a broad front, impressions of the presidency as an overburdened and beleaguered office were reconsidered. In the latest of the post-Progressive assessments, the president's strategic advantages as a unitary actor have been factored in and the structural implications of the system have been recalibrated accordingly. The president now appears, for better or worse, to be an imposing figure quick to seize the initiative and difficult for others to check.[17]

There is no gainsaying the fact that this running commentary on the problems and prospects of presidential agency has yielded important and timely insights. And yet, if we reflect back on the rapid succession of revisions and follow their many twists and turns, we may become aware as well of the inbred nature of this conversation and of the limits of the concerns that animated the discussion in the first place. In retrospect, it is striking that each of these assessments of the efficacy of the presidency rested on a slightly different characterization of the political system in which presidential power is exercised. Thus, it is hard to tell whether we have over the years generated an understanding of presidential efficacy that is more refined and more generally applicable, or merely catalogued different prospects as they have been brought into view by historical changes in the political system itself.

This, in turn, points to another limitation, one that speaks to the basic conception of political agency employed in these assessments. By first positing a system and then trying to generalize about the efficacy of presidential action within it, scholars have in effect sidelined serious consideration of whether the exercise of presidential power has systemic political effects of its own. The questions that have been asked—about whether presidents are at an advantage or disadvantage vis-à-vis other actors with whom they must engage, or about whether personal or structural factors are more important in determining how much incumbents get done—are geared to set parameters; they test presidential capacities in a political system that is given, not the president's capacities to change the system or the implications of one president's actions for the prospects of the next.

In this respect, the seminal case of Franklin Roosevelt has proven less exemplary than exceptional. Everyone knows that Roosevelt's leadership had a profound effect on the political assumptions and aspirations of his successors, but few scrutinize the efforts of those successors in the same manner with an eye to determining the systemic political effects of *their* leadership. No doubt George W. Bush's leadership will have an effect on the political assumptions and aspirations of his successor that will be very different from Roosevelt's, but that does not mean it will be negligible. On the contrary, it is hard to think of any more significant factor bearing on the next presidency than the problem of coming to terms with what Bush has done. So long as inquiry into the impact of presidential action is not brought to bear on change in the political situation itself, treatments of the agency question must remain attenuated and incomplete.

Power or Authority. A more complete view of presidential agency awaits a change in the terms of the discussion, and the place to begin is with the preoccupations that the Progressives brought to the question at the dawn of the modern age. The Progressives wanted a more powerful presidency, which is to say they assumed that the president was not powerful enough. By reducing efficacy to a problem of power and directing scholars to try to figure out just how much power modern presidents really have, they muddied the waters considerably. A less loaded approach to presidential agency would strip away the Progressives' assumptions and preoccupations and consider the issue in a more rudimentary form.

The immediate effect of a stripped-down view of presidential agency is to shift attention from the question of institutional power to the question of political authority. The power question was rooted in the Progressives' concern with the capacity of incumbents to get things done and in their interest in figuring out the conditions under which incumbents might do more. The authority question takes its point of departure from the historical observation that virtually all incumbents do quite a lot. The Constitution gives the president considerable power and, one way or another, the exercise of that power changes things. Authority speaks to the political warrants for change that presidents bring to the exercise of this power, to the leadership claims incumbents can make on their own behalf for intruding upon the status quo and rearranging national politics. These warrants relate the politics of the recent past to a political project for the moment at hand. They indicate to allies and opponents alike what is at stake in the incumbent's efforts to follow through, and thus they set the terms in which presidential action will be assessed. The priority of authority lies in determining how the exercise of presidential power will be perceived and interpreted politically.

A high-stakes, high-impact intervention in national politics is all but mandated by the power and independence of the president's constitutional position. All presidents are charged to form and operate administrations of their own. In swearing to "execute the office of President of the United States," incumbents take personal responsibility for politically sweeping and inherently disruptive actions. By simply filling the top administrative positions and assuming control over the executive branch in their own right, presidents alter political prospects and determine winners and losers. With every succeeding choice of personnel and policy, they intrude more deeply into a polity rife with contending ambitions and alternative plans for the uses of power. As the only officers who represent the polity as a whole—as officers who hold powers independently and are readily held to account for the state of national affairs—presidents cannot help but be politically catalytic. National debate is continually reorganized around the implications of the courses of action they choose, and the contest for future advantage is correspondingly transformed. For presidents themselves, the political struggle is, first and foremost, to control the terms of this debate and vindicate the premises of their actions.

Whether we look back at the full sweep of presidential history or more narrowly at the struggles of incumbents in our day, the lesson is the same: The institutional power of American presidents almost always exceeds their political authority; it is easier for presidents to do things than it is for them to sustain warrants for the actions they take and the changes they instigate. Presidential agency—the efficacy of political action in the presidential office—is primarily a legitimation problem. Incumbents are engaged in a contest to control the meaning of actions that are inherently disruptive of the status quo ante. The president who successfully solves this problem will wield a form of authority that is difficult to resist; and those who follow in the office will be constrained in their own efforts by the new terms of legitimate national government secured by their predecessor. Presidents who fail to solve this problem will find their pretensions besieged; their actions will confer significant advantages on their competitors and authorize the pursuit of political alternatives. Either way, the struggle of American presidents to assert authority for their course and sustain authority for their actions will drive American politics to new ground.

Rudiments of the Problem. If we can generalize about the legitimation problem, we will have gone a long way toward reformulating the study of presidential agency and, with it, our understanding of the presidency in the development of American politics. Does the problem have discernible determinants, characteristic historical configurations, and corresponding consequences for the political system as a whole? Returning to our stripped-down view with these considerations in mind, it will be observed that the president not only swears to "execute the office" but also to "preserve, protect, and defend the Constitution." This makes the presidency at once a disruptive, order-shattering institution and a conservative, order-affirming one. If the legitimation problem is to be solved, the incumbent must somehow be able to reconcile the inherently disruptive effects of presidential actions with some larger, order-affirming purpose, and the best way to do that is to create a new order whose altered condition is identified with certain fundamentals emblematic of the body politic. In effect, each incumbent bids to exercise the powers of the presidency by manipulating warrants available in the moment at hand to disrupt, affirm, and reconstruct the political order. Legitimation is a difficult problem for presidents because the order-shattering, order-affirming, and order-creating components of their leadership position seldom pull in tandem and often work at cross-purposes. A clue to the contingent political conditions that facilitate a successful resolution of the problem may be found in a rhetorical trope commonly employed by our most effective political leaders:

Abraham Lincoln: "Our republican robe is soiled and trailed in the dust. Let us repurify it and wash it white in the spirit, if not the blood, of the Revolution. . . . If we do this, we shall not only have saved the Union; but we shall have so saved it, as to make it, and keep it, forever worthy of the saving."[18]

Franklin Roosevelt: "[The] rulers of the exchange of mankind's good have failed through their own stubbornness and their own incompetence. . . . The money changers have fled from their high seats in the temple of our civilization. We may now restore that temple to the ancient truths."[19]

Ronald Reagan: "Isn't our choice really not one of left or right, but of up or down? Down through the welfare state to statism, to more and more government largesse accompanied always by more government authority, less individual liberty, and ultimately totalitarianism. . . . The alternative is the dream conceived by our Founding Fathers, up to the ultimate in individual freedom consistent with an orderly society.[20]

As this rhetoric indicates, the presidents who have been most effective in asserting authority and resetting the terms and conditions of legitimate national government have shared similar circumstances. They all came to power in a position to repudiate forthrightly basic commitments of ideology and interest that they had inherited from their immediate predecessors, and they all justified their disruptions of the status quo ante as essential to retrieving core American values that had allegedly been lost or squandered in the indulgences of the received order. When received political priorities are most fully discredited and the president stands foursquare against them, the power and authority of the office are most fully and effectively aligned. In these circumstances, order shattering *becomes* order affirming, and the exercise of presidential power can effect an extensive reconstruction of the terms and conditions of legitimate national government.

By the same token, the weaker the authority to repudiate inherited commitments, the more difficult it will be for a president to resolve the legitimation problem. To the extent that presidents are committed by the circumstances of their rise to power to carry established political commitments forward, or are otherwise constrained by the perceived legitimacy of the received order of things, political disruption of the status quo ante will be harder to justify and the prospects for regenerating political order through the exercise of presidential power will become more remote. Without the authority to repudiate, presidents lose their advantage in matching meaning to effects, or to put it another way, competitors in the contest for meaning have an easier time second-guessing presidential action and defining it in terms all their own.

Consider in this regard the plight of our second president, John Adams. Adams's political legitimacy upon taking office was so closely tied to his affiliation with his predecessor that he felt constrained to forgo forming an administration of his own and simply kept George Washington's cabinet in place. Presidential power in this instance was held hostage to the promise of continuity, and as the state of national affairs turned more critical, resistance to Adams's leadership stiffened from within the executive branch itself. Moreover, when Adams finally did assert control in his own right and set his own course, his leadership was repudiated by key allies within his own ranks, and an insurgent opposition was able to take advantage of the political disarray with the promise of a thorough housecleaning. This president was not powerless to act, nor was his exercise of power without transformative political effect, but the effect of wielding presidential power in these circumstances was to undercut the political ground on which he stood. Adams was unable to forthrightly repudiate the political regime he had inherited, or, in the end, to forthrightly affirm it. His actions thus called into question the political foundations of his presidency and passed to others control over the meaning of those actions. Success and failure begin to appear here as variations on a logic of political agency, a logic that opens to historical scrutiny the presidency's unrelenting rearrangement of political expectations, political assumptions, and political possibilities. The core issue is the authority of the president to sustain the politically disruptive effects of exercising the independent powers of the office. The structural bias of the office seems to favor the opposition stance, if only because political opposition to received interests and values makes it easier to assert the political independence inherent in the president's constitutional position and to sustain the disruptions that attend it. But not all presidents come to power from the opposition. The paradox of presidential agency in American political history is precisely this: The repudiator tends to create political order, while the stalwart tends to undermine it. In both instances, the disruptive impact of presidential action is registered on the commitments of the political regime at large, as they are called into question and reconstructed over time.

PERIODIZATION:
RETHINKING PRESIDENTIAL HISTORY

The Progressives sought to reorganize American government around a new kind of presidency, and analysts ever since have demarcated the relevant history of the office to take account of their handiwork. According to Theodore Lowi, the changes in American government and politics that accompanied the development of the modern presidency were so sweeping as to amount to the founding of a "second republic."[21] Or as Fred Greenstein put it, "The transformation of the office has been so profound that the modern presidencies have more in common with one another in the opportunities they provide and the demands they place on their incumbents than they have with the entire sweep of traditional presidencies from Washington's to Hoover's."[22] Assumptions like these have structured the field of presidential studies as we know it today. They divide presidential history into a modern period and a traditional period; they set the modern presidents apart from the traditional presidents developmentally as creatures of a different sort; they pull the modern presidents together analytically as a coherent group for comparison. Analysts are directed in this way to evaluate Progressive aspirations and achievements, and the early American presidents are rendered largely irrelevant to an understanding of how the office works today.

If nothing else, the passage of time has begun to put some strains on this periodization scheme. In light of changes in politics, in society, in the economy, and in world affairs, the view forward from the benchmark of 1939—when the Executive Reorganization Act institutionalized presidency-centered government—no longer looks all of a piece, and as the circumstances of modern presidents have grown more variable, a simple modern-traditional dichotomy seems to have less purchase. An open-ended classification of post–New Deal presidents as "modern" now reaches across developments as diverse as the dismantling of racial apartheid and the rise of multiculturalism, the collapse of the Democratic South and the rise of the Republican South, the end of liberal domination and the rise of a conservative insurgency, the displacement of convention nomination for presidential candidates by primary nominations, the displacement of labor-intensive campaigning by capital-intensive campaigning, the decline and resurgence of political parties, a continuing revolution in the means and techniques of public communication, the expansion and politicization of the offices of the White House at the expense of institutions designed for neutral management, the decline of the industrial economy and the rise of a service economy, the rise and collapse of a Keynesian consensus on the workings of the economy, the globalization of corporate power and governance, the beginning and the end of the Cold War, the political and economic integration of Europe, and the proliferation of nonstate actors and terrorist threats.

To try to accommodate historical changes of this variety and magnitude within a single heuristic is to risk creating more confusion than clarity. In fact, in the absence of more attention to questions of periodization, presidency studies are apt to get tangled up in their own insights. Current criticisms of Neustadt's midcentury analysis of presidential power are suggestive in this regard. Scholars today are quick to take Neustadt to task for overstating the importance of informal bargaining skills in determining a president's prospects and for understating the significance of the president's formal advantages in acting unilaterally.[23] And yet, when Neustadt wrote about the politics of leadership, bargaining skills may well have been at a premium, for, as we now know, the middle of the twentieth century was an unusual period of political consensus on the basic contours of economic and foreign policy. It is entirely possible that under midcentury conditions the perceived political costs to presidents of trying to impose their preferences unilaterally outweighed the prospective benefits. It is equally plausible that unilateral action has become a more attractive strategy for presidents as conflict among elites over fundamentals has grown more intense. In this case, Neustadt's analysis would still stand as a period piece revealing a particular relationship between political conditions and leadership strategies, and the debate about which of these perspectives is more correct would lose much of its heat.

There is no one best way to deal with the analytic limitations of the modern-traditional divide. Because the developments to be accounted for since the rise of the modern presidency are so varied and extensive, lots of different schemes, each attending to a different dimension of historical change, might now be appropriate. The most straightforward approach, of course, would be simply to update the modern-presidency construct with a new analytic model that at once delimits the politics of the recent past and captures the implications of newly emergent power relations within the government. Along these lines, scholars have tried in various ways to set the parameters of a "postmodern presidency."[24] Other efforts along these same lines jettison the "modern" label in favor of more substantive contrasts between contemporary politics and politics in the recent past. Samuel Kernell, for example, identified the years after World War II as a period of "institutional pluralism" in which structural conditions favored a bargaining style of leadership like the one described by Neustadt; he then marked changes in power relationships that displaced institutional pluralism with an institutional system characterized more by egocentric entrepreneurship, and he related that new system to the more combative and plebiscitary style of leadership in vogue today.[25] This is important work, but it is work aimed quite self-consciously at extending the original conversation. It draws the history of the modern presidency forward by marking recent structural changes as they affect power relations within the government and the attendant repertoire of resources, motivations, and strategies. It sets up contrasts across a new period divide and comparisons among the leaders of more recent times. The original methodology of grouping together incumbents who are historically proximate to one another and share similar opportunities and constraints remains intact.

Secular Time or Political Time. Other dimensions of change in contemporary presidential politics are hard to capture in this way. At least as conspicuous as the reconfiguration of power relations over the past several decades is the reconfiguration of ideological and programmatic conflict. Drawing out the implications of the former for presidential politics may be a relatively simple matter of updating the standard historical template used to analyze the modern presidency, but drawing out the implications of the latter is not. Presidents of the same period may share similar resources and strategic incentives, but they do not share the same relationship to the ideological and programmatic conflicts of their day. Those relationships tend to change significantly from one incumbent to the next, and largely in reaction to what came immediately before. If we are to capture the significance for presidential politics of change on this dimension, we will need to set aside the historical assumptions behind the modern presidency construct and begin to rethink presidential history altogether.

The logic of presidential agency or effective political action that we began to sketch above points the way. Taking its cues from the legitimation problem and the struggle for authority, it identifies presidents as catalysts of ideological and programmatic change. Moreover, this legitimation problem is integral to the constitutional construction of the presidency; it is not a new problem but one that has been a part and parcel of presidential politics from the start. Thus, if we want to figure out how presidents have been reconfiguring ideological and programmatic conflict in our own time, it makes sense to take a long look back at how they have done so all along. A history of political authority in the American presidency will look very different from the history of political power in the American presidency. It will break down the period divisions that have consigned the presidents of earlier eras to contemporary irrelevance and open the full range of presidential experiences to reexamination.

Scholars have shown that as power structures for presidential action evolve, new strategies and tactics for the exercise of leadership displace the old. But a long look back at the changing structure of political authority reveals development of a different sort. Authority structures for presidential action recur in rough sequences over broad stretches of time, each tending to drive a characteristic kind of political change. If considerations of power track institutional resources and strategies as they evolve in secular time, considerations of authority track warrants for action and contests over its meaning as they recur in what we might call "political time."

Political time is the medium through which presidents encounter received commitments of ideology and interest and claim authority to intervene in their development. Political time has a narrative structure: Presidents bid for authority by reckoning with the work of their predecessors, locating their rise to power within the recent course of political events, and addressing the political expectations that attend their intervention in these affairs. To paraphrase Lincoln, political time is the president's construction of "where we are" as a polity and "whither we are tending," a construction designed to authorize a certain course of political action in the moment at hand.[26] The rhythms and demarcations of political time are thus very much expressions of the presidency itself, of a political imperative inherent in the office prompting each incumbent to attempt to control the terms in which the exercise of its powers will be understood.

Jimmy Carter, heir to an aging liberal establishment, told the American people that there were "no easy answers" to the problems of the day and that the issues plaguing liberalism had to be addressed by getting into the government smart people who could deal with those issues in all their complexity.[27] It is hard to imagine a more delicate or tenuous premise for sustaining the bluntly disruptive political effects of presidential action, but in the circumstances, it is also hard to imagine what a political affiliate of the liberal regime could have said that would have been more compelling. Carter's successor, a radical critic of the liberal regime and leader of the insurgent opposition, promised the American people a "New Beginning" that would proceed on the devastatingly simple premise that "government is not the solution to our problems; government is the problem."[28] Carter's determination in action to fix what he saw as liberalism's problems demoralized its friends and energized its foes; Reagan's repudiative stance drew upon Carter's failure and saddled the very word "liberalism" with a stigma of illegitimacy. Different as they were from one another, these bids for leadership authority find parallel expression in the more distant past, and not just in the warrants for action claimed but also in the political effects registered. The similarities so readily drawn impressionistically between Jimmy Carter and Herbert Hoover, between Ronald Reagan and Franklin Roosevelt, or for that matter between George W. Bush and Lyndon Johnson can be anchored analytically in leadership dynamics that unfold in political time.

Political time is reset periodically by a great repudiator, like Reagan, who carries an insurgent opposition to power. These presidents disavow commitments of ideology and interest integral to the operations of the received order of things, and in directing their own powers against them, they redefine the terms and conditions of legitimate national government. Political time passes from there through various episodes in which leaders affiliated with the new regime offer to affirm, extend, and complete work on the established agenda, and opposition leaders test the vulnerabilities of the established commitments and the potential for repudiating them outright. Analytically speaking, presidents located in different historical periods at parallel moments in these interactive sequences of political time are likely to be more similar to one another in the leadership challenges they face and the political effects they register than they are to the presidents located within their own period of secular political development.

The comparisons set up by periodizing presidential history in this way allow us to generalize about the politics presidents make. Episodes of affiliated leadership will tend to foment factional divisions among those tied to the established order of things, and over successive episodes they will tend to plunge these establishments into crises of legitimacy. This is because the exercise of presidential power invariably alters the political commitments these presidents are pledged to affirm and carry forward, and because the premise of affiliation becomes more attenuated, and the promise of reaffirmation harder to sustain, as the nation drifts away from the circumstances in which those commitments were originally made. Successive episodes of opposition leadership, on the other hand, will tend over time to launch more robust and politically effective assaults on the established regime because the opposition stance frees the incumbent to exploit factional disaffection and agenda fatigue within the establishment, and because these opportunities expand as that establishment ages and frays.

The period breaks of political time thus become marked by extremes of presidential performance and political effect: John Adams and Thomas Jefferson, John Quincy Adams and Andrew Jackson, James Buchanan and Abraham Lincoln, Herbert Hoover and Franklin Roosevelt, Jimmy Carter and Ronald Reagan. This repeated historical coupling of an affiliated leader who appears to exemplify incompetence, if not political paralysis, in the presidency with an opposition leader who appears to exemplify political mastery is in fact indicative of the persistent and dramatic effect presidents have on the development of American politics. Interactive and catalytic, these pairings are less about differences of strategic acumen in deploying the institutional resources of the day than they are about shifting structures of political authority as they alter the legitimation problem and the prospects for its resolution. These changing prospects have driven a process of regime degeneration and regeneration that demarcates American political history into a Jeffersonian era (1800–1828), a Jacksonian era (1828–1860), a Republican era (1860–1932), a New Deal era (1932–1980), and a conservative era (1980–).[29] Presidents, as agents of this process, periodically set up nationwide crises of political legitimacy and resolve them in the production of new and relatively durable political orders. The starkly contrasting performance pairs that punctuate American presidential history are one of the premier expressions of how the American political system works.

CONSTITUTIONALISM:
RETHINKING THE IMPLICATIONS
OF PRESIDENTIAL EMPOWERMENT

The Progressives' vision of a new democracy led by a more powerful presidency was tied to a sharp critique of constitutional determinism. These reformers rejected out of hand the idea that Americans were stuck with the governing arrangements with which they began. In place of a formally fixed and politically limiting structure, they posited an "organic" or "living" Constitution. It was their belief that government— American government in particular—should not be burdened by outmoded constraints but should be continually alive with possibilities, that it should take its cues from public opinion and demonstrate the flexibility to do what the people demand. Woodrow Wilson, who at one point in his career despaired at the formality and rigidity of the constitutional separation of powers, ultimately came around to accepting the Constitution insofar as its interpretation was "sufficiently broad and elastic to allow for the play of life and circumstance."[30] Henry Jones Ford put the Progressives' case more directly when he described presidential power as "the work of the people breaking through the constitutional form."[31]

Post-Progressive scholarship has been far more circumspect about the effects of playing fast and loose with the fundamentals of the government's design, and constitutional determinism has emerged as an overriding theme in contemporary assessments of presidency-centered government. A reconsideration of this sort was already evident in Neustadt's *Presidential Power,* which elaborated upon the structural implications of the Constitution's arrangement of "separate institutions sharing powers."[32] Neustadt charged incumbents with an existential task: They were urged to orchestrate a concert of action in a system of government that institutionalized conflict and resistance, a system that they could not alter in any enduring way and that was all but certain to thwart them.

Recent scholarship has gone much further. Terry Moe has questioned whether presidents have strong incentives to bridge the separated design as Neustadt directed, and he sees little prospect that they will aspire to reinvent themselves as an American version of British prime ministers. He points out that once Americans decided to vest the presidency with more resources and greater responsibility, all the incentives of the constitutional structure encouraged incumbents to press to the limit their own institutional prerogatives while minimizing the intrusions of their constitutional competitors into the executive branch. To the extent that Congress has determined to keep itself in the game, the results for modern American government have been an organizational nightmare.[33]

More pointed still is the charge that the belief in constitutional flexibility and adaptability that the Progressives brought to the construction of the modern presidency has had grave developmental consequences of its own. Along these lines, Jeffrey Tulis has called attention to just how incompatible the Progressives' vision was with the original design of American government. Tulis grants that there was much to recommend the creation of a new, presidency-centered, opinion-based government at the turn of the twentieth century, but he also points out that such a government would have required a very different constitution if it were to work in accordance with the new standards of democracy it professed. As it happened, the structures and practices of this new presidency were simply layered over the original constitutional design, and that, Tulis argues, has left modern American government caught between two largely antithetical standards of accountability, neither of which is likely to be met in practice.[34]

Just how flexible is the U.S. Constitution? Are there limits to its highly touted adaptability? How much change can that foundational framework accommodate before it becomes hopelessly compromised and the various ideals loaded upon it begin to work at cross-purposes? Of all the questions to be raised about the presidency in American political development, these are the most fundamental, and the analytic tools introduced in this essay for thinking about political agency and presidential history bear on them in their own distinctive way.

The Modern Presidency in Political Time. The perspective of political time highlights important constitutional functions that, though they are nowhere stipulated in the document itself, have been performed by the presidency from the very beginning. Particularly striking is the way the institution has operated in American history as a built-in mechanism for periodically "reconstituting" the system politically. The struggles of incumbents to assert political authority and sustain their legitimacy as they exercise the powers of the office all but guarantee that the terms and conditions of legitimate national government will be subject to constant manipulation and that received political commitments will over time be pressed to the limits of their governing capacities. The interesting thing is that when, under the pressure of these manipulations, governing commitments have been rendered hopelessly confused and compromised, these same struggles have exposed them to repudiation and invited a new incumbent to construct them afresh.

The framers of the Constitution were acutely aware of the historic propensity of republican governments to fall prey to the tumult of sectarian pursuits, and when they set out to design their own republic, they were determined to arrest that degenerative tendency. The paradox revealed by the perspective of political time is that their handiwork institutionalized a version of the very process they sought to avoid. Their fragmented system of separated powers and checks and balances did make it difficult to dislodge commitments once they had taken hold, but the political impact of presidential succession was underestimated, as was its bearing on the legitimation problem and the difficulties of controlling the disruptive political effects of the exercise of presidential power.[35] No one suspected that the Constitution would itself channel American politics through extended sequences of sectarian fragmentation and political atrophy or that the officer chiefly responsible for protecting and defending it would become the catalytic agent leading its gradual political breakdown and periodic transformation. Nonetheless, the Constitution has endured for so long because it has not held on to governing commitments in perpetuity but has, rather, made its political purposes periodically vulnerable to wholesale replacement.

Progressives like Henry Jones Ford were clearly drawing on one part of this history when they envisioned presidents as empowered by the people to "break through" received arrangements and establish new forms of government. Certain manifestations of this built-in mechanism of political regeneration, like the outstanding performances of Jackson and Lincoln, are hard to miss, and it is easy to understand why they might have captured the Progressives' imagination. Less obvious perhaps is how this mechanism might be compromised by trying to tap the creative, revitalizing energy displayed historically in a few presidencies through reforms that would make all presidents more powerful. Lincoln and Jackson are poor models for building a "better" presidency because their stunning successes were inextricably linked to the political disintegration and leadership failures that had preceded them. Far from providing a paradigmatic model of what every president should be, theirs were but two among several highly interdependent expressions of what the American presidency is and of how it operates in political time. A constitution in which every president can do what Lincoln did would be very different from the one that gave us Lincoln; indeed, it would hardly be a constitution at all.

No doubt the Progressives thought that presidential empowerment would make the whole system operate differently. They imagined processes of change and adaptation that would be more continuously effective, a political system that would operate more organically in sync with its environment, a form of leadership that would be more responsive, flexible, and efficacious in its management of governmental affairs. They can hardly be faulted for believing that the substantive challenges to be faced by American government in the future would be categorically different from those of the past, that the stakes of enlightened policy making and hands-on management would be higher, or that constitutional arrangements might need to be altered to operate accordingly. But the legitimation problem ingrained in the presidency at the start was not resolved by giving the institution more resources and enhancing its power, and the struggle for political authority that is ongoing within the institution has left it something of a square peg in the round hole of the Progressive design. The presidency continues to drive American politics toward flashpoint crises of legitimacy before wrenching it in a new direction, and that does not comport at all well with the vision of pragmatic adaptation and responsible management that has fueled the presidency's empowerment. The Progressives forced a marriage between presidential leadership and modern American government, and there are good reasons to wonder whether it has brought out the best in either.

There are, in fact, two different ways of looking at this incongruous overlay of elements at work in presidential politics today, and it is hard to say which raises more serious questions about the enduring vitality of our constitutional system. On the one hand, the primordial struggle for authority ingrained in the institution undercuts the capacities of the modern presidency to smooth the management of the affairs of state. To the extent that the Progressives were correct in their assessment of what contemporary American government demands—to the extent that new forms of leadership are anticipated by governing arrangements in which power is more densely concentrated, more thoroughly interconnected, more consequential—a presidency caught up in the rhythms of political time is likely to appear increasingly anachronistic.

On the other hand, the empowerment of the presidency for more continuous hands-on management might have unintended consequences of its own, consequences that threaten to derail the long-term cycles of renewal on which the American system has depended in the past. Consider first that presidents whose warrants for political disruption are, by historical standards, weak or problematic are now able to do more. Though they may not command any more political authority than their counterparts in political time, they have more power for independent action and are harder for others to stymie institutionally. A second implication cuts the other way: The leaders whose warrants for political disruption are, by historical standards, the most expansive will be able to do less. Those few who are authorized to repudiate the system and reconstruct it will find themselves surrounded by the new trappings of responsible system management and more easily called to account to received standards of good government. Reforms aimed at smoothing the path of change and authorizing presidents to cope more effectively with the governing challenges of the modern era may, in these ways, work to diminish the regenerative potential of presidential power while at the same time increasing its risks.

Rather than foreclosing attention to the fact that the presidency is in many ways a very different institution than it was at the outset, the perspective of political time captures critical aspects of presidential leadership that have been lost in the contemporary discussions of what those differences imply. It does so by retrieving political dynamics that have been with us from the start, drawing them forward through the contemporary period, and reflecting modern expectations back upon them. A third look at the presidency in American political development is complete only when it joins the other two, for it is through the alignment of different developmental currents that we stand to gain the sharpest assessment of where things now stand and where this polity might be headed.

2. Presidential Leadership in Political Time

This is the oldest of the five essays collected in this volume, but though it was a very early articulation of the political time thesis, it nicely captures its historical range.[1] The original version was written in the early 1980s as a reflection on the long course of liberal leadership that had begun in the New Deal and had recently come to an end in the Reagan Revolution. Reagan's repudiation of liberal priorities in government and his call for a "New Beginning" seemed to have put the entire sequence of liberal political development in a new light. It occurred to me that the Democratic leaders of the liberal era could be aligned with Democratic leaders of the Jacksonian era to reveal parallel sets of leadership opportunities, ambitions, and challenges as they had shifted in rough sequence through each of these periods. Pointing in the end to an intimate connection between Carter's travails and Reagan's success, the essay set a research agenda that would explore typical leadership contexts that recur across the full sweep of presidential history and would consider the systemic effects of action within those contexts as they unfold in political time.

When a presidency succeeds, our natural inclination is to laud the special talents and skills the incumbent brought to the office; when things go wrong, we look for strategic missteps and character flaws. There is something comforting in these judgments, for they preserve our confidence in the office of the presidency and in the American political system at large no matter what the fallout from the particular incumbents who pass through them. Our implicit assumption is that presidents, as incumbents of the same office, are tested in similar ways and are thus equally free to show us if they have the right stuff. So long as performance is tied in this way to the incumbent's personal attributes, success is always a possibility; it awaits only the right combination of character, agility, and acumen. So long as there are some success stories to point to, there is little reason to question the operations of the system itself. Woodrow Wilson captured the spirit of these evaluations at the dawn of the Progressive era when he proclaimed, "The American president is at liberty . . . to be as big a man as he can."[2]

But what if this system does not present each incumbent with the same test? What if the political demands on incumbents change in significant ways even within the same historical period? What if the leadership capacities of the office vary widely from one administration to the next? Much of what we take to be evidence of character and strategic acumen might actually be an expression of changing relationships between the presidency and the political system, and if this is the case, the workings of this system might be more deeply implicated in leadership failure and its fallout than we are wont to admit.

This essay explores these possibilities. It steps out of the narrow historical frame in which presidents present themselves to us, one after another in a linear succession, and examines more closely the changing political contours of the field of action on which successive leadership efforts play out. Taking a look back at the broad sweep of American political history, it brings into view a recurrent sequence of change—of political breakthroughs, followed by political breakups, followed by political breakdowns—and it identifies typical reconfigurations of the relationship between the presidency and the political system along the way.

American political history has been punctuated by many beginnings and many endings. Periods are marked by the rise to power of an insurgent political coalition that secures its dominance over national affairs for an extended period of time. The dominant coalition perpetuates its position by gearing the federal government to favor a particular approach to public policy questions. The political-institutional regimes they establish tend to have staying power because the Constitution, with its separation of powers and checks and balances, makes concerted change of the sort needed to dislodge these arrangements difficult and rare. Once established, however, coalition demands gradually sap the energies of these regimes. From the outset, conflicts among interests within the dominant coalition threaten to cause political disaffection and weaken regime support. Then, beyond the problems posed by conflicts among established interests, more basic questions arise concerning the nature of the interests themselves. Not only does the nation change in ways that the old ruling coalition finds increasingly difficult to address, but as disaffection within the coalition makes the mobilization of political support more difficult, the regime becomes increasingly dependent on sectarian interests with myopic demands and momentary loyalties. Generally speaking, the longer a regime survives, the more its approach to national affairs is likely to become encumbered and distorted. As its political energies dissipate, its hold on power thwarts efforts to address the manifest governing demands of the day.

Looking across these sequences reveals several distinct contexts for presidential leadership. Situations might be distinguished by whether or not the president is affiliated with the dominant political coalition. Looking at the post–New Deal period of liberal political dominance, regime outsiders like Republicans Dwight D. Eisenhower and Richard Nixon might be said to have faced a different political problem in leading the nation than regime insiders like John F. Kennedy and Lyndon B. Johnson. Leadership situations also might be distinguished in "political time," that is, by when in the sequence of sectarian unraveling the president engages the political-institutional order. Thus, presidents Franklin D. Roosevelt, John F. Kennedy, and Jimmy Carter—all Democrats who enjoyed Democratic majorities in Congress—may be said to have faced different problems in leading the nation as they were arrayed along the sequence of political change that encompassed the generation and degeneration of the liberal order.

It is not difficult to relate this view of the changing relationship between the presidency and the political system to certain outstanding patterns in presidential leadership across American history. First, the presidents who traditionally make the historians' roster of America's greatest political leaders—George Washington, Thomas Jefferson, Andrew Jackson, Abraham Lincoln, and Franklin D. Roosevelt—all came to power in an abrupt break from a long-established political order, and each led an infusion of new political interests into control of the federal government.[3] Second, after the initial break with the past and the consolidation of a new system of governmental control, a general decline in the political effectiveness of regime insiders is notable. Take, for example, the sequence of Jeffersonians. After the galvanizing performance of Jefferson's first term, we observe increasing political division and a managerial-style presidency under James Madison. Asserting the sanctity of an indivisible Republican majority, James Monroe opened his administration to unbridled sectarianism and oversaw a debilitating fragmentation of the federal establishment. A complete political and institutional breakdown marked the shortened tenure of John Quincy Adams.

But is it possible to go beyond these general observations to a more systematic analysis of the politics of leadership? What are the characteristic political challenges that face a leader at any given stage in a regime sequence? How is the quality of presidential performance affected by the changing shape of the political order? To what extent are the political sequences we observe constituted and driven by the leadership pretensions and follow-through actions of presidents themselves? These questions call for an investigation that breaks presidential history into regime segments and then compares leadership problems and presidential performances at similar stages in regime development across historical periods. Taking different regimes into account simultaneously, this essay will group presidents together on the basis of the parallel positions they hold in political time.

The analysis focuses on three pairs of presidents drawn from the New Deal and Jacksonian regimes: Franklin D. Roosevelt and Andrew Jackson; John F. Kennedy and James K. Polk; and Jimmy Carter and Franklin Pierce. All were Democrats and thus affiliated with the dominant coalition of their respective periods. None took a passive, caretaker view of his office. Indeed, each aspired to great national leadership. Paired comparisons have been formed by slicing into these two regime sequences at corresponding junctures and exposing a shared relationship between the presidency and the political system.

We begin with two beginnings—the presidency of Roosevelt and its counterpart in political time, the presidency of Jackson. These are not random success stories, nor are there common character traits or shared skills that clearly set them apart as paragons of political leadership in the American system. What they shared was a moment in political time. They came to power upon the displacement of a long-established governing coalition. In those circumstances, the leadership opportunity was not so much to make the system work as to remake it altogether, and that prospect engaged these presidents in remarkably similar political struggles. Leadership became a matter of securing the political and institutional infrastructure for a new set of governing commitments. Although separated by more than a century of history, these presidents both grappled with the distinctive politics of regime construction.

Beyond the challenge of regime construction lie ever-more-perplexing problems of regime management. The overriding political imperatives for affiliates of an established order are to maintain and vindicate the governing commitments of the dominant coalition. That entails serving the interests of the faithful, keeping the agenda timely and responsive to changing demands, and ameliorating factional divisions within the ranks. Whereas reconstructive leaders battle over the government's fundamental commitments of ideology and interest, regime managers are at pains to avoid such debates. They are caught up in the challenges of making good on received commitments and holding things together, on service delivery and conflict control. Our examination of these managerial dilemmas focuses on Kennedy and his counterpart in political time, Polk.

Finally, we come to the problem of establishing a credible leadership posture in an enervated regime. Carter and Pierce came to power at a time when the dominant coalition had degenerated into myopic sects that appeared impervious to the most basic problems facing the nation. Neither of these presidents was able to engage the political system at the level of managing coalition interests. Each found himself caught up in the widening disjunction between established power and political legitimacy. Their affiliation with the old order in a new age turned their respective bids for leadership into awkward and superficial struggles to escape the stigma of their own irrelevance, and their hapless struggles for credibility fueled radical insurgencies.

All six of these presidents had to grapple with the erosion of political support that inevitably comes with executive action. But while this problem plagued them all, the initial relationships between the leaders and their supporters were not the same, and the terms of presidential interaction with the political system changed sequentially from stage to stage. Looking within these pairs, we can identify performance challenges that are shared by leaders who addressed the political system at a similar juncture. Looking across the pairs, we observe an ever-more-constricted universe for political action, an ever-more-complicated leadership posture, an ever-more-attenuated opportunity for success. Last but not least, the catalytic effects of presidential leadership itself are marked all along the way.

JACKSON AND ROOSEVELT: POLITICAL UPHEAVAL AND THE CHALLENGE OF REGIME CONSTRUCTION

The presidencies of Andrew Jackson and Franklin D. Roosevelt were both launched on the heels of a major political upheaval. Preceding the election of each, a party long established as the dominant and controlling power within the federal government had begun to flounder and fragment in an atmosphere of national crisis. Finally, the old ruling party suffered a stunning defeat at the polls, losing its dominant position in Congress as well as its control of the presidency. Jackson and Roosevelt assumed the office of chief executive with the old ruling coalition thoroughly discredited by the electorate and, at least temporarily, displaced from political power. They each led a movement of general discontent with the previously established order of things into control of the federal establishment.

Of the two, Jackson's election in 1828 presents the crisis of the old order in a more purely political form. New economic and social conflicts had been festering in America since the financial panic of 1819, but it was the confusion and outrage unleashed by the election of 1824 that gave Jackson's campaign its special meaning. In that earlier election, the Congressional Caucus collapsed as the engine of national political unity. The once-unrivaled party of Jefferson disintegrated into warring factions, and after an extended period of political maneuvering, an alliance between John Quincy Adams and Henry Clay secured Adams a presidential victory in the House of Representatives despite Jackson's pluralities in both popular and electoral votes. The Adams administration was immediately and permanently engulfed in charges of conspiracy, intrigue, and profligacy in high places. Jackson, the hero of 1815, became a hero wronged in 1824, and having saved the government once in a battle against the British at New Orleans, he was prompted by this political defeat to save it again, this time from itself. The Jackson campaign of 1828 launched a broadside assault on the degrading "corruption of manners" that had consumed Washington and on the conspiracy of interests that had captured the federal government from the people.[4]

In the election of 1932, the collapse of the old ruling party dovetailed with and was overshadowed by the Depression. The Democratic Party of 1932 offered nothing if not hope for economic recovery, and Roosevelt's candidacy found its special meaning in that prospect almost in spite of the candidate's own rather conservative campaign rhetoric. The Depression had made a mockery of President Herbert Hoover's early identification of his party with prosperity, and the challenge of formulating a response to the crisis broke the Republican ranks and threw the party into disarray. The Roosevelt appeal was grounded not in substantive proposals or even in partisan ideology but in a widespread perception of Republican incompetence, even intransigence, in the face of national economic calamity. As future secretary of state Cordell Hull outlined Roosevelt's leadership situation in January 1933: "No political party at Washington [is] in control of Congress or even itself. . . . there [is] no cohesive nationwide sentiment behind any fundamental policy or idea today. The election was an overwhelmingly negative affair."[5]

Thus, Jackson and Roosevelt each engaged a political system cut from its moorings by a wave of popular discontent. Basic commitments of ideology and interest were suddenly thrown into question. New commitments were as yet only vague appeals to some essential American value (republican virtue, economic opportunity) that had been lost in the indulgences of the old order. With old political alliances in disarray and new political energies infused into Congress, these presidents had an extraordinary opportunity to set a new course in public policy and to redefine the terms of legitimate national government. They recaptured the experience of being first.

But such a situation is not without its characteristic leadership challenge. The leader who is propelled into office by a political upheaval in governmental control ultimately must confront the imperatives of establishing a new order in government and politics. Naturally enough, this challenge is presented by the favored interests and residual institutional supports of the old order, and once it has been posed, the unencumbered leadership environment that was created by the initial break with the past quickly fades. As the stakes of change are more starkly revealed, presidents in these circumstances are faced with the choice of either abandoning their revolution or consolidating it with structural reforms. Situated just beyond the old order, presidential leadership crystallizes as a problem of regime construction.

The leader as regime builder grapples with the fundamentals of political regeneration—recasting institutional relationships within the government and building a new governing coalition. The president must undermine the institutional support for opposition interests, restructure institutional relations between state and society, and secure electoral dominance. Success in these tasks is hardly guaranteed. Lincoln was assassinated just as the most critical questions of party building and institutional reconstruction were to be addressed. That disaster ushered in a devastating confrontation between his successor and Congress and left the emergent Republican regime hanging in a politically precarious position for the next three decades. Even Jackson and Roosevelt—America's quintessential regime builders—were not uniformly successful. Neither could keep the dual offensives of party building and institutional reconstruction moving together long enough to complete the work on both.

Andrew Jackson

Republican renewal was the keynote of Andrew Jackson's first term. The president was determined to ferret out the political and institutional corruption that he believed had befallen the Jeffersonian regime. This meant purging incompetence and profligacy from the civil service, initiating fiscal retrenchment in national projects, and reviving federalism as a system of vigorous state-based government.[6] Jackson's appeal for a return to Jefferson's original ideas about government certainly posed a potent indictment of the recent state of national affairs and a clear challenge to long-established interests. But there was a studied political restraint in his initial program that defied the attempts of his opponents to characterize it as revolutionary.[7] Indeed, while holding out an attractive standard with which to rally supporters, Jackson was careful to yield his opposition precious little ground upon which to mount an effective counterattack. He used the initial upheaval in governmental control to cultivate an irreproachable political position as the independent voice of the people, a crusader determined to restore the nation's integrity.

Significantly, the transformation of Jackson's presidency from a moral crusade into a radical program of political reconstruction was instigated, not by the president himself, but by the premier institution of the old regime, the Bank of the United States.[8] At the time of Jackson's election, the bank was long established as both the most powerful institution in America and the most important link between state and society. It dominated the nation's credit system, maintained extensive ties of material interest with political elites, and actively involved itself in electoral campaigns to sustain its own political support. It embodied all the problems of institutional corruption and political degradation toward which Jackson addressed his administration. The bank was a concentration of political and economic power able to tyrannize over people's lives and to control the will of their elected representatives.

During his first years in office, Jackson spoke vaguely of the need for some modification of the bank's charter. But since the charter did not expire until 1836, there appeared to be plenty of time to consider appropriate changes. Indeed, although Jackson was personally inclined toward radical hard-currency views, he recognized the dangers of impromptu tinkering with an institution so firmly entrenched in the economic life of the nation and hesitated at embracing untested alternatives. Moreover, Jackson foresaw an overwhelming reelection endorsement for his early achievements and knew that to press the bank issue before the election of 1832 could only hurt him politically. After routing Henry Clay, the architect of the bank and the obvious challenger in the upcoming campaign, Jackson would have a free hand to deal with the institution as he saw fit.

But Jackson's apparent commitment to some kind of bank reform and the obvious political calculations surrounding the issue led the bank's president, Nicholas Biddle, to join Clay in a preelection push to recharter the institution without any reforms a full four years before its charter expired. Biddle feared for the bank's future in Jackson's second term. Clay needed to break Jackson's irreproachable image as a national leader and to expose his political weaknesses. An early recharter bill promised to splinter Jackson's support in Congress. If the president signed the bill, his reputation as a reformer would be destroyed; if he vetoed it, the shock to the system would rally anti-Jackson sentiment.

As expected, the recharter bill threw Jackson enthusiasts into a quandary and passed through Congress. The president saw the bill not only as a blatant attempt by those attached to the old order to destroy him politically, but also as proof certain that the bank's political power threatened the very survival of republican government. He accepted the challenge and set out to destroy the bank. Pushed beyond the possibility of controlling the modification of extant institutions without significant opposition, Jackson stiffened his repudiative stance and pressed for an irrevocable break with established governmental arrangements. The 1828 crusade for republican renewal became in 1832 an all-fronts offensive for the establishment of an entirely new political and institutional order.

The president's veto of the recharter bill clearly marked this transition. The political themes of 1828 were turned against the bank with a vengeance. Jackson defined his stand as one that would extricate the federal government from the interests of the privileged and protect the states from encroaching federal domination. He appealed directly to the interests of the nation's farmers, mechanics, and laborers, claiming that this great political majority stood to lose control over the government to the influential few. This call to the "common man" for a defense of the Republic had long been a Jacksonian theme, but now it carried the portent of sweeping governmental changes. Jackson not only was declaring open war on the premier institution of the old order, he was challenging long-settled questions of governance. The U.S. Supreme Court, for example, had affirmed the constitutionality of the bank thirteen years earlier. Jackson's veto challenged the assumption of executive deference to the Court and asserted presidential authority to make an independent and contrary judgment about judicial decisions. Jackson also challenged executive deference to Congress, one of the central political principles of the Jeffersonian regime. His veto message went beyond constitutional objections to the recharter bill and asserted the president's authority to make an independent evaluation of the social, economic, and political implications of congressional action. In all, the message was a regime builder's manifesto that looked toward the fusion of a broad-based political coalition, the shattering of established institutional power relationships between state and society, and the transformation of governing arrangements within the federal government itself.

Of course, regime construction requires more than a declaration of presidential intent. Jackson had his work cut out for him at the beginning of his second term. His victory over Clay in 1832 was certainly sweeping enough to reaffirm his leadership position, and having used the veto as a campaign document, Jackson could claim a strong mandate to complete the work it outlined. But the veto had also been used as an issue by Clay, and the threat to the bank was fueling organized political opposition in all sections of the country.[9] More important still, the Senate, whose support had been shaky enough in Jackson's first term, moved completely beyond his control in 1833, and his party's majority in the House returned in a highly volatile condition. Finally, the bank's charter still had three years to run, and bank president Biddle had every intention of exploiting Jackson's political vulnerabilities in hope of securing his own future.

Jackson seized the initiative. He set out to neutralize the significance of the bank for the remainder of its charter and to prevent any new recharter movement from emerging in Congress. His plan was to have the deposits of the federal government removed from the bank on his own authority and transferred to a select group of politically friendly state banks. The president would thus circumvent his opponents and, at the same time, offer the nation an alternative banking system. The new banking structure had several potential advantages. It promised to work under the direct supervision of the executive branch, to forge direct institutional connections between the presidency and local centers of political power, and to secure broad political support against a revival of the national bank.

The plan faced formidable opposition from the Treasury Department, the Senate, and, most of all, from the Bank of the United States. Biddle responded to the removal of federal deposits with an abrupt and severe curtailment of loans. By squeezing the nation into a financial panic, the bank president hoped to turn public opinion against Jackson. The Senate followed suit with a formal censure of the president, denouncing his pretensions to independent action on the presumption of a direct mandate from the people.

The so-called Panic Session of Congress (1833–1834) posed the ultimate test of Jackson's resolve to forge a new regime. Success hinged on consolidating the Democratic Party in Congress and reaffirming its control over the national government. The president moved quickly to deflect blame for the panic onto the bank. Destroying Biddle's credibility, he was able by the spring of 1834 to solidify Democratic support in the House and gain an endorsement of his actions (and implicitly, his authority to act) from that chamber. Then, undertaking a major party-building effort at the grass roots in the midterm elections of 1834, Jackson and his political lieutenants were able to secure a loyal Democratic majority in the Senate. The struggle was over, and in a final acknowledgment of the legitimacy of the new order, the Democratic Senate expunged its censure of the president from the record.

But even as Congress was falling into line, the limitations of the president's achievement were manifesting themselves throughout the nation at large. Jackson had shattered the old governmental order, consolidated a new political party behind his policies, secured that party's control over the entire federal establishment, and redefined the position of the presidency in its relations with Congress, the courts, the states, and the electorate. But his institutional alternative for reconstructing financial relations between state and society—the state deposit system—was proving a dismal failure.

In truth, Jackson had latched onto the deposit banking scheme out of political necessity as much as principle. The president had been caught between his opponents' determination to save the bank and his supporters' need for a clear and attractive alternative to it. Opposition to Biddle and Clay merged with opposition to any national banking structure, and the interim experiment with state banking quickly became a political commitment. Unfortunately, the infusion of federal deposits into the pet state banks fueled a speculative boom and threatened a major financial collapse.

Hoping to stem the tide of this disaster, the Treasury Department began to choose banks of deposit less for their political soundness than for their financial soundness, and Jackson threw his support behind a gradual conversion to hard money. In the end, however, the president was forced to accept the grim irony of his success as a regime builder. Congress had moved solidly behind him, but in so doing members had begun to see for themselves the special political attractions of the state deposit system. With the passage of the Deposit Act of 1836, Congress expanded the number of state depositories and explicitly limited executive discretion in controlling them.[10]

Jackson reconstructed American government and politics; through his leadership, new commitments of ideology and interest were woven into the very fabric of national institutions. Notably, however, reconstructive leadership did not solve the nation's problems. Jackson merely substituted one irresponsible and uncontrollable financial system for another. Jackson's chosen successor, Martin Van Buren, understood this all too well as he struggled to extricate the federal government from the state banks in the midst of the nation's first great depression.

Franklin D. Roosevelt

As a political personality, the moralistic, vindictive, and tortured Jackson stands in marked contrast to the pragmatic, engaging, and buoyant Franklin D. Roosevelt. Yet their initial victories over long-established ruling parties and the sustained popular enthusiasm that accompanied those triumphs offered similar political opportunities and propelled each into grappling with a similar set of leadership challenges. By late 1934, Roosevelt himself seemed to sense the parallels. To Vice President John Nance Garner he wrote, "The more I learn about Andy Jackson, the more I love him."[11]

The interesting thing about this remark is its timing. In 1934 and 1935, Roosevelt faced mounting discontent with the emergency program he had implemented during his early days in office from the favored interests of the old order. Moreover, he saw that the residual bulwark of institutional support for that order was capable of simply sweeping his programs aside. Like Jackson in 1832, Roosevelt was being challenged either to reconstruct the political and institutional foundations of the national government or to abandon the insurgent energy and leadership initiative that he had carried into power.

The revival of the economy had been the keynote of Roosevelt's early program.[12] Although collectivist in approach and bold in their assertion of a positive role for the federal government, the policies of the early New Deal did not present a broadside challenge to long-established political and economic interests. Roosevelt adopted the role of a bipartisan national leader reaching out to all interests in a time of crisis. He carefully courted the southern Bourbons, who controlled the old Democratic Party, and incorporated big business directly into the government's recovery program. The problem was not that Roosevelt's program ignored the interests attached to and supported by the governmental arrangements of the past, but that it implicated those interests in a broader coalition. The New Deal also bestowed legitimacy on the interests of organized labor, the poor, and the unemployed, and that left southern Bourbons and northern industrialists feeling threatened and increasingly insecure.

This sense of unease manifested itself politically in the organization of the American Liberty League in the summer of 1934. The league mounted an aggressive assault on Roosevelt and the New Deal, but Roosevelt's party received a resounding endorsement in the midterm elections, actually broadening the base of enthusiastic New Dealers in Congress. The congressional elections vividly demonstrated the futility of political opposition, but in the spring of 1935 a more potent adversary arose within the government itself. The Supreme Court, keeper of the rules for the old regime, handed down a series of anti–New Deal decisions. The most important of these nullified the centerpiece of Roosevelt's recovery program, the National Industrial Recovery Act. With the American Liberty League sorting out friend from foe and the Court pulling the rug out from under the cooperative approach to economic recovery, Roosevelt stiffened his repudiative stance and turned his administration toward structural reform. If he could no longer lead all interests toward economic recovery, he could still secure the interests of a great political majority within a new governmental order.

Roosevelt began the transition from national healer to regime builder with a considerable advantage over Jackson. He could restructure institutional relations between state and society simply by reaching out to the radical and irrepressibly zealous Seventy-Fourth Congress (1935–1937) and offering it sorely needed coherence and direction. The result was a "second" New Deal. The federal government extended new services and permanent institutional supports to organized labor, the small businessman, the aged, the unemployed, and, later, the rural poor. At the same time, the president revealed a new approach to big business and the affluent by pressing for tighter regulation and graduated taxation.[13]

In their scope and vision, these achievements far surpassed the makeshift and flawed arrangements that Jackson had improvised to restructure institutional relations between state and society in the bank war. But Roosevelt's comparatively early and more thoroughgoing success on this score proved a dubious advantage in subsequent efforts to consolidate the new order. After his overwhelming reelection victory in 1936, Roosevelt pressed a series of consolidation initiatives. Like Jackson in his second term, he began with an effort to neutralize the remaining threat within the government.

Roosevelt's target, of course, was the Supreme Court. He was wise not to follow Jackson's example in the bank war by launching a direct ideological attack on the Court. After all, Roosevelt was challenging a coequal branch of government and could hardly succeed in labeling an arm of the Constitution a threat to the survival of the Republic. The president decided instead to kill his institutional opponent with kindness. He called for an increase in the size of the Court, ostensibly to ease the burden on the elder justices and increase the efficiency of the federal judiciary. Unfortunately, the real stakes of the contest never were made explicit, and the chief justice deflected the attack by simply denying the need for help. More importantly, the Court, unlike the bank, did not further exacerbate the situation. Instead, it reversed course in the middle of the battle and indicated its willingness to accept the policies of the second New Deal.

The Court's turnabout was a great victory for the new regime, but it eliminated even the implicit justification for Roosevelt's proposed judicial reforms. With the constituent services of the New Deal secure, Congress had little reason to challenge the integrity of the Court. Roosevelt, however, found himself bound by his own arguments about the administrative inefficiencies of the Court and suspicious of tactics that seemed to preserve claims of judicial supremacy for the future. He did not withdraw his proposal. Although stalwart liberals stood by the president to the end, traditional Democratic conservatives deserted him. A bipartisan coalition came together in opposition to Roosevelt, defeated the "court-packing" scheme, and divided the ranks of the New Deal coalition. It was a rebuke every bit as portentous as the formal censure of Jackson by the Senate.

With Roosevelt, as with Jackson, the third congressional election of his tenure called forth a major party-building initiative. Stung by the Court defeat, the president moved to reaffirm his hold over the Democratic Party and to strengthen its liberal commitments. But this effort too was handicapped by the sweeping character of Roosevelt's early successes. Unlike Jackson in 1834, Roosevelt in 1938 could not point to any immediate threat to his programmatic commitments. A liberal program was already in place, the Court had capitulated, and despite deep fissures manifested during the Court battle, the overwhelming Democratic majorities in Congress gave no indication of abandoning the New Deal. Even the more conservative southern delegations in Congress maintained majority support for Roosevelt's domestic reform initiatives.[14] Under these conditions, party building took on an aura of presidential self-indulgence. Although enormously important from the standpoint of future regime coherence, at the time it looked like heavy-handed and selective punishment for the ungrateful defectors. In this guise, it evoked little popular support, let alone enthusiasm.

The party-building initiative failed. Virtually all of the conservative Democrats targeted for defeat were reelected, and the Republicans showed a resurgence of strength. As two-party politics returned to the national scene, the division within the majority party between the old southern conservatism and the new liberal orthodoxy became more ominous than ever.

Despite these setbacks, Roosevelt's effectiveness as a regime builder was not completely exhausted. A final effort at strengthening the new order institutionally met with considerable success. In 1939, Roosevelt received congressional approval for a package of administrative reforms that promised to bolster the position of the president in his relations with the other branches of government. Following the precepts of his Commission on Administrative Management, the president asked for new authority to control the vastly expanded federal bureaucracy and for new executive offices to provide planning and direction for governmental operations. Congress responded with a modest endorsement. While deflating Roosevelt's grand design, it clearly acknowledged the new governing demands of the enlarged federal bureaucracy and system of national services he had forged. The establishment of the Executive Office of the President closed the New Deal with a fitting symbol of the new state of affairs.[15]

As is often noted, the New Deal reforms did not solve the economic problems underlying the Depression. The outbreak of World War II was far more effective in that. Roosevelt did, however, redefine the terms and conditions of legitimate national government. It would be a long time before a president called into question the expansive national commitments supported by his liberal regime.

POLK AND KENNEDY: THE DILEMMAS
OF INTEREST MANAGEMENT IN AN
ESTABLISHED REGIME

The administrations of Jackson and Roosevelt shared much in both the political conditions of leadership and the challenges undertaken. The initial upheaval, the ensuing political confusion, and the enduring popular enthusiasm for reform set the stage for America's quintessential regime-building presidencies. Opposition from the favored interests of the old order and their residual institutional supports eventually pushed these presidents from an original program to meet the immediate crisis at hand into structural reforms that promised to place institutional relations between state and society on an entirely new footing. After a second landslide election, Jackson and Roosevelt each moved to consolidate his new order by eliminating the institutional opposition and forging a more coherent base of party support. As the nation redivided politically, a new set of governing commitments took hold, a new ruling coalition emerged to back them up, and the presidency itself gained a new position of power.

It is evident from a comparison of these performances that where Rooseveltian regime building was triumphant, Jacksonian regime building faltered, and vice versa: Roosevelt left institutional relations between state and society thoroughly reconstructed, but his party-building initiative fell flat and the achievement on that score was flawed; Jackson left institutional relations between state and society in a dangerous disarray, but his performance and achievement as a party builder remain unparalleled. These differences would have important implications for the future operations of these new regimes. But the more important point for our purposes lies elsewhere. It is that few presidents have the incentive to address fundamental commitments of ideology and interest or the opportunity to secure new commitments through institutional reconstruction and party building. Most presidents must use their skills and resources—however extensive those may be—to work within an already established governmental order.

Successful regime builders leave in their wake a more constricted political universe for presidential action. To their partisan successors, in particular, they leave the difficult task of keeping faith with a ruling coalition in changing times. In established regimes, majority-party presidents come to power as representatives of the dominant political alliance and they are expected to offer a representative's service in delegate style. Commitments of ideology and interest are all too clear, and the fusion of national political legitimacy with established power relationships argues against any attempt to tinker with the basics of government and politics. These leaders are challenged not to break down the old order and forge a new one, but to complete the agenda, adapt the vision, and defuse the potentially explosive choices among competing obligations. If they are to whip up national enthusiasm behind their leadership, they must do so on other fronts that promise to unite all supporters. Presidents in these circumstances are partners to a highly structured regime politics, and to make the partnership work, they must anticipate and control impending disruptions.

The presidencies of Polk and Kennedy clearly illustrate the problems and prospects of leadership circumscribed by the challenge of managing an established regime. Each of these men came to the presidency after an interval of opposition-party control and divided government. The intervening years had seen some significant changes in the tenor of public policy, but there had been no systemic transformations in government or politics. Ushering in a second era of majority-party government, Polk and Kennedy promised to revive the commitments and revitalize the vision of the regime founder.

Neither Polk nor Kennedy could claim the leadership of a major party faction. Indeed, their credibility as regime managers rested in large part on their second-rank status in regular party circles. Each honed skills for allaying mutual suspicions among the great centers of party strength. Their nominations to the presidency were the result of careful posturing around the conflicts that divided contending party factions. What they lacked in deep political loyalties, they made up for with their freedom to cultivate the support of all interests.

Once the office was won, the challenge of interest management was magnified. Each of these presidents had accepted one especially controversial commitment (Texas annexation, civil rights) that held majority support within the party as a necessary part of the regime's updated agenda. Their ability to lend their support to their party's most divisive enthusiasm without losing their broad base of credibility within it was fitting testimony to their early education in the art of aggressive maintenance. But their mediating skills did not alter the fact that each had taken on an issue that had long threatened to split the party apart. In addition, Polk and Kennedy each won astonishingly close elections. There was no clear mandate for action, no discernible tide of national discontent, no mass repudiation of what had gone before. The hairbreadth Democratic victories of 1844 and 1960 suggested the opposition could continue to make a serious claim to the presidency, and that reinforced in these incumbents an already highly developed sense of executive dependence on all parts of the party coalition. With maintenance at a premium and with an ideological rupture within the ranks at hand, Polk and Kennedy carried the full weight of the leadership dilemma that confronts the majority-party president of an established regime.

James K. Polk

For the Democratic Party of 1844, the long-festering issue was the annexation of Texas, with its implicit threat of prompting a war of aggression for the expansion of slave territory.[16] Even Jackson, an ardent nationalist, had seen Texas as forbidden fruit. Despite his passion for annexation, Old Hickory steered clear of the issue during the last years of his presidency for fear that it would divide along sectional lines the national party he had just consolidated.[17] Democratic loyalists followed Jackson's lead until 1843, when the partyless "mongrel president" John Tyler, desperate to build an independent political base of support for himself, latched onto the annexation issue and presented a formal proposal on the subject to Congress. With Texas finally pushed to the forefront, expansionist fever heated up in the South and the West, and antislavery agitation accelerated in the North.

Jackson's political nightmare became reality on the eve of his party's nominating convention in 1844. Van Buren, Jackson's successor to the presidency in 1837 and still the nominal head of the Democratic Party, risked an all-but-certain nomination by coming out against the "immediate" annexation of Texas. The New Yorker's pronouncement fused a formidable opposition in the southern and western wings of the party and left the convention deadlocked through eight ballots. With Van Buren holding a large bloc of delegates but unable to get the leaders of the South and West to relinquish the necessary two-thirds majority, it became clear that only a "new man" could save the party from disaster. That man had to be sound on Texas without being openly opposed to Van Buren. On the ninth ballot, James Knox Polk became the Democratic nominee.

Polk was a second-choice candidate, and he knew it. As leader of the Democratic Party in Tennessee, he had the unimpeachable credential of being a stalwart friend of Andrew Jackson. He had served loyally as floor leader of the House during the critical days of the bank war, and he had gone on to win his state's governorship. But after Polk tried and failed to gain his party's vice presidential nomination in 1840, his political career fell on hard times. Calculating his strategy for a political comeback in 1844, Polk made full use of his second-rank standing in high party circles. Again he posed as the perfect vice presidential candidate and cultivated his ties to Van Buren. Knowing that this time Van Buren's equivocation on the Texas issue would make his nomination more difficult, Polk also understood the special advantages of being a Texas enthusiast with Van Buren connections. As soon as that calculation paid off, Polk ventured another. In accepting the presidential nomination, he pledged that, if elected, he would not seek a second term. Although he thus declared himself a lame duck even before he was elected, Polk reckoned that he would not serve any time in office at all unless the frustrated party giants in each section of the nation expended every last ounce of energy for the campaign, which they might not do if it meant foreclosing their own prospects for eight years.[18]

The one-term declaration was a bid for party unity and a pledge of party maintenance. But the deepening divisions that were exposed at the convention of 1844, and their uncertain resolution in a Texas platform and a dark-horse nomination, suggested that the party was likely to chew itself up under a passive caretaker presidency. If Polk was to avoid a disastrous schism in the party of Jackson, he would have to order, balance, and service the major contending interests in turn. He would have to enlist each contingent within the party in support of the policy interests of all the others. Polk submerged himself in a high-risk strategy of aggressive maintenance in which the goal was to satisfy each faction of his party enough to keep the whole from falling apart. The scheme was at once pragmatic and holistic, hardheaded and fantastic. More than that, it almost worked.

The president opened his administration (appropriately enough) with a declaration that he would "know no divisions of the Democratic party." He promised "equal and exact justice to every portion."[19] His first action, however, indicated that the going would be rough. Scrutinizing the cabinet-selection process, Van Buren judged that New York (whose electoral votes had put Polk over the top) had not had its interests sufficiently recognized. The frustrated ex-president thought he saw a determination on the new president's part to turn the party toward the slave South. Polk moved immediately to appease Van Buren with other patronage offers, but relations between them did not improve. From the outset Van Buren's loyalty was tinged with a heavy dose of suspicion.

The outcry over patronage distribution indicated that any action the president took would evoke charges of favoritism. Van Buren's was but the first in an incessant barrage of such charges.[20] But Polk was not powerless in the face of disaffection. He had an irresistible agenda for party government to bolster his precarious political position.

Polk's program elaborated the theme of equal justice for all coalition interests. On the domestic side, he reached out to the South with support for a lower tariff, to the Northwest with support for land-price reform, to the Northeast by endorsing a warehouse storage system advantageous to import merchants, and to the old Jacksonian radicals with a commitment to a return to hard money and a reinstatement of the independent Treasury. (Van Buren had dedicated his entire administration to establishing the independent Treasury as a solution to Jackson's banking dilemma, but his work had been undermined in the intervening four years.) It was in foreign affairs, however, that the president placed the highest hopes for his administration. Superimposed on his carefully balanced program of party service in the domestic arena was a missionary embrace of Manifest Destiny. Reaching out to the South, Polk promised to annex Texas; to the Northwest, he promised to secure the Oregon Territory; and to bind the whole nation together, he made a secret promise to himself to acquire California. In all, the president would complete the Jacksonian program of party services and fuse popular passions in an irresistible jingoistic campaign to extend the Jacksonian Republic across the continent.

Driven by a keen sense of the dual imperatives of maintenance and leadership, Polk embarked on a course of action designed to transform the nation without changing its politics. Party loyalty was the key to success, but it would take more than just a series of favorable party votes to make this strategy of aggressive maintenance work. The sequence, pace, and symbolism of Polk's initiatives had to be assiduously controlled and coordinated with difficult foreign negotiations so that the explosive moral issues inherent in the program would not enter the debate. Sectional paranoia and ideological heresies had to be held in constant check. Mutual self-interest had to remain at the forefront so that reciprocal party obligations could be reinforced. Polk's program was much more than a laundry list of party commitments. If he did not achieve everything he promised in the order he promised it, he risked a major party rupture. Here, at the level of executive management and interest control, the president faltered.

After the patronage tiff with Van Buren demonstrated Polk's problems with the eastern radicals, disaffection over the Oregon boundary settlement with Great Britain exposed his difficulties in striking an agreeable balance between western and southern expansionists. The president moved forward immediately and simultaneously on his promises to acquire Oregon and Texas. In each case he pressed an aggressive, indeed belligerent, border claim. He demanded "all of Oregon" (extending north to the 54°40' parallel) from Great Britain and "Greater Texas" (extending south below the Nueces River to the Rio Grande) from Mexico.

The pledge to get "all of Oregon" unleashed a tidal wave of popular enthusiasm in the Northwest. But Great Britain refused to play according to the presidential plan, and a potent peace movement spread across the South and the East out of fear of impending war over the Oregon boundary. Polk used the belligerence of the "54°40' or fight" faction to counter the peace movement and to prod the British into coming to terms, but he knew he could not risk war on that front. An impending war with Mexico over the Texas boundary promised to yield California in short order, but a war with both Mexico and Great Britain threatened disaster.

When the British finally agreed to settle the Oregon boundary at the forty-ninth parallel, Polk accepted the compromise. Then, after an appropriate display of Mexican aggression on the Texas border, he asked Congress for a declaration of war against that nation. Abandoned, the 54°40' men turned on the president, mercilessly accusing him of selling out to the South and picking on defenseless Mexico instead of standing honorably against the British. A huge part of the Oregon Territory had been added to the Union, but a vociferous bloc of westerners now joined the Van Burenites in judging the president to be willfully deceptive and dangerously prosouthern. Polk had miscalculated both British determination and western pride. His accomplishment deviated from the pace and scope of his grand design and in so doing undermined the delicate party balance.

Polk's designs were further complicated by the effects of wartime sensibilities on his carefully balanced legislative program. The independent Treasury and warehouse storage bills were enacted easily, but old matters of principle and simple matters of interest were not enough to calm agitated eastern Democrats. They demanded the president's assurance that he was not involved in a war of conquest in the Southwest. Polk responded with a vague and evasive definition of war aims. There was little else he could do to ease suspicions.

More portentous still was the influence of the tariff initiative on wartime politics. Polk had to court northwestern Democrats to make up for expected eastern defections on a vote for a major downward revision of rates. To do so, he not only held out his promised land-price reform as an incentive to bring debate to a close, he also withheld his objections to a legislative initiative brewing among representatives of the South and the West to develop the Mississippi River system. The northwesterners swallowed their pride over Oregon in hopeful expectation and threw their support behind the tariff bill.

After the tariff bill was enacted, Polk vetoed the internal improvement bill. It had never been a part of his program, and it was an offense to all orthodox Jacksonians. Needless to say, the deviousness of the president's maneuverings was an offense to the West that all but eclipsed the veto's stalwart affirmation of Jacksonian principles. To make matters worse, the land bill failed. The president made good his pledge to press the measure, but he could not secure enactment. Burned three times after offering loyal support to southern interests, the northwesterners no longer were willing to heed the counsels of mutual restraint. The president's effort to bring the war to a quick and triumphant conclusion provided them with their opportunity to strike back.

The war with Mexico was in fact only a few months old, but that already was too long for the president and his party. To speed the peace, Polk decided to ask Congress for a $2 million appropriation to settle the

Texas boundary dispute and to pay "for any concessions which may be made by Mexico."[21] This open offer of money for land was the first clear indication that the United States was engaged in—perhaps had consciously provoked—a war of conquest in the Southwest. With it, the latent issue of 1844 manifested itself with a vengeance. Northern Democrats, faced with the growing threat of antislavery agitation at home, saw unequal treatment in the administration's handling of matters of interest, intolerable duplicity in presidential action, and an insufferable southern bias in national policy. They were ready to take their stand on matters of principle.

It is ironic that Polk's implicit acknowledgment of the drive for California, with its promise of fulfilling the nationalist continental vision, would fan the fires of sectional conflict. Surely he had intended just the opposite. The president was, in fact, correct in calculating that no section of the party would oppose the great national passion for expansion to the Pacific. But he simply could not stem the tide of party disaffection in the East, and unfulfilled expectations fueled disaffection in the West. He was thus left to watch in dismay as the disaffected joined forces to take their revenge on the South.

Northern Democrats loyally offered to support the president's effort to buy peace and land but added a demand that slavery be prohibited from entering any of the territory that might thus be acquired. This condition, known as the Wilmot Proviso after Pennsylvania Democrat David Wilmot, splintered the party along the dreaded sectional cleavage. An appropriation bill with the proviso passed in the House, but it failed in the Senate when an effort to remove the proviso was filibustered successfully. Now it was Polk's turn to be bitter. In a grim confession of the failure of his grand design, he claimed that he could not comprehend "what connection slavery had with making peace with Mexico."[22]

Ultimately Polk got his peace with Mexico, and with it he added California and the greater Southwest to the Union. He also delivered on tariff revision, the independent Treasury, the warehouse storage system, Oregon, and Texas. Interest management by Polk had extorted a monumental program of party service from established sources of power in remarkably short order. Indeed, except for the conclusion of peace with Mexico, everything had been put in place between the spring of 1845 and the summer of 1846. But the Jacksonian party was ruptured in the very course of enacting its national vision. Polk's monument to Jacksonian nationalism proved to be a breeding ground for sectional heresy.

The shortfall in Polk's efforts at interest management manifested itself in political disaster for the Democratic Party. By the fall of 1846, the New York party had divided into two irreconcilable camps, with Van Buren leading the radicals who were sympathetic to the Wilmot Proviso and opposed to the administration. While the president maintained an official stance of neutrality toward the schism, party regulars rallied behind Lewis Cass, a westerner opposed to the proviso. Cass's alternative—"popular" or "squatter sovereignty" in the territories—promised to hold together the larger portion of the majority party by absolving the federal government of any role in resolving the questions of slavery extension and regional balance that were raised by Polk's transformation of the nation. When the Democrats nominated Cass in 1848, the Van Buren delegation bolted the convention. Joining "Conscience Whigs" and "Liberty Party" men, they formed the Free Soil Party, dedicated it to the principles of the Wilmot Proviso, and nominated Van Buren as their presidential candidate.[23]

After the convention, Polk abandoned his studied neutrality. In the waning months of his administration, he withdrew administration favors from Free Soil sympathizers and threw his support behind the party regulars.[24] But it was Van Buren who had the last word. Four years after putting aside personal defeat, loyally supporting the party, and helping elect Polk, he emerged as the leader of the "heretics" and ensured Cass's defeat.

John F. Kennedy

John F. Kennedy had every intention of spending eight years in the White House, but this ambition only compounded the dilemma inherent in his leadership position. Kennedy's presidential campaign harkened back to Rooseveltian images of direction and energy in government. It stigmatized the Republican interregnum under Eisenhower as a lethargic, aimless muddle, and it roused the people with a promise to "get the country moving again." At the same time, however, the party of Roosevelt maintained its awkward division between northern liberals and southern conservatives. Kennedy assiduously courted both wings, and the narrowness of his victory reinforced his debts to each. The president's prospects for eight years in the White House seemed to hinge on whether or not he could, in his first four, vindicate the promise of vigorous national leadership without shattering an already fractured political base.

Kennedy's "New Frontier" was eminently suited to the demands of aggressive maintenance. It looked outward toward placing a man on the moon and protecting the free world from communist aggression. It looked inward toward pragmatic adaptations and selective adjustments of the New Deal consensus. Leadership in the international arena would fuse the entire nation together behind bold demonstrations of American power and determination. Leadership in the domestic arena would contain party conflict through presidential management and executive-controlled initiatives.

This leadership design shared more in common with Polk's pursuits than a frontier imagery. Both presidents gave primacy to foreign enthusiasms and hoped that the nation would do the same. Facing a politically divided people and an internally factionalized party, they set out to tap the unifying potential of America's missionary stance in the world and to rivet national attention on muscle-flexing adventures on the world stage. By so doing, they claimed the high ground as men of truly national vision. At the same time, each countered deepening conflicts of principle within the ruling coalition with an attempt to balance interests at home. They were engaged in a constant struggle to mute the passions that divided their supporters and stem the tide of coalition disaffection. Resisting the specter of irreconcilable differences within the ranks, Polk and Kennedy held out their support to all interests and demanded in return that each agree to allow the executive to determine the range, substance, and timing of policy initiatives.

Of course, there were notable differences in the way these presidents approached regime management. Kennedy, who was not unaware of Polk's failings, avoided Polk's tactics.[25] Polk had gone after as much as possible as quickly as possible for as many as possible in the hope that conflicts among interests could be submerged through the ordered satisfaction of each. Kennedy seemed to feel that conflicts could be avoided best by refraining from unnecessarily divisive action. He was more circumspect in his choice of initiatives and more cautious in their pursuit. The task of balancing interests was translated into legislative restraint, and aggressive maintenance into carefully contained advocacy. Kennedy's "politics of expectation" kept fulfillment of the liberal agenda at the level of anticipation.[26]

At the heart of Kennedy's political dilemma was the long-festering issue of civil rights for black Americans. Roosevelt had seen the fight for civil rights coming, but he had refused to make it his own, fearing the devastating effect it would have on the precarious sectional balance in his newly established party coalition.[27] Harry S. Truman had seen the fight break out and temporarily rupture the party in 1948.[28] His response was a balance of executive action and legislative caution. When the Republicans made gains in southern cities during the 1950s, the prudent course Truman had outlined appeared more persuasive than ever. But by 1961, black migration into northern cities, Supreme Court support for civil rights demands, and an ever-more-aggressive civil rights movement in the South had made it increasingly difficult for a Democratic president to resist a more definitive commitment.

In his early campaign for the presidential nomination, Kennedy developed a posture of inoffensive support for civil rights.[29] While keeping himself abreast of liberal orthodoxy, he held back from leadership and avoided pressing the cause upon southern conservatives. Such maneuvering became considerably more difficult at the party convention of 1960. The liberal-controlled platform committee presented a civil rights plank that all but committed the nominee to take the offensive. It pledged presidential leadership on behalf of new legislation, vigorous enforcement of existing laws, and reforms in congressional procedures to remove impediments to such action. Adding insult to injury, the plank lent party sanction to the civil rights demonstrations that had been accelerating throughout the South.

Although the Democratic platform tied Kennedy to the cause that had ruptured the party in 1948, it did not dampen his determination to hold on to the South. Once nominated, he reached out to the offended region and identified himself with more traditional Democratic strategies. Indeed, by offering the vice presidential nomination to Lyndon Johnson, he risked a serious offense to his left wing. Not only was Johnson the South's first choice and Kennedy's chief rival for the presidential nomination, but his national reputation was also punctuated by conspicuous efforts on behalf of ameliorative civil rights action in the Senate. Kennedy himself seems to have been a bit surprised by Johnson's acceptance of second place. The liberals were disheartened.[30] Together, however, Kennedy and Johnson were to make a formidable team of regime managers. Riding the horns of their party's dilemma, they balanced the boldest Democratic commitment ever on civil rights with a determination not to lose the support of its most passionate opponents. Their narrow victory owed as much to those who were promised a new level of action as to those promised continued moderation.

The president's inaugural and State of the Union addresses directed national attention to imminent international dangers and America's world responsibilities. Civil rights received only passing mention. Stressing the need for containment in the international arena, these speeches also reflected the president's commitment to containment in the domestic arena. In the months before the inauguration, Kennedy had decided to keep civil rights off the legislative agenda. Instead, he would prod Congress along on other liberal issues such as a minimum wage, housing, aid to education, mass transit, and health care. The plan was not difficult to rationalize. If the president pressed for civil rights legislation and failed, his entire legislative program would be placed in jeopardy, and executive efforts on behalf of blacks would be subject to even closer scrutiny. If he withheld the civil rights issue from Congress, southerners might show their appreciation for the president's circumspection. His other measures thus would have a better chance for enactment, and blacks would reap the benefits of these programs as well as of Kennedy's executive-centered civil rights initiatives.

Accordingly, Kennedy avoided a preinaugural fight in the Senate to liberalize the rules of debate. The liberalization effort failed. He did lend his support to a liberal attempt to expand the House Rules Committee, but this was a prerequisite to House action on Kennedy's chosen legislative program. The Rules Committee effort succeeded, but the new committee members gave no indication of an impending civil rights offensive.[31]

Feelings of resentment and betrayal among civil rights leaders inevitably followed the decision to forgo the bold legislative actions suggested in the party platform. Poised to affirm commitments to all regime interests, the administration seemed determined to avoid a debate on fundamentals. The question was whether the promise of aggressive executive action could allay resentment, persuasively demonstrate a new level of commitment to civil rights, and still contain the threatened political rupture. The administration moved forward on several fronts. The centerpiece of its strategy was to use the Justice Department to promote and protect black-voter-registration drives in the South. This approach promised to give blacks the power to secure their rights and also to minimize the electoral costs of any further Democratic defections among southern whites. In other initiatives, the president liberalized the old Civil Rights Commission and created a Committee on Equal Employment Opportunity to investigate job discrimination. When liberals in Congress moved to eliminate the poll tax, the president lent his support. When demonstrations threatened to disrupt southern transportation terminals, Attorney General Robert Kennedy enlisted the cooperation of the Interstate Commerce Commission in desegregating the facilities. When black applicant James Meredith asserted his right to enroll at the University of Mississippi, the administration responded with protection and crisis mediation. Even more visibly, the president appointed a record number of blacks to high civil service positions.

Kennedy pressed executive action on behalf of civil rights with more vigor and greater effect than any of his predecessors. Still, civil rights enthusiasts were left with unfulfilled expectations and mounting suspicions. Ever mindful of the political imperatives of containing advocacy, the president was trying not only to serve the interests of blacks but also to manage those interests and acknowledge the interests of civil rights opponents as well. Indeed, there seemed to be a deceptive qualification in each display of principle. For example, the president's patronage policies brought blacks into positions of influence in government, but they also brought new segregationist federal judges to the South. The FBI provided support for the voter-registration drive, yet it also tapped the phone of civil rights activist Martin Luther King, Jr. The poll tax was eliminated with administration support, but the administration backed away from a contest over literacy tests. Kennedy liberalized the Civil Rights Commission, but he refused to endorse its controversial report recommending the withholding of federal funds from states that violated the Constitution. While he encouraged the desegregation of interstate transportation terminals, the president put off action on a key campaign pledge to promote the desegregation of housing by executive order. (When the housing order was finally issued, it adopted the narrowest possible application and was not made retroactive.) And although the administration ultimately saw to the integration of the University of Mississippi, the attorney general first tried to find some way to allow the racist governor of the state to save face.

Executive management allowed Kennedy to juggle contradictory expectations for two years. But as an exercise in forestalling a schism within the ranks, the administration's efforts to control advocacy and balance interests ultimately satisfied no one and offered no real hope of resolving the issue at hand. The weaknesses in the president's position became more and more apparent early in 1963 as civil rights leaders pressed ahead with their own timetable for action.

While civil rights leaders clearly needed the president's support, they steadfastly refused to compromise their demands or to relinquish de facto control over their movement to presidential management. The president and his brother became extremely agitated when movement leaders contended that the administration was not doing all that it could for blacks. Civil rights groups, in turn, were outraged at the implications that the movement represented an interest like any other and that claims of moral right could be pragmatically "balanced" against the power of racism and bigotry in a purely political calculus. Independent action had already blurred the line between contained advocacy and reactive accommodation in the administration's response to the movement. Continued independence and intensified action promised to limit still further the president's room to maneuver and to force him to shift his course from interest balancing to moral choice.

The first sign of a shift came on 28 February 1963. After a season of rising criticism of presidential tokenism, embarrassing civil rights advocacy by liberal Republicans in Congress, and portentous planning for spring demonstrations in the most racially sensitive parts of the South, the president recommended some mild civil rights measures to Congress. His message acknowledged that civil rights was indeed a moral issue and indicated that it could no longer be treated simply as another interest. But this shift was one of words more than action. Kennedy did not follow up his legislative request in any significant way.

Although civil rights agitation was clearly spilling over the channels of presidential containment, the prospect for passing civil rights legislation in Congress had improved little since the president had taken office. Kennedy's circumspect attitude on civil rights matters during the first two years of his administration had been only moderately successful in winning support from southern Democrats for his other social and economic measures. Several of the administration's most important successes—minimum-wage, housing, and area-redevelopment legislation—clearly indicated the significance of southern support. On the other hand, the president had already seen southern Democrats defect in droves to defeat his proposed Department of Urban Affairs, presumably because the first department head was to be black.[32] If Kennedy could no longer hope to contain the civil rights issue, he still faced the problem of containing the political damage that would inevitably come from spearheading legislative action.

Kennedy's approach to this intractable problem was to press legislation as an irresistible counsel of moderation. This meant holding back still longer, waiting for the extreme positions to manifest themselves more fully, and then offering real change as the only prudent course available. He did not have to wait long. A wave of spring civil rights demonstrations that began in Birmingham, Alabama, and extended throughout the South brought mass arrests and ugly displays of police brutality to the center of public attention. Capitalizing on the specter of social disintegration, the administration argued that a new legislative initiative was essential to the restoration of order and sought bipartisan support for it on this basis. Congressional Republicans were enlisted with the argument that the only way to get the protesters off the streets was by providing them with new legal remedies in the courts. Kennedy then seized an opportunity to isolate the radical Right. On the evening of the day that Governor George Wallace made his symbolic gesture in defiance of federal authority at the University of Alabama (physically barring the entrance of a prospective black student), the president gave a hastily prepared but impassioned television address on the need for new civil rights legislation.

In late June the administration sent its new legislative proposal to Congress. The bill went far beyond the mild measures offered in February. It contained significantly expanded voting-rights protections and for the first time called for federal protection to enforce school desegregation and to guarantee equal access to public facilities. But even with this full bow to liberal commitments, the struggle for containment continued. The administration tried to counter the zeal of urban Democrats by searching for compromise in order to hold a bipartisan coalition of civil rights support. When civil rights leaders planned a march on Washington in the midst of the legislative battle, the president tried without success to dissuade them.

Containing the zeal of the Left was the least of the president's problems. Kennedy had continually struggled to moderate his party's liberal commitments and thus avoid a rupture on the right. Now, as a landmark piece of civil rights legislation inched its way uncertainly through Congress, the president turned to face the dreaded party schism. His popularity had plummeted in the South. George Wallace was contemplating a national campaign to challenge liberal control of the Democratic Party, and an ugly white backlash in the North made the prospects for such a campaign brighter than ever. As the Republican Party itself prepared for a sharp move to the right under the banner of Barry Goldwater, civil rights leaders feared that the political logic of Democratic accommodation might once again rear its ugly head and that the president's determination might wane as the inevitable legislative showdown in the Senate heated up. Conservative reaction, party schism, and the need to hold a base in the South were foremost in the president's thinking as he embarked on his fateful trip to Texas in November 1963.

PIERCE AND CARTER: ESTABLISHING CREDIBILITY IN AN ENERVATED REGIME

For Polk and Kennedy, leadership was circumscribed by the dilemmas of interest management and the test of aggressive maintenance. With a hands-on assertion of executive authority, each determined to orchestrate the redemption of political promises, to control the course and pace of regime development, to hold the old coalition together as best they could through changing times. Their political strategies involved them in convoluted manipulations calculated to accommodate conflicting interests while upholding controversial commitments and staving off a schism within the ranks. Grounded in established power, leadership cast a dark cloud of duplicity over its greatest achievements.

Indeed, it would be difficult to choose the greater of these two performances. Polk was able to deliver on an extraordinary array of policy promises, but his success was premised on excluding the basic moral issue inherent in these policies from the arena of political debate. Kennedy delivered little in the way of outstanding policy, but he eventually came around to acknowledging the great moral choice he confronted, and he ultimately made a moral decision of immense national significance. Despite these manifest differences, Polk's and Kennedy's limited claims to greatness actually rest on similar responses to the dilemmas of interest management. These presidents began with a credible claim to executive control and a promise of respectful service to all the interests of the majority party. Within two years, however, the delicate interest balance they had been at pains to maintain began to unravel, and the effort to stave off coalition disaffection became a matter of limiting the effects of an open rupture. When interest management could no longer hold the old majority coalition together, these presidents took their stand with their party orthodoxies and moved to secure the greater part.

The irony in these performances is that while upholding their respective regime commitments and vindicating their party orthodoxies, Polk and Kennedy raised serious questions about the future terms of regime survival and left orthodoxy itself politically insecure. Because Polk's nationalism and Kennedy's liberalism ultimately came at the expense of the old majority coalitions, a new appeal to the political interests of the nation seemed imperative. In vindicating orthodoxy, Polk and Kennedy set in motion a pivotal turn toward sectarianism in regime development.

For the Jacksonian Democrats, the turn toward sectarianism grew out of a political defeat. The election of 1848 exposed the weaknesses of stalwart Jacksonian nationalism and spurred party managers to overcome the political damage wrought by sectional divisiveness. In 1850, Democratic votes secured passage of a bipartisan legislative package designed to smooth the disruptions that had rumbled out of the Polk administration.[33] This incongruous series of measures, collectively labeled the Compromise of 1850, repackaged moderation in a way that many hoped would isolate the extremes and lead to the creation of a new Union Party. But the dream of a Union Party failed to spark widespread interest, and Democratic managers grasped the sectarian alternative. Using the compromise as a point of departure, they set out to reassemble the disparate parts of their broken coalition. While supporting governmental policies that were designed to silence ideological conflict, they renewed a partnership in power with interests at the ideological extremes.[34]

For the New Deal regime, the turn came on the heels of a great electoral victory. Running against a Republican extremist, Lyndon Johnson swept the nation. But the disaffection stemming from the Kennedy administration was clearly visible: Southern Democrat Johnson lost five states in his own region to the Republican outlier. In 1965 and 1966, Johnson tried to forge a new consensus with policies that would redeem the nation's commitments in foreign policy while submerging political conflict in a vast expansion of interest services. His attempt to trump the New Deal with a Great Society without, at the same time, relinquishing the fight against communism to the hard Right left the liberal regime disoriented and overextended. His hopes for superseding the old Democratic Party with a "party for all Americans" did more to scatter political loyalties than to unify them.[35]

By the time of the next incarnation of majority-party government (1852 and 1976, respectively), the challenge of presidential leadership had shifted categorically once again. By 1852, the nationalism of Jackson had degenerated into a patchwork of suspect compromises sitting atop a seething sectional division. By 1976, the liberalism of Roosevelt had become a grab bag of special-interest services all too vulnerable to political charges of burdening a troubled economy with bureaucratic overhead. Expedience eclipsed enthusiasm in the bond between the regime and the nation. Supporters of orthodoxy were on the defensive. The energies that once came from advancing great national purposes had dissipated. A rule of myopic sects defied the very notion of governmental authority.

Expedience also eclipsed enthusiasm in the bond between the majority party and its president. Franklin Pierce and Jimmy Carter each took the term "dark horse" to new depths of obscurity. Each was a minor local figure, far removed from the centers of party strength and interest. Indeed, each hailed from the region of greatest erosion in majority-party support. Pierce, a former governor of New Hampshire, was called to head the Democratic ticket in 1852 after forty-eight convention ballots failed to yield a consensus on anyone who might have been expected to actually lead the party. His appeal within regular party circles (if it may be so called) lay first in his uniquely inoffensive availability, and second in his potential to bring northeastern Free Soil Democrats back to the standard they had so recently branded as proslavery. Carter, a former governor of Georgia, was chosen to head the Democratic ticket in 1976 after mounting a broadside assault on the national political establishment. To say that he appealed to party regulars would be to mistake the nature of his campaign and to exaggerate the coherence of the Democratic organization at that time. Still, Carter offered the Democrats a candidate untainted by two decades of divisive national politics and capable of bringing the South back to the party of liberalism.

The successful reassembling of broken coalitions left Pierce and Carter to ponder the peculiar challenge of leading an enervated regime. These presidents engaged the political system at a step removed from an assertion of managerial control over the interests with which they were affiliated. Because they were tenuously attached to a governmental establishment that itself appeared barren of any interest in addressing the most pressing problems of the day, their leadership turned on a question so narrow that it really is prerequisite to leadership—that of their own credibility. Despite determined efforts to establish credibility, neither Pierce nor Carter could reconcile his own awkward position in the old order with the awkward position of the old order in the nation at large. Caught between the incessant demands of regime interests and festering questions about the governing assumptions that had supported those interests in the past, neither could find secure ground on which to make a stand to limit the inevitable political fallout that comes from executive action. What began in expedience simply dissolved into irrelevance.

Franklin Pierce

In 1852, Franklin Pierce carried twenty-seven of the thirty-one states for a hefty 250 out of 296 electoral votes.[36] In the process, the Democratic Party strengthened its hold over both houses of Congress. But the Pierce landslide was more apparent than real, and the election was anything but a mandate for action. As a presidential candidate, Pierce had simply endorsed the past work of a bipartisan group of Senate moderates. His campaign was confined to a declaration of support for the Compromise of 1850 as the "final" solution to the slavery issue and a pledge to resist any further agitation on this, the issue that underlay all other national concerns. The Pierce campaign was nothing if not a dutiful bow to senatorial authority and moderate political opinion.

It is possible that the new president might have enhanced his position at the start of his term by taking a second bow to the center and placing the full largesse of his office at the disposal of the Senate moderates. But there were other aspects of the election that argued against this approach. Pierce had actually received less than 51 percent of the popular vote. He had won the presidency not because the moderate center of national opinion had rallied to his standard, but because the party managers working in the field had reassembled support at the political extremes. To these extremes, the Compromise of 1850 was a source of suspicion rather than satisfaction; it was a matter of reluctant acquiescence rather than loyal support.

Pierce was sensitive to the precariousness of his victory but thought the logic of his situation was fairly clear. He believed that the election of 1848 had demonstrated that it was not enough for the Democratic Party to stand with the moderates and let the extremes go their own way. As he saw it, the narrow victory of 1852 had amply demonstrated the electoral imperative of consolidating party loyalties at the extremes. Pierce refused to ignore these renewed displays of Democratic support—however reluctantly given—in the vague hope that the centrists of both parties might join him in a national coalition government. He decided to reach out to the old party coalition and to try to heal the wounds of 1848 once and for all.

In a bold bid for leadership, Pierce held himself aloof from the moderate Democratic senators and set out to rebuild the political machinery of Jacksonian government under presidential auspices. As the mastermind of a party restoration, he hoped to gain a position of respectability in his dealings with Congress, to take charge of national affairs, and ultimately—in 1856—to claim the mantle of Andrew Jackson. The basic problem with this plan for establishing a credible leadership posture was that no interest of any significance depended on the president's success. Pierce had exhausted his party's national strength and legitimacy simply by letting the various party leaders elect him. These leaders had no stake in following their own creation and no intention of suspending their mutual suspicions in order to enhance the president's position. Pierce quickly discovered that his claims to the office of Jackson had no political foundation and that by asserting his independence at the outset, he had robbed the alternative strategy—a bow to senatorial power—of any possible advantage.

As a political vision, Pierce's goal of resuscitating the old party machinery was ideologically and programmatically vacuous. It was conceived as a purely mechanical exercise in repairing and perfecting the core institutional apparatus of the regime and thereby restoring the regime's operational vitality. There was no reference to any of the substantive concerns that had caused the vitality of the party apparatus to dissipate in the first place. Those concerns were simply to be forgotten. Pierce recalled Polk's dictum of "equal and exact justice" for every portion of the party, but not the wide-ranging appeal to unfinished party business that had driven Polk's administration. He held up to the nation the vision of a perfect political machine purged of all political content.[37]

The rapid unraveling of the Pierce administration began with the president's initial offer to forget the Free Soil heresy of 1848 and provide all party factions in the North their due measure of presidential favor for support given in 1852. Much to the president's dismay, many of the New York Democrats who had remained loyal in 1848 refused to forgive the heretics and share the bounty. The New York party disintegrated at a touch, and the Whigs swept the state's elections in 1853.

Within months of his inauguration, Pierce's strategy for establishing leadership credibility was in a shambles. The president's key appointment to the collectorship of the Port of New York had yet to be confirmed by the Senate, and if the party leaders withheld their endorsement—a prospect that Pierce's early standoffishness and the New York electoral debacle made all too possible—the rebuke to the fledgling administration would be disastrous. But Pierce had not only placed himself at the mercy of the Senate, he had also placed the Senate at the mercy of the radical states' rights advocates of the South. This small but potent faction of southern senators felt shortchanged by the distribution of patronage in their own region and resolved to use the president's appeal for the restoration of Free Soilers as a basis for seeking their revenge. They characterized the distribution of rewards in the North as representing a heightened level of commitment to the Free Soil element, and they challenged their more moderate southern cohorts to extract an equal measure of new commitment for their region as well.

The radical southerners found their opportunity in Illinois senator Stephen Douglas's bill to organize the Nebraska Territory. Douglas pushed the Nebraska bill because it would open a transcontinental railroad route through the center of his own political base. His bill followed the orthodox party posture, a posture confirmed in the Compromise of 1850, by stipulating that the new territory would be organized without reference to slavery and that the people of the territory would decide the issue. Southerners who ostensibly had accepted this formula for settling new lands by electing Pierce in 1852 were offended by his northern political strategy in 1853 and felt compelled to raise the price of their support in 1854. They demanded that the Douglas bill include a repeal of the Missouri Compromise of 1820 and thus explicitly acknowledge that slavery could establish itself permanently in any part of the national domain. Douglas evidently convinced himself that the expected benefits of his Nebraska bill were worth the price extracted by the South. After all, it could be argued that the repeal would only articulate something already implicit in the squatter sovereignty doctrine. The change in the formal terms of sectional peace would be more symbolic than real. Whatever his rationale, Douglas accepted the repeal, and by dividing the Nebraska Territory in two (Nebraska and Kansas), he hinted that both sections might peacefully lay claim to part of the new land.

In January 1854, less than a year into Pierce's administration, Douglas led his southern collaborators to the White House to gain a presidential endorsement for the Kansas-Nebraska bill. With Douglas's railroad and the confirmation of Pierce's New York collector nominee hanging in the balance, the cornerstone of the Pierce presidency was placed on the line. Confronted with his very first legislative decision, the president was being told to disregard the one clear pledge he had made to the nation, the electoral pledge not to reopen the issue of slavery. If he chose to stand by this pledge now, he stood to lose all credibility within his party. If he endorsed the handiwork of the party leaders instead, he stood to lose all credibility in the nation at large. Pierce chose to stand with the party leaders. He convinced himself that the Kansas-Nebraska bill was faithful enough to the spirit of the Compromise of 1850 and offered to help Douglas convince the northern wing of the party. The collector of the Port of New York was confirmed.

Between March 1853 and January 1854, Pierce had tried and failed to prove himself to his party on his own terms; between January and May 1854, he struggled to prove himself to his party on the Senate's terms. The president threw all the resources of the administration behind passage of the Kansas-Nebraska bill in the House. Despite a Democratic majority of 159 to 76, he fought a no-win battle to discipline a party vote. Midway into the proceedings, 66 of the 90 northern Democrats stood in open revolt against this northern Democratic president. Even a no-holds-barred use of presidential patronage persuaded only 44 finally to give their assent. Instead of perfecting a political machine, Pierce found himself defying a political revolution. Presidential power helped secure passage of the bill, but only with the support of southern Whigs. Forty-two northern Democrats openly voted no. Not one northern Whig voted yes.[38]

During the winter of 1854, Pierce lost his claim to credibility in the nation at large. Stigmatized and exhausted by its efforts to muscle Douglas's bill through, the administration turned to reap northern revenge for the broken pledge of 1852. The Democrats lost every northern state except New Hampshire and California in the elections of 1854. A huge Democratic majority in the House was wiped out, and the curious new amalgamation of political forces that was preparing to take over harbored the makings of radical insurgency. Adding to the rebuke was the threat of civil war in the territories. Free Soil and slave factions rushed into Kansas and squared off in a contest for control. The president called for order, but the call was ignored.

Pierce never gave up hope that his party would turn to him. But once the North rejected his administration, the South had no more use for him, and the party Pierce had so desperately wanted to lead became increasingly anxious to get rid of him. Ironically, when faced at midterm with the unmitigated failure of his leadership and his political impotence, Pierce seemed to gain a sense of higher purpose for the first time. He threw his hat into the ring for a second term with a spirited defense of the Kansas-Nebraska Act and a biting indictment of the critics of the Missouri Compromise repeal. He appealed to the nation to reject treason in Kansas. He wrapped his party in the Constitution and cast its enemies in the role of uncompromising disunionists bent on civil war.[39]

This was the president's shining hour. Rejecting the specter of party illegitimacy and the stigma of his own irrelevance, standing firm with the establishment against the forces that would destroy it, Pierce pressed the case for his party upon the nation and, with it, his own case for party leadership. Still, there was no rally of political support. The party took up the "friends of the Constitution" sentiment, but it hastened to bury the memory of the man who had articulated it. Pierce's unceasing effort to prove his significance to those who had called him to power never bore fruit. The Democratic convention of 1856 was an "anybody but Pierce" affair.

Jimmy Carter

There is no better argument for Jimmy Carter's mugwumpish approach to political leadership than the example of Franklin Pierce's unmitigated failure. No sooner had Pierce identified his prospects for gaining credibility as a national leader with the revitalization of the old party machinery under presidential auspices than he fell victim to party interests so fractious that the desperate state of national affairs was all but ignored. Gripped by myopic sects, the party of Jackson proved itself bankrupt as a governing instrument. Its operators were no longer capable of even recognizing that they were toying with moral issues of explosive significance for the nation as a whole. Pierce's plan for claiming party leadership first and then taking charge of the nation dissolved with its initial action, pushing the president down a path as demoralizing for the nation as it was degrading to his office. The quest for credibility degenerated into saving face with the Senate over patronage appointments, toeing the line on explosive territorial legislation for the sake of Douglas's railroad, and forswearing a solemn pledge to the electorate.

It was Jimmy Carter's peculiar genius as a presidential candidate to treat his remoteness from his party and its institutional power centers as a distinctive asset rather than a conspicuous liability in his quest for a credible leadership posture. Carter called attention to moral degeneration in government and politics, made it his issue, and then compelled the political coalition that had built that government to indulge his criticisms of their handiwork. In a style reminiscent of Andrew Jackson, Carter identified himself with popular disillusionment with political insiders, entrenched special interests, and the corruption of manners that had consumed Washington. He let the liberals of the Democratic Party flounder in their own internal disarray until it became clear that liberalism could no longer take the political offensive on its own terms. Then, in the 1976 Florida primary, Carter pressed his southern advantage. The party either had to fall in line behind his campaign against the establishment or risk another confrontation with the still-greater heresies of George Wallace's latest presidential run.

The obvious problem in Carter's approach to the presidency was that while it claimed a high moral stance of detachment from the establishment, it also positioned itself within the established governing coalition. This awkward stance afforded Carter neither the regime outsider's freedom to oppose established interests nor the regime insider's freedom to promote them. The tension in Carter's campaign between an effort to reassemble the core constituencies of the traditional Democratic coalition and his promise to reform the governmental order that served it suggested the difficulties he would face establishing a credible leadership posture in office. Carter's narrow victory in the election magnified those difficulties by showing the regime's supporters in Congress to be a good deal more secure politically than their strange new affiliate in the executive mansion.

On what terms, then, did Carter propose to reconcile his outsider's appeal with his position within the old order? The answer of the campaign lay in Carter's preoccupation with problems of administrative form, procedure, and discipline rather than in the substantive content of the old order. It was not bureaucratic *programs,* Carter argued, but bureaucratic *inefficiency* that left the people estranged from their government. It was not the system per se that was at fault but the way it was being run. In the eyes of this late-regime Democrat, the stifling weight and moral decay of the federal government presented problems of technique and personnel rather than problems of substance.

Like Jackson's early efforts, Carter's reform program called for governmental reorganization, civil service reform, and fiscal retrenchment. But coming from an outsider who was nominally affiliated with the old order, it was hard to capitalize on the political force and ideological energy of this program for revitalization. What Jackson presented as an ideological indictment of the old order and a buttress for supporters newly arrived in power, Carter presented as institutional engineering plain and simple. Carter's Jackson-like appeal to the nation translated into an ideologically passionless program for reorganizing the old order without challenging any of its core concerns.[40]

It is in this respect that the shaky ground on which Carter staked his credibility as a leader begins to appear a good deal more like that claimed by Franklin Pierce than their different party postures would at first lead us to suppose. Both pinned their hopes on the perfectibility of machinery. Carter would do for the bureaucratic apparatus of the liberal regime what Pierce had intended to do for the patronage apparatus of the Jacksonian regime—repair the mechanical defects and realize a new level of operational proficiency. With their perfection of the apparatus, they hoped to save the old regime from its own self-destructive impulses and, at the same time, eliminate the need to make any substantive choices among interests. Political vitality was to be restored simply by making the engines of power run more efficiently.

Sharing this vision, Pierce and Carter also shared a problem of action. Neither could point to any interest of political significance that depended on his success in reorganization. Carter's plan for instilling a new level of bureaucratic discipline was not the stuff to stir the enthusiasm of established Democrats, and once the plan became concrete action, there was plenty for party interests to vehemently oppose. Carter's vision of institutional efficiency dissolved in a matter of weeks into institutional confrontation.

The Carter administration immediately engaged the nation in an elaborate display of symbolism that was designed to build a reservoir of popular faith in the president's intentions and confidence in his ability to change the tenor of government.[41] The economic difficulties the old regime faced in simply maintaining its programmatic commitments at current levels dampened whatever enthusiasm there was for reaching out to coalition interests with bold new programs in traditional Democratic style. The impulse to lead thus focused on an early redemption of the pledge to be different. With his "strategy of symbols," the president bypassed Congress and claimed authority in government as an extension of his personal credibility in the nation at large.

The first material test of this strategy came in February 1977 when Carter decided to cut nineteen local water projects from the 1978 budget. As mundane as this bid for leadership was, it placed the disjunction between the president's appeal to the nation and his political support in government in the starkest possible light. For the president, the water projects were a prime example of the wasteful and unnecessary expenditures inherent in the old way government did business. The cuts offered Carter a well-founded and much-needed opportunity to demonstrate to the nation how an outsider with no attachments to established routines could bring a thrifty discipline to government without really threatening any of its programmatic concerns. Congress—and, in particular, the Democratic leadership in the Senate—saw the matter quite differently. The president's gesture was received as an irresponsible and politically pretentious assault on the bread and butter of congressional careers. Its only real purpose was to enhance the president's public standing, yet its victims were those upon whom presidential success in government must ultimately depend. The Democratic leaders of the Senate pressed the confrontation. They reinstated the threatened water projects on a presidentially sponsored public works jobs bill. Carter threatened to stand his ground, and majority-party government floundered at the impasse.

As relations with the Democratic Congress grew tense, the president's bid for national leadership became even more dependent on public faith and confidence in his administration's integrity. By standing aloof from "politics as usual," the administration saddled itself with a standard of conduct that any would find difficult to sustain. A hint of shady dealing surfaced in the summer of 1977 around Bert Lance, Carter's director of the Office of Management and Budget, and by the fall, the symbolic supports of Carter's leadership were a shambles.

Like the water projects debacle, the Lance affair is remarkable for its substantive insignificance. The administration's "scandal" amounted to an investigation of financial indiscretions by one official before he took office. But the Carter administration was nothing if not the embodiment of a higher morality, and the budget director was the president's most important and trusted political appointee. The exposé of shady dealings on the part of the man whose hand was on the tiller of the bureaucratic machine not only indicted the administration on the very ground where it had asserted a distinctive purpose but also made a sham of the Democratic Senate's nomination-review process. Shorn of its pretensions to set a higher standard of conduct, the outsider status of the administration became a dubious asset. Attention now was directed to the apparent inability of the outsider to make the government work and address the nation's manifest problems.

Despite these first-year difficulties in establishing a credible leadership posture on his own terms, Carter still refused to abdicate to the party leaders. Indeed, as time went on, the intransigence of the nation's economic difficulties seemed to stiffen the president's resistance to social-policy enthusiasms he felt the nation could no longer afford to support. There was to be no alliance between Carter and Senator

Edward "Ted" Kennedy to recapitulate the Pierce-Douglas disaster. But what of the prospects for continued resistance? The core constituencies of the Democratic Party—blacks and organized labor in particular—found the president's program of governmental reorganization and fiscal retrenchment tangential to their concerns at best. They had little use for a Democratic president who seemed to govern like a Republican, and their disillusionment added to the dismay of the congressional leadership. Stalwart liberals admonished the president not to forsake the traditional interests but to rally them and, in Ted Kennedy's words, "sail against the wind."[42] If the shaky state of the economy made this message a perilous one for the president to embrace, his awkward political position made it an equally perilous one to ignore.

Following the Lance affair, Carter did attempt to dispel disillusionment with an appeal to the neoliberal theme of consumerism. He had identified himself with consumer issues during his campaign and opened the second year of his administration with a drive to establish a consumer-protection agency. The proposal could hardly be said to address the demands of the old Democratic constituencies, but it had enthusiastic backing from new consumer groups, a general appeal in the nation at large, and support from the Democratic leadership in Congress. Even more attractive was the fact that it posed little additional cost to the government. In consumer protection, Carter found all the makings of a great victory, one that would not only wash away the memory of the first year but also define his own brand of political leadership. But the legislation failed, and with it his prospects for leadership all but collapsed.

Indeed, this defeat underscored the paradox that plagued Carter's never-ending struggle for credibility. Opposition fueled by business interests turned the consumer-protection issue against the administration with devastating effect. Identifying governmental regulation of industry with the grim state of the national economy, business made Carter's neoliberalism appear symptomatic of the problem and counterproductive to any real solution.[43] Carter's own critique of undisciplined governmental expansion actually became the property of his critics, and the distinctions he had been at pains to draw between himself and the old liberal establishment became hopelessly blurred. While this most distant of Democratic presidents was alienating the liberal establishment by his neglect of its priorities, he was being inextricably linked to it by an insurgent conservative assault on the manifest failings of the New Deal liberal regime as a whole. Carter's liberalism-with-a-difference simply could not stand its ground in the sectarian controversies that racked the liberal order in the 1970s. It was as vulnerable to the conservatives for being more of the same as it was to the liberals for being different.

As tensions between the old-regime politics and new economic realities intensified, all sense of political definition was eclipsed. Notable administration victories—the Senate's ratification of a bitterly contested treaty with Panama, the endorsement of a version of the much-heralded administrative reorganization, the negotiation of an accord between Israel and Egypt—offered precious little upon which to vindicate the promise of a rehabilitation of the liberal order. Moreover, the president's mugwumpish resolve to find his own way through deepening crises increasingly came to be perceived as rootless floundering. His attempt to assert forceful leadership through a major cabinet shake-up in the summer of 1979 only added credence to the image of an administration out of control. His determination to support a policy of inducing recession to fight inflation shattered the political symbolism of decades past by saddling a Democratic administration with a counsel of austerity and sacrifice and passing to the Republicans the traditional Democratic promise of economic recovery and sustained prosperity.

The administration was aware of its failure to engage the political system in a meaningful way well before these momentous decisions. By early 1979, the president had turned introspective. It was readily apparent that his credibility had to be established anew and that it was imperative to identify the administration with some clear and compelling purpose. Carter's response to the eclipse of political definition was not, of course, a Pierce-like defense of the old order and its principles. It was, if anything, a sharpened attack on the old order and a renewed declaration of presidential political independence.

In what was to be his most dramatic public moment, Carter appeared in a nationally televised appeal to the people in July 1979 with a revised assessment of the crisis facing the nation.[44] This new bid for leadership credibility opened with a candid acknowledgment of widespread disillusionment with the administration and its "mixed success" with Congress. But the president detached himself from the "paralysis and stagnation and drift" that had marked his tenure. He issued a strong denunciation of the legislative process and reasserted his campaign image as an outsider continuing the people's fight against a degenerate politics. Attempting to restore the people's faith in themselves and to rally them to his cause, Carter all but declared the bankruptcy of the federal government as he found it. Thirty months in office only seemed to reveal to him how deeply rooted the government's incapacities were. It was the system itself, not simply its inefficiencies, that the president now placed in question.

Trying once again to identify his leadership with the alienation of the people from the government, Carter again exposed himself as the one with the most paralyzing case of estrangement. The awkward truth in this presidential homily lent credence to the regime's most vehement opponents by indicting the establishment controlled by the president's ostensible allies. On the face of it, Carter had come to embrace a leadership challenge of the greatest moment, but beneath the challenge lay the hopeless paradox of his political position. The Democratic Party tore itself apart in a revolt against him and the sentiments he articulated. It rejected his message, discredited his efforts, and then, in its most pathetic display of impotence, revealed to the nation that it had nothing more to offer. Carter finally may have seen the gravity of the problems he confronted, but as the people saw it, he was not part of the solution.

PRESIDENTIAL LEADERSHIP
IN POLITICAL TIME

Presidential leadership is often pictured as a contest to determine whether the incumbent has the stuff to make the system work. Timeless forces of political fragmentation and institutional intransigence threaten to frustrate the would-be leader at every turn. Success is reserved for the exceptional individual. It takes a person of rare political skill to control this system and manipulate the government in politically effective ways. It takes a person of rare character to give those manipulations constructive purpose and national resonance.

The problem is that this picture presents a rather one-sided view of the interaction between the president and the political system. It is highly sensitive to differences among individual incumbents, but it tends to obscure differences in the political situations in which they act. If presidential leadership is indeed something of a struggle between the individual and the system, it must be recognized that the system changes as well as the incumbent. The changing universe of political action is an oft-noted but seldom explored dimension of the leadership problem.

While changes in the political conditions and challenges of presidential leadership have been incessant, they have not been entirely erratic. A broad view of American political development reveals recurrent sequences of political change; leadership problems are reconfigured in typical ways along these sequences, and each configuration yields a corresponding pattern in presidential performance. Presidential history in this reading has been episodic rather than evolutionary, with leadership opportunities gradually dissipating after an initial upheaval in political control over government. Presidents intervene in—and their leadership is mediated by—the generation and degeneration of political orders. The clock at work in presidential leadership keeps political time.

The leaders who stand out at a glance—Washington, Jefferson, Jackson, Lincoln, and Roosevelt—are closer to each other in the political conditions of leadership than they are to any of their respective neighbors in historical time. In *political* time all were first. As the analysis of the Jacksonian and New Deal regimes has shown, successive incarnations of majority-party government produced progressively more-tenuous leadership situations. Presidents approached ever-more-perplexing problems of regime governance with ever-more-superficial political options; regime supporters approached ever-more-perplexing leadership choices with ever-less forbearance.

The regime builders rode into power on an upheaval in governmental control and tested their leadership in efforts to secure the political and institutional infrastructure for a new governing coalition. Their success created a new establishment, thrust their partisan successors into the position of regime managers, and posed the test of maintenance. These efforts, in turn, had consequences of their own, eventually saddling the regime with more controversial promises, more extensive commitments, and deeper divisions. Ultimately, visions of regime management dissolved into politically vacuous mechanical contrivances, and leadership was forestalled by the political difficulties of simply establishing presidential credibility.

Political time does not turn presidents into automatons or negate the substantive significance of the choices they make. As we have seen, Polk and Kennedy responded differently when their efforts at interest management began to unravel. Pierce and Carter made different choices as well, particularly as they became more deeply implicated in the crisis of political legitimacy engulfing their presidencies. The unique character of each president in these pairs is displayed all the more vividly by the different options they pursued in trying to address their shared political problem. But these differences only serve to underscore more basic points: Political time is a powerful determinant of leadership authority, of the range of options, of the prospects for success, and of the practical impact of the exercise of presidential power on the political system at large.

Situating presidents in political time provides a truer measure of the way our political system works and of how our leaders interact with it. Presidents within the same historical period grapple with radically different political challenges. Success in one instance constricts options in the next. Many of the political challenges periodically thrust upon our presidents are inherently intractable, and the dynamics of leadership are such that some presidents are thrust into political circumstances that are wholly untenable. Perhaps the most sobering observation of all is that the great performances—the ones that get held up as a standard for others to emulate—have been the most wrenching in their assault on the system. All told, the relationship between the presidency and the American political system is not at all a comforting one. It is always paradoxical and often perverse.

3. The Politics of Leadership at the End of the Twentieth Century

This essay brings the perspective of political time to bear on the last four leaders of the twentieth century: Jimmy Carter, Ronald Reagan, George H. W. Bush, and Bill Clinton. It is a version of an article first published in the wake of the presidential election of 2000 under the title "Continuity and Change in the Politics of Leadership."[1] For this collection, I have incorporated into the essay a four-cell typology of the political structures of presidential leadership that I had been developing in various other forums since 1986.[2] It was striking to me that the last four presidents of the twentieth century neatly filled out the cells of this typology. Notwithstanding all the changes that modern political development had carried in its train, the same structures of leadership we find recurrent in the nineteenth century were still clearly discernible at the end of the twentieth, and their corresponding political effects were still very much in evidence. At the same time, it hardly seemed plausible to me that the developments that had transformed American government and politics so profoundly over the course of the twentieth century would have no bearing at all on political prospects for presidential leadership. In reflecting the experiences of these four presidents back on earlier renditions of each type, I wanted to pay particular attention to how factors specific to politics in the late twentieth century might be altering the political expression of these familiar and recurrent forms. The case of George H. W. Bush, for example, brought to light new strains developing in the premises of one type—leadership as orthodox innovation. On the other hand, the case of Bill Clinton suggested how contemporary conditions might play to the advantage of another type, which I call preemptive leadership. Though the fundamentals had not changed, it was possible at this time to tease out of modern politics developments that seemed to point to a different future.

The final presidency of the twentieth century must surely rank among the strangest. The incumbent was steward of a nation that had emerged triumphant from its global struggle with communism; he was the leader of a superpower that was unchallenged in the world and enjoying a respite of relative peace. Moreover, under his tutelage the federal government seemed, for the first time in decades, to be putting its fiscal house in order, and the engines of prosperity had kicked into high gear. For all appearances, Bill Clinton led in the best of times. Yet his turned out to be one of the most volatile presidencies in memory.

Observers described the Clinton years as a national spectacle in which larger-than-life antagonists locked horns in mortal combat and slugged it out before a bemused, if largely passive, citizen audience.[3] The president provoked a series of stinging indictments and suffered a string of stunning reversals, but efforts to isolate him and finally to evict him from office never quite succeeded. A wily combatant in his own right, the president parried each assault and evaded the knockout blow. If, in the end, the stigma of the Clinton wars was sufficient to dispel the aura of national well-being and handicap the campaign of his designated successor, Clinton's reputation as the champion prizefighter of late-century politics seems secure. He was not a particularly resolute leader nor an especially productive one, but leadership in America seemed at this moment to have devolved into a struggle for survival, and, if nothing else, Clinton was a survivor.

What are we to make of this? What does the Clinton presidency tell us about the development of American government and politics at the close of the twentieth century? No doubt, part of the story lies in changes that had been in the works for many years, in new rules of the game whose implications for leadership were simply being drawn out more clearly in the Clinton years. Political scientists had long been pointing to such changes. Since the 1970s, they had been highlighting the emergence of a new universe of political and institutional action and calling attention to its effects on the politics of leadership.[4] Jimmy Carter, Ronald Reagan, George H. W. Bush, and Bill Clinton were all products of a primary system of candidate selection, which tended to vent the most passionate interests in the electorate and to turn politicians throughout the system into masters of their own political machinery. Once in the White House, these presidents took possession of an office bolstered by a host of new resources, one that now supported an extensive political operation devoted exclusively to promoting their ambitions, enhancing their personal control, and bringing their messages directly to the people. These developments, in turn, went hand in hand with others: a breakdown of consensus in social, economic, and foreign policy; a weakening of institutional ties that had previously bound elites together; a proliferation of political entrepreneurs in the other branches able to operate with considerable independence from secure positions of their own; a new style of investigative journalism and new communications technologies that lent themselves to exposé, confrontation, and scandalmongering; and last but not least, a concentration of interest pressures and their financial resources in professional organizations located at the seat of power.

It is not difficult to imagine how developments such as these might magnify conflicts at the center, enlist public opinion at large in the political battles framed there, and generate extraordinary political tumult even in extraordinarily good times.[5] Moreover, Clinton's survival under nearly constant siege suggests the sorts of leadership skills demanded by American government at this new stage in its historical evolution. His empathetic television persona, his "continual campaign," his preoccupation with managing public opinion, his protean political vision—all seem perfectly adapted to the "egocentric" politics of the day.[6] In the tactical challenges he faced, Clinton appeared as the most perfect expression to date of what scholars had dubbed the "postmodern" presidency; in the strategic resources he brought to bear on these challenges he seemed to epitomize what they had called the "personal" president.[7]

But for all that might be drawn from this portrait, the picture remains unsatisfying and incomplete. Neither the emergence of a new strategic environment for the exercise of power nor the display of new tactics probes very deeply into what politics was about during the Clinton years. Turning this president's experience in office into just another expression of secular changes ongoing within American politics side-steps direct consideration of his avowed political purposes, of the distinctive challenges his leadership posed to the political system at the moment he confronted it, of the commitments of ideology and interest at stake for others in his following through. The Clinton wars were about more than recent trends in the techniques of governing; they were also, primarily, about control of the national political agenda. The tumult of these years was less about Clinton's personal fate than about the fate of the political project he had presented to the nation.

There is no denying that Carter, Reagan, Bush, and Clinton shared a certain strategic environment for action that distinguished them as a group from presidents in earlier times. It is just as clear, however, that these presidents came into office with very different political projects in mind and that in acting on these ambitions each passed to his successor a leadership challenge very different from the one with which he himself had begun. Much of what Clinton's experience has to tell us about the development of American government and politics is bound up in the substantive character of the political contest that propelled this sequence of leadership efforts and in the framing of each effort in reaction to those that preceded it. To understand Clinton, we need to understand his position in this sequence, and that means taking stock of the different claims each of the presidents of the late twentieth century made on his own behalf, of the different kinds of political change each sought to bring about, and of the different ways in which the efforts of each to make good on those claims altered the political environment.

This essay proceeds with two goals in mind. The first is to distinguish the leadership challenges of the last four presidents of the twentieth century and the patterns of change associated with them. The relationship between the president and political system may change significantly from one incumbent to the next, but a broad look back at the history of leadership efforts indicates the basic range and structure of these relationships. It will be seen that each of last four presidents of the twentieth century exhibits a typical configuration of the politics of leadership and that these configurations have recurred in rough sequence across broad stretches of history. In each configuration a different kind of leadership challenge is posed, a different kind of political contest is set up, and a different kind of impact is registered. To draw out these dynamics, the analysis will identify each of the presidents of the late twentieth century with incumbents in similar circumstances in earlier periods and examine common features in the politics of leadership on display.

The second goal of the essay is to reckon with the fact that American government and politics were in many respects very different for these incumbents than for those in prior periods. Once the dynamics of leadership characteristic of each recurrent type configuration have been brought into view, each of the last four performances of the twentieth century will be reconsidered for aspects that appear to reflect the newly emergent strategic and tactical environment that these incumbents shared. The effect of contemporary conditions on the politics of leadership may actually be sharpened in this way, for it will not necessarily appear all of a piece. Rather, we should be able to point to effects that vary in relation to the substantive political ambitions in play.

RECURRENT STRUCTURES OF
POLITICAL AUTHORITY

Presidents change things, and they need to justify the changes they instigate. In one way or another, each incumbent must speak in a timely fashion to the state of the federal government's basic commitments of ideology and interest and suggest how proposed actions will bear on them. Presidents will face different challenges in doing so insofar as each confronts pressure on those commitments from late-breaking events, from the passage of time, and from the impact of prior leadership efforts.

These differences are reflected in what we observe retrospectively as the regime-based structure of American political history, the recurrent establishment and disintegration of relatively durable sets of commitments across broad swaths of time. The traditional demarcations distinguish the rise and decline of Federalist nationalism between 1789 and 1800, of Jeffersonian democracy between 1800 and 1828, of Jacksonian democracy between 1828 and 1860, of Republican nationalism between 1860 and 1932, and of New Deal liberalism between 1932 and 1980. Each regime can be identified with the empowerment of an insurgent political coalition whose reconstruction of basic governing commitments endured through various subsequent configurations of party power. Just as America's fragmented constitutional system has made sweeping political change rare and difficult to achieve, it has worked to perpetuate the ideological formulas and programmatic arrangements of the few insurgencies that have succeeded. To this extent at least, the regime structure of American political history may be considered one of the chief byproducts of the constitutional structure of American government. More specifically, it is a chief byproduct of the political impact of presidential leadership. Leadership efforts are themselves formative of these sequences; they shape and drive the observed patterns of political reconstruction and political decay.

The relevant mechanism is the struggle for leadership authority, the attempt of each incumbent to address and resolve the legitimation problem that lies at the heart of presidential action. As the exercise of presidential power is inherently disruptive of the status quo ante, and as the president is a state official pledged to "preserve, protect, and defend" values emblematic of the body politic, each bid for authority is, in effect, an effort to try to reconcile the order-shattering prospects of presidential action with the order-affirming purposes of the office. Authority takes the form of a timely set of warrants addressed to the circumstances that brought the president to power, warrants that promise to justify and sustain the exercise of presidential power. If these warrants are effective, they will secure the legitimacy of the changes they instigate and vindicate the president's leadership.

Warrants are not freely chosen. They are fashioned under constraints, and some prove sturdier than others. Most, in fact, fall short of the mark. In each case, however, the bid for authority structures the ensuing political contest as actors throughout the system react to the order-shattering effects and order-affirming pretensions of the president's actions. Though the failures lend a very different meaning to the result than do the successes, they are just as important for their effect in altering the distribution of advantages throughout the political system.

Typical political configurations of the legitimation problem are represented in Table 3.1. The structure of authority in presidential leadership is framed here by two basic considerations. First is whether the president comes to power politically affiliated with or opposed to the dominant ideological and programmatic commitments of the era. As presidential power is inherently disruptive of the status quo ante, we might expect that, other things being equal, affiliated leadership is going to be harder to sustain than opposition leadership. The other factor in play has to do with the state of the regime's commitments at the time of the president's rise to power. This admits of more nuance, but one questions is overriding: Are the dominant ideological and programmatic commitments of the era resilient, in the sense that they still hold out credible solutions to the problems of the day and constrain the alternatives put forth by regime opponents? Or have these commitments become vulnerable in the course of events to charges of bankruptcy, as might be indicated by newfound support for an insurgent opposition out to challenge their legitimacy directly? Affiliated leaders will be more authoritative in political action to the extent that received commitments are resilient, and opposition leaders will be more authoritative in political action to the extent that received commitments are vulnerable.

Table 3.1. Recurrent Structures of Political Authority

| | | Incumbent's Political Identity | |
		Affiliated	*Opposed*
Regime Commitments	*Vulnerable*	Politics of disjunction	Politics of reconstruction
	Resilient	Politics of articulation	Politics of preemption

The cells of Table 3.1 indicate the characteristic politics presidents make. As detailed below, the last four presidents of the twentieth century moved one after the other through the four cells of this typology. Carter, Reagan, Bush, and Clinton each came to power in a different relationship to the political system and with a distinctly configured leadership posture. Accordingly, each put forth a different claim to leadership authority, set up a different sort of political contest, and had a qualitatively different political effect. Together they drove an interactive sequence of political change. Comparing the efforts of these presidents with the efforts of presidents in similar circumstances in past political sequences confirms the typical effects emblematic of the circumstances and of the systemic impact of the presidential leadership on American politics overall. To the extent that we identify deviations or refinements in the late-century iterations of these types, we should be able to speak as well to how secular changes in American government over the course of the twentieth century seem to be affecting the politics presidents make.

JIMMY CARTER AND THE
POLITICS OF DISJUNCTION

In 1976, it was still possible to think of a Democratic presidential victory as a restoration of the normal state of affairs that had been ushered in by Franklin D. Roosevelt, the New Deal, and the establishment of a liberal political regime. Richard Nixon's 43 percent victory in 1968, George McGovern's anomalous candidacy in 1972, the strengthening in 1974 of the Democratic Party's long-unbroken control of Congress—all suggested that the recent Republican interregnum of Nixon and Gerald Ford might be, like Dwight D. Eisenhower's in the 1950s, a pause in preparation for the next leap forward on the liberal agenda. But as Jimmy Carter reassembled the national political alliance that had defined the government's basic commitments of ideology and interest since the New Deal, confidence in liberal solutions to the nation's problems was fast fading. Already torn by the political turmoil of the civil rights movement and the Vietnam War, the governing establishment of the liberal regime returned to power in 1977 with its basic assumptions exposed and vulnerable. The once solidly Democratic South was up for grabs, the Cold War foreign policy consensus was a shambles, and changes in the international economic environment had begun to raise questions about the basic governing formulas on which the expansion of liberal programs had been premised. Fiscal Keynesianism—the management of taxes and government expenditures to balance stable economic growth with maximum employment—strained under the multiple burdens of an energy crisis, stagflation, aggressive foreign economic competition, and defensive blue-collar unions. Radical conservatism, which had been but a minor annoyance when Barry Goldwater ran for president in 1964, was resurgent in 1976 and was better positioned than ever to peg liberal government itself as the source of the nation's burgeoning problems.

Carter was elected, at least in part, because he understood exactly what was at stake for liberal government in the 1970s. He had tempered his promise of another round of reforms on the order of Lyndon B. Johnson's Great Society with concerns about cost and efficiency, and he had made the repair and rehabilitation of the beleaguered apparatus of liberal government his priority. Against the increasingly strident attacks of Republicans, Carter insisted that "the problem is not that our program goals are unworthy or that our bureaucrats are unfit." Rather, he said, the problems of the day stemmed from "the inefficient operations" of the federal government.[8] Carter argued that the processes of government had over the years gotten so bogged down in red tape that liberal programs and priorities were no longer being implemented effectively. The president maintained that these problems were technical, not fundamental, that liberal government could be made to work again by reforming its methods of operation. His knowledge of the latest management and budgeting techniques would, he promised, breathe new life into the substantive commitments of the liberal order.[9]

Several things can be said about Carter's hapless struggle to make good on this promise. First, his was a subtle and complicated message. A candidate who recognizes serious problems in the governing establishment while promising continuity in basic governing commitments sets up a delicate balancing act. Throughout his campaign for the White House, Carter was hounded by the press to explain how he could solve the governmental problems he had identified without threatening basic liberal commitments. His standard reply was enigmatic: There were "no easy answers."

The second thing to be said is that no American president has been able to bring about a change of the sort Carter outlined. The historical record is full of examples of presidents who have offered and conscientiously tried to rehabilitate old and battered political establishments. In this regard, Carter's failure is of a piece with those of John Adams, John Quincy Adams, Franklin Pierce, James Buchanan, and Herbert Hoover. All were nominal affiliates of long-established political regimes, regimes that had in the course of events come to appear less as legitimate guides to new governing solutions and more as central parts of the governing problem. In each case, the basic commitments of ideology and interest with which the president was affiliated had become vulnerable to direct attack from the most radical segments of his opposition, and the president responded with a promise to fix things up.

These presidents employed very different leadership resources and acted in accordance with very different norms and techniques of governing. They brought to office assorted attributes of character and skill, and they pursued a variety of strategies in their relationships with Congress, their party, and the public. But none was able to make good on his purpose of orchestrating the repair and rehabilitation of a political establishment in trouble. Although the promise has been made repeatedly, and the American electorate has repeatedly responded to it, the task of breathing new life into an old order seems to be beyond the political capacities of the presidential office.

It is instructive that each of these presidents was singled out in his time and is still often treated today as a political incompetent, plain and simple. The problem, Americans like to tell themselves, is that these men lacked the political skills needed to make the presidency work and to succeed as a leader. Carter was accused of being too technocratic in his approach to policy and politics, of leading like an engineer, of having too narrow an interest in the details of government, of becoming consumed by the nation's problems and never getting on top of them. Some observers called him "Jimmy Hoover" to dramatize his incompetence and drive home his resemblance to the last engineer to make it to the White House.[10]

The Carter-Hoover comparison was used at the time to prove that engineers make bad politicians and to suggest that someone with more political savvy might have done a better job. But once it is recognized that technocratic appeals to repair and rehabilitate government tend to appear at similar junctures in the development of political regimes, the charges of personal incompetence lose much of their bite, and the political appeal of such leaders comes more clearly into focus. The technocratic approach to leadership authority—the tendency to submerge problems of substance in the mechanics and processes of government— is especially well suited to the election of a leader affiliated with a vulnerable regime. When Carter told the American people that there were "no easy answers" to the problems of the day and that they needed a leader who was smart enough to tackle those problems in all their complexity, he was offering the liberal establishment its best hope for survival and offering the rest of the nation an alternative to the more radical solution being promulgated by the regime's insurgent opponents. As a political appeal, Carter's "no easy answers" smoothed over long-simmering tensions within the ranks of the Democratic Party and held off, at least momentarily, the Republicans' broadside assault on the substantive commitments of the liberal regime. Late-regime affiliates rest their authority to lead on their technical competence precisely because the more basic commitments of ideology and interest with which their regimes are associated have already been thrown into question. Appeals of this sort seem destined to recur in American politics so long as political regimes linger beyond their ability to generate compelling substantive responses to the governing challenges of the day.

The problem is not that these presidents offered the wrong message for their times. The problem is that the best case for leadership in these circumstances is a weak one, the most tenuous of all for sustaining political authority in the American presidency. The pattern of failure has been remarkably similar for late-regime affiliates. Almost immediately, such presidents have found themselves caught between the stark demands of their supporters for regime maintenance and the blunt charges of regime bankruptcy coming from their opponents. The subtleties that made their promise of repair and rehabilitation attractive during the campaign appear quite different under the political pressures of governing. Hard choices need to be made, and fundamental questions about the legitimacy of the establishment press in on each. Holding the most equivocal of warrants for changing things, such presidents quickly lose control over the meaning of their own actions.

All told, affiliation with a vulnerable regime might serve as a working definition of the impossible leadership situation. Open recognition of serious problems within the establishment coupled with a promise of continuity leaves the incumbent little authority with which to sustain the inherently disruptive and highly politicizing effects of presidential action. Initiatives that reach out to allies, that appear to affirm or extend established commitments, are portrayed by opponents as symptoms of the nation's problems. Actions that confront allies or that appear to challenge substantive commitments alienate the natural base of support and leave the president politically isolated. Unable either to forthrightly repudiate or to forthrightly affirm their political inheritance, presidents tend by their actions to plunge the nation deep into a crisis of political legitimacy. Presidential control of the terms of national political debate tends to evaporate almost immediately in these circumstances and never recover. The systemic political effect is disjunctive. These leadership efforts sever the last connections between legitimacy and received commitments and ideology and interest and pass control over the meaning of the situation to the regime's most implacable opponents.

Whatever else the altered circumstances of late-twentieth-century politics may have done, they did not alter the basic dynamics of leadership in Carter's situation in any categorical sense. In its basic outlines, Carter's hapless struggle for credibility was both typical of late-regime affiliates and unique among recent presidents. Still, it is possible to point to certain aspects of Carter's performance that do speak to the effects of secular change in American government and politics, and though those aspects did not prove in any way decisive, their significance for the future is worth pondering. Most notable in this regard is that in comparison with other late-regime affiliates, Carter was far more the independent political entrepreneur. He had built his own political organization to contest and win the Democratic nomination in 1976, and in weathering the crises of his White House years, he was able to draw on extensive staff resources for governing and technical resources for communication that were directly under his control in the White House.

For a president caught in a legitimation crisis, any additional capacities for entrepreneurial maneuvering must be counted a clear plus, and President Carter used those capacities aggressively to try to jettison the baggage that was weighing him down, to distance himself from the faltering liberalism with which he was nominally affiliated. His effort in this regard far surpassed anything attempted by the late-regime affiliates who preceded him. A century and a half earlier, John Quincy Adams had found himself completely immobilized by the crisis of legitimacy that gripped his administration during its first year. Franklin Pierce had quickly lost control of his party and found himself subordinated to its most controversial elements. Herbert Hoover had felt compelled to wrap himself more tightly in Republican orthodoxy even as his own actions began to depart from it. Carter, however, responded to his increasingly precarious political position with ever-more-vigorous assertions of his political independence. A symbolic assault on the congressional pork barrel during his first year in office was followed up by the president's stunning midterm critique of the entire governing establishment.[11] Late in his term, Carter went so far as to reverse liberal priorities in fiscal and monetary policy, and then, when his renomination was challenged, he went on to trounce the liberal's standard bearer, Senator

Edward "Ted" Kennedy, in a bruising primary campaign. By using the newfound capacities of his office to defy the constraints imposed by his party's liberalism, Carter demonstrated the vastly expanded range of independent action now available to a late-regime affiliate. The Democratic Party of 1980 affirmed traditional liberal commitments in its national platform, but it nominated a candidate who had committed the nation to fiscal austerity and a defense buildup.

Even in the final moments of his reelection campaign, Carter was testing the newfound capacities of his office to alter his leadership prospects. His ability to focus all eyes on his efforts to engineer a release of American hostages held by Iran nearly succeeded in changing the subject entirely and, with that, the political standard by which he might be judged. But his capacity to go it alone still had clear limits. Though he had defeated Ted Kennedy for the nomination in 1980, he was compelled in the end to acknowledge his inability to stand apart. As he put it to the party faithful assembled at the Democratic convention, "Ted, your party needs you, and I need you."[12] In 1980, Carter accepted renomination by the party of liberalism, and he dutifully campaigned to save the legacy of Roosevelt, Kennedy, and Johnson from an insurgency that would overthrow it. His independence turned out to be a distinction without a difference.

RONALD REAGAN AND THE
POLITICS OF RECONSTRUCTION

Although the leadership position of late-regime affiliates has repeatedly proven untenable, the political effect of these presidents has nonetheless been profound. Time and again, presidents who have offered personal competence and technocratic repair as premises for action have, in effect, called attention to the government's paralysis and become the leading symbols of political collapse. In their fitful struggles for credibility, late-regime affiliates unwittingly deepen the sense of systemic political failure and confirm the insurgents' message that the old order is indeed beyond all hope. A politics of disjunction authorizes the regime's most implacable opponents to sweep away the dogmas of the past and apply an entirely new governing formula.

Notwithstanding his vigorous assertions of independence, Carter had just such an effect. His vulnerabilities placed his successor, Ronald Reagan, in the situation that has traditionally proven the most favorable to political mastery in the American presidency. As the leader of an insurgency that had been targeting the liberal regime's most basic commitments, candidate Reagan had little patience with Carter's efforts to distance himself from its failures. He deftly turned the president's difficulties into proof that something fundamental was wrong with liberal government. Reagan forthrightly declared the old order bankrupt and held its defenders directly responsible for a national crisis. As he put it to the Republican national convention in 1980, "The major issue in this campaign is the direct political, personal, and moral responsibility of the Democratic Party leadership—in the White House and in the Congress—for this unprecedented calamity which has befallen us."[13] Or as he declared in his first inaugural address, "In the present crisis, government is not the solution to our problems; government is the problem."[14] Taking direct aim at the governing regime that liberalism had created, Reagan proposed to cast aside the assumptions of the past and start afresh.

At the time, Reagan was called "The Great Communicator," and his magnetic political appeal was attributed to his long years of experience in radio, the movies, and television. The distinctive talents he had honed as a professional actor were described as perfectly suited to the new resources and leadership opportunities of contemporary American politics. But a striking fact of American history is that nearly all presidents who have come to power in situations like this have proven to be great communicators. The presidents who traditionally appear on lists of America's most effective political leaders—Thomas Jefferson, Andrew Jackson, Abraham Lincoln, and FDR—were, like Reagan, opposition leaders standing steadfast against already discredited political regimes. These were men of very different background, character, and political skill. They employed very different resources and acted in accordance with very different norms and techniques of governing. What they shared was a moment in a political sequence in which presidential authority is at its most compelling, a moment when opponents stand indicted in the court of public opinion and allies are not yet secure enough in their new positions of power to compete for authority. It is in such rare circumstances that the bluntly disruptive political effects of presidential action are most easily justified and sustained.

Considering these reconstructive presidents as a group suggests several things about the political capacities of the American presidency. First, it suggests that presidential mastery of American politics depends above all on the widespread perception of a systemic political collapse. Presidents have been able to fend off detractors and establish a new course only when they have been perceived as the only alternative to national ruin. The masters of presidential politics were all immediately preceded by a president like Carter—that is, by a late-regime affiliate who struggled fitfully with a complicated message of support for a faltering regime. John Adams and Thomas Jefferson, John Quincy Adams and Andrew Jackson, James Buchanan and Abraham Lincoln, Herbert Hoover and Franklin Roosevelt, Jimmy Carter and Ronald Reagan— these repeated historical pairings of apparent political paralysis in the presidency followed by the sudden appearance of a masterful politician suggest nothing so much as an intimate connection between manifest incapacity and towering success in presidential leadership.

Note further that the presidents who have most fully mastered the problems of sustaining leadership authority and orchestrating political change have been not only great communicators but also great repudiators. They have come to office promising to root out the entrenched remnants of the discredited past and to recapture some essential American values lost or squandered in the indulgences of the old order. Determined ideologues, they have successfully employed this repudiative leadership stance to identify their political ideas with the high duty of restoring the moral integrity of the nation. In this vein, Lincoln told the people that their "republican robe" had been "soiled and trailed in the dust" by a conspiracy of entrenched elites and that the people needed to "wash it white in the spirit, if not the blood, of the Revolution."[15] FDR spoke of chasing the "money changers" from their high seats of power and of restoring the "ancient truths" of American civilization.[16] Reagan posed a choice not between "left or right" but between "up or down"— "down through the welfare state to statism" or "up to the ultimate in individual freedom" as "conceived by our Founding Fathers."[17] Reaching back to emblematic values allegedly squandered in the indulgences of the old order, each was able to harness the disruptive, order-shattering effects of the exercise of presidential power to an order-affirming purpose and to engage in an extensive reconstruction of the terms and conditions of legitimate national government. No one understood better than Reagan the transformative political effect of bringing the order-shattering and order-affirming elements of presidential action into alignment. As he put it in his farewell address: "They called it the Reagan Revolution. Well, I'll accept that, but for me it always seemed more like the great rediscovery, a rediscovery of our values and our common sense."[18]

This historically contingent authority to repudiate forthrightly the legacy of the immediate past must be counted the most precious leadership resource an American president can have in orchestrating political change. It is the key to the resolution of the legitimation problem, to the establishment of a new common sense. Presidents without it are bound to find themselves at cross purposes; unable to justify their own disruptive effects, they get caught up in the many checkpoints of the American constitutional system and find their authority besieged. The authority to repudiate unleashes the inherent independence of the presidential office, facilitating an exercise of power that will remake the system in the incumbent's own image. It holds detractors at bay, sustains the most profound disruptions and transformations of the American polity, and, with its open-ended promise of establishing something categorically different, it even submerges differences among the president's own followers as to what that something different might be.

The singular success of this leadership stance indicates once again that the presidency is not a place for complicated messages. The presidency's political interventions are too blunt and unsettling for a subtle and nuanced claim of legitimacy; the only irresistible appeal has been the blunt, repudiative one. This is one of the more sobering observations to be drawn from American presidential history, especially so for those who believe that the problems facing American government in modern times are growing increasingly complicated. As we have seen in the case of the late-regime affiliates, presidential leadership is not very effective as a problem-solving instrument. That point is reinforced in the case of reconstructive leaders. Such incumbents have repeatedly demonstrated the potency of the repudiative posture in redefining the terms and conditions of legitimate national government, but they have not proved much more adept than other presidents at actually resolving the practical problems that brought them to office: Jefferson's leadership left the nation weaker than it had been before in the face of the international difficulties that brought him to power; Jackson rode to power on anxieties produced by the economic dislocations of 1819, but his alternative financial arrangements fueled a speculative binge of their own; Lincoln's leadership failed to end the forcible subjugation of blacks in the South; FDR's New Deal failed to pull the nation out of the Depression. What these leaders did that their predecessors could not was to reformulate the nation's political agenda, to galvanize support for the release of governmental power on new terms, and to move the nation past the old problems, eyeing a different set of possibilities altogether. After Reagan, liberalism would be saddled with the stigma of "tax and spend"; indeed, "liberal" became "the L word," its full expression banished from legitimate political discourse. In its place, a new conservative agenda was associated with fundamental American values, and future Democratic candidates were left to scramble for new terms of opposition.

Reagan rode to reelection in 1984 saying that he had reset the clock, that he had made it "morning again in America." By recasting the federal government around a new constellation of ideological and programmatic commitments, reconstructive leaders recapture the sense of beginning anew, of starting over in a durable new regime. But there is more involved in resetting the political clock in America than simply declaring it so. Reconstructive leaders are party builders; they use their authority to consolidate a coalition that will support the new agenda and dominate electoral politics. On this score, Reagan played true to form. Capitalizing on prior Republican efforts, he expanded the coalition to blue-collar workers, anchored it in a southern base, and tightened its organization overall.[19] In conjunction with party building, reconstructive leaders have also traditionally moved forcibly to dislodge from government the residual institutional supports for the priorities of the past. Jackson's repudiation of entrenched elites took institutional form in the destruction of the Second National Bank; Lincoln's repudiation of the "slave-power conspiracy" took institutional form in the destruction of slavery itself; and FDR's repudiation of "economic royalists" took institutional form as a frontal assault on the independence of the U.S. Supreme Court. Bank war, Civil War, Court battle—these blunt confrontations with the institutional infrastructure of the old order have been the reconstructive presidents' special province in regenerating and redirecting American politics. For the most part, the positive and constructive task of fleshing out the new regime has fallen to Congress. The American presidency has proven most effective politically as the battering ram, as a negative instrument for displacing entrenched governing elites, destroying the institutional arrangements that support them, and clearing the ground for something new.

It is on this count that Reagan's reconstruction takes on a decidedly postmodern character, for most of what he accomplished was conceptual. Just as surely as distinctive ambitions and achievements set Reagan apart from other recent incumbents, a comparison with earlier reconstructive presidencies highlights the limits of his success in forcibly dislodging the residual institutional infrastructure of the old order and clearing the ground of obstructions to his alternative. After delivering a stunning first-year jolt to old priorities in taxation, spending, and regulation, the Reagan administration found itself mired in an institutional standoff with a divided Congress. Most telling in this regard was the early rejection by the newly empowered Republican Senate of administration hints of an assault on the cornerstone of liberal government, Social Security. Unable to press the case against liberalism's core programmatic commitments to a decisive institutional breakthrough, the Reagan reconstruction was thrown back on more indirect means. In place of the frontal attack, the president opted for a long-term strangulation of activist government.

An exploding budget deficit became the chief transformative instrument. The deficit promised to reconstruct the regime gradually by restricting new federal initiatives, leaving old commitments to atrophy, and propelling a search in the states and private sector for alternative solutions to governing problems. By saddling later presidents with a monumental governing problem, the deficit condemned liberalism to die slowly of neglect.[20] And yet by projecting reconstruction over a longer term and by not decisively eliminating any of liberalism's governmental services or institutional supports, Reagan did less than other reconstructive leaders to foreclose alternatives and determine the precise shape of the new order.

Ironically, Reagan's reconstructive achievement seems to have been limited by some of the same features of contemporary American government that had bolstered Carter's more independent stance. In a governmental system in which both Congress and the presidency have come under the control of relatively autonomous political entrepreneurs, it is more difficult for a reconstructive leader to mobilize the requisite number of supporters behind a systemic political transformation. Insurgents quickly find themselves less dependent on one another than on the governmental services they can provide individually to their various constituencies. The greater autonomy of all political institutions and actors, the tighter integration of administrative services and supports into interest networks of social and economic power, and the consequent weakening of collective, cross-institutional resolve at the political center all constitute new encumbrances on presidentially led political reconstructions of American government. The result in Reagan's case was a reconstruction that, by historical standards, played out as more rhetorical than institutional, its comparatively shallow foundations laid on an ideological aversion to red ink.

GEORGE H. W. BUSH AND THE
POLITICS OF ARTICULATION

The American presidency has been least effective as an instrument for political leadership when the president is, like Jimmy Carter, saddled by a set of politically vulnerable governing commitments and compelled to try to rehabilitate the faltering regime that supports them. The American presidency has been most effective as an instrument for political leadership when the incumbent is, like Ronald Reagan, opposed to a set of politically vulnerable governing commitments and free to hammer away at the interests, institutions, and ideas that gave them vitality. Between these extremes lie two other leadership postures that, although they exhibit a bit more historical variation, have nonetheless framed distinctive political contests.

One is well represented by George H. W. Bush, a president who came to power affiliated with a set of governing commitments that he affirmed forthrightly as providing a clear and compelling guide to future action. "There's a general thrust and President Reagan set that," Bush said. "We're not coming in to correct the ills of the past. We're coming in to build on a proud record that has already been established."[21] Bush presented himself to the nation in 1988 as a faithful son of the Reagan Revolution, an orthodox innovator pledged to continue work on an agenda that was his rightful inheritance. When Democratic candidate Michael Dukakis spoke of the need for a change after eight years of Republican leadership, the Republican convention that nominated Bush responded with the refrain "We *are* the change," meaning that the Reagan Revolution was ongoing, that the Democrats' "change" was really a retreat back to the discredited past, and that the task at hand was to complete the transformation Reagan had set in motion.

On the face of it, the leadership claims of orthodox innovators seem as clear, simple, and compelling as those of the reconstructive leaders whose achievements they vow to elaborate. Unlike late-regime affiliates, the orthodox innovator's warrants for action are not complicated or strained by questions about the adequacy of the governing formulas with which they are associated. Instead, these presidents present themselves as stalwart regime boosters, preachers to the choir. They stand foursquare on their robust inheritance and make straightforward pledges to deliver on the regime's most basic commitments of ideology and interest.

There is some notable variation in what actually gets done in this regard. Orthodox innovators who have come to office directly on the heels of a reconstructive leader have had a hard time building on their inheritance. Like Bush, James Madison, Martin Van Buren, and Harry S. Truman, each stood directly in the shadow of a reconstructive leader and was plagued by the comparison. These presidents appeared as mere stand-ins for the reconstructive leader, surrogates meant to extend their reign. Actually, these presidents grappled with a very different leadership problem.[22] Practically speaking, they had to turn their predecessor's legacy into a workable system of government, and that more sober business had little of the blunt appeal of their predecessor's transformative charge.

By contrast, America's greatest orthodox innovators have entered office with a bit more distance from the reconstructive leader. James Monroe, James K. Polk, Theodore Roosevelt, and Lyndon Johnson all spurred great bursts of orthodox innovation and erected grand superstructures on the regime's foundations. All were stalwart regime boosters, but they drew on more fully developed senses of what a second round of orthodox innovations should look like. Headstrong with confidence in the shape of things to come, these presidents came closest to realizing the premise of orthodox innovation as a culmination of the work of the past and a demonstration of the enduring vitality of established commitments. The expectation of a second-round breakthrough of this sort has figured more prominently in the presidency of Bush's son, George W. Bush, where the way forward appeared clearer and where the Republican Party controlled, at least intermittently, both houses of Congress.

Notwithstanding these variations, orthodox innovators share a set of problems in sustaining leadership authority and effectively orchestrating political change, and the distinctive political contest they set up deepens our insight into the political capacities of the office they inhabit. Though these presidents bring to office strong warrants for action, the warrants are wholly affirmative. Expectations run high for robust action, but these presidents represent robust establishments, and that makes it hard for them to sustain the inevitable disruptions that accompany the exercise of power. The difficulty is inherent in the idea of orthodox innovation itself, of negotiating changes that will faithfully affirm prior commitments. Exactly what these commitments entail, how they are to be adapted to new conditions, what else they can accommodate—these are questions that belie the simplicity of the premise of following through. Different factions of the faithful will understand these matters differently. Faced with the dilemmas of interest management, these presidents are likely to find it easier and more politically attractive to vent the robust self-confidence of the regime in muscle flexing abroad, to look outward to "new frontiers" and "new world orders" that will realize the nation's Manifest Destiny.

With every action these presidents take, their particular views of what received commitments entail become more distinct. Orthodox innovators cannot escape the dilemma that their decisions enact but one version of the established faith, and as they draw their rendition out, they are likely to stir doubts and qualms among their own followers. Moreover, try as they might to explain themselves to the faithful—to convince the faithful that they are fair managers of their interests and consistent ministers of their creed—orthodox innovators have no good defense against charges from within their own ranks that they misinterpreted or mishandled their charge. When authority is wholly affirmative, disruption is debilitating. These presidents remain but one of several leaders of the regime, each of whom can speak with some authority about what its real commitments are. Ultimately, it is these "followers" who set the boundaries of appropriate regime policy, and they tend to do so at their president's expense. Typically, orthodox innovators find themselves increasingly isolated and ultimately discredited by their own ostensible allies.

George H. W. Bush's leadership was classic in this regard. In 1990, he led America to victory in a splendid little war in the Arabian Gulf and soared to unimaginable heights of political popularity in its wake, but his political authority was soon torn to shreds over a matter of political faith. Bush had launched his 1988 presidential campaign with an iron-clad profession of his orthodoxy in representing the faith: "Read my lips: No New Taxes."[23] After a year and a half of trying to work within that constraint, the president ultimately felt compelled to chart his own course toward fulfillment of the conservative agenda. He broke his pledge in order to gain from the Democratic Congress another objective of the Reagan Revolution, a strong deficit-reduction plan. Instantly, he was denounced by conservative Republicans for his betrayal of the tax pledge, and ultimately he was challenged for renomination on that ground by ultraconservative Pat Buchanan. Unlike Carter, Bush did not press his case for independence any further. To gain renomination, he felt compelled to negotiate a humiliating retreat. Awkwardly bowing to the resilience of his party's orthodoxy, he announced that he had come to agree with the Republican faithful that his most significant domestic achievement had been a mistake, and he pledged that he would, if re-elected, replace his entire economic management team. Not only did Bush repudiate his own administration's handiwork in order to salvage his credentials as an orthodox affiliate of the Reagan regime, but he also allowed the stalwarts who had denounced him to take control of the convention that was to renominate him. Commentators spoke at the time of his de facto abdication of leadership.[24]

Bush had indeed tied himself in a knot, but it was hardly a unique one. Of the twenty-four American presidents before him who had come to power affiliated with an established set of governing commitments, only four—James Madison, James Monroe, Ulysses S. Grant, and William McKinley—were reelected to second terms. The first two pre-dated the rise of organized opposition, and the third was reelected with much of his opposition under force of arms. Moreover, the seven presidents in American history who voluntarily withdrew from second-term bids were all orthodox innovators.[25] Whatever might be said about

Bush's lack of charisma or resolve, orthodox innovators like him have wielded a form of political authority that has always tended to dissolve in its own accomplishments. The difficulties Bush encountered in trying to sustain his leadership authority are emblematic of the problems inherent in trying to exercise the independent powers of the presidential office in ways consistent with an established orthodoxy.

Bush's leadership was perhaps most typical in its practical political effects. The characteristic political effect of orthodox innovation has been schismatic. The actions of these presidents spark debilitating debates among regime affiliates over the true meaning of the faith, and the more they get done, the deeper these factional disputes tend to cut. By the end of their elected terms, even the greatest of the orthodox innovators—Monroe, Polk, Theodore Roosevelt, and Lyndon Johnson—found that they had built a house of cards. In erecting an imposing policy monument to political orthodoxy, each fractured his political base and put regime supporters at odds with one another. Purely constructive warrants for political leadership—warrants that are intended to affirm and extend the received order—may accomplish a lot in terms of public policy, but in the process the establishments that support them tend to succumb, at least momentarily, to internal bickering and factional splintering.

Developments in American government and politics over the course of the twentieth century would seem only to exacerbate the leadership problems that attend orthodox innovation. The tension in this leadership stance comes, on the one hand, from the president's identification with an established and collective political project, and, on the other, from the president's constitutional independence and personal responsibility for uses of power. Institutional developments that expand the resources of the executive office, accentuate its independence, and highlight the personal aspects of leadership cannot but compound the problem of sustaining a collective political identity in the course of exercising presidential power.

Several particulars of Bush's efforts to pose as a faithful son of the Reagan Revolution illustrate the point quite plainly. First, back in 1980, when Bush was waging a campaign in the Republican primaries for the presidential nomination, he publicly denounced Reagan's ideas as "voodoo economics" and a "free lunch" approach. Having drawn himself out in this most modern way at the outset of the Reagan Revolution, it was hard for Bush to put forward the face of a stalwart later on. Even after eight years as Reagan's vice president, doubts about Bush's faith in the new orthodoxy ran deep among true believers, and his best efforts to dispel these doubts—like his ludicrously ironclad pledge on taxes at the 1988 Republican national convention—strained his identity to the point of caricature. Second, once in office Bush found himself hounded by the media for his reluctance to articulate his own vision for the nation. The "vision thing," as it became known, reflected the contemporary demand for a more personal form of leadership, the expectation that each president will stand for personally distinctive priorities and purposes. But the idea of a personal vision runs contrary to a leadership project whose chief warrants entail adherence to an established orthodoxy; it was an expectation that could not but put this president at cross-purposes. Finally, it is notable that the budget deal that proved so costly to Bush's political authority is widely viewed in retrospect as an exemplary act of responsible problem solving and effective national management. To the extent that the enhanced resources of the modern presidency have been designed with the values of responsible national management in view, they too are likely to compete with and complicate the task of leaders who come to power as stewards of a robust ideological movement.

The highly personalized politics of today presents a minefield of dangers for the orthodox innovator. Leaders saddled with a faltering political project, as Carter was, may appreciate the newfound autonomy; leaders who draw authority more directly from their attachment to the established orthodoxy will not. In the more party-centered politics of the nineteenth and early twentieth centuries, orthodox innovators were better able to submerge their own identities in the collective identities of the political organizations they presumed to represent. Not so today. The postmodern presidency seems to have turned this most common of leadership stances into something of an anachronism.

BILL CLINTON AND THE
POLITICS OF PREEMPTION

In his rise to power, it was clear that Bill Clinton was not, like Ronald Reagan, the great repudiator of a governing regime in collapse. Nor was he, like George H. W. Bush, the faithful son of an unfinished revolution. A Democrat seeking the presidency in the post-Reagan era, Clinton set out to preempt the Republican revolution by promising a "third way."

To talk about a third way in 1992 was to acknowledge the Democrats' three consecutive losses to liberal-bashing Republicans and to attempt to adjust the Democratic alternative to the new political standards that had been established by the Reagan Revolution. The idea was to dispel the aura of illegitimacy that had surrounded the Democratic Party's posture in national politics since the Carter debacle and to redefine the choices at hand so that the Republicans no longer posed the only alternative to discredited liberalism. The third way cast off a defense of liberalism and found its traction in opposition to the new orthodoxy of the day. The practical problems Clinton addressed were not those of a regime with which he was politically affiliated; they were those of a regime that had pushed his allies to the sidelines. His was a bid to get back in the game.

The candidate did not hesitate to peg the nation's woes to twelve years of Republican rule or to exploit divisions arising within the Republican coalition. He committed himself to a "new course" that would "put people first." He fixated on the challenge of economic management, decried the limits of the governing formulas offered by orthodox conservatives, and promised that he could do better. At the same time, however, Clinton acknowledged the Republicans' redefinition of the terms and conditions of legitimate national government. He candidly told his fellow Democrats what they could no longer ignore, that liberalism was no longer trusted as an ideology of national stewardship and that the path back to power lay in grappling candidly with that fact. To escape the burdens of older Democratic identities, Clinton rejected the liberal label outright, turned a cold shoulder to familiar icons of the Left, and openly proclaimed himself the leader of a "New Democratic Party."

By actively disassociating himself from the standard that Reagan had so effectively driven from the field, Clinton promised to take the discussion of political alternatives beyond what he called "the stale, safe, rhetoric of the past."[26] But where he was going was never entirely clear. His new party was, he said, "neither liberal nor conservative but both and different."[27] The third way insisted that government was not the root of all evil, but at the same time it granted that "the era of big government is over."[28] Deflecting the Reagan critique became a matter of splitting the difference: "Government is not the problem, and government is not the solution."[29]

This message was neither clear nor straightforward; it was at once pointedly critical and oddly equivocal. Candid in its acknowledgement of the Democrats' new status as an opposition and bold in its reformulation of their message, Clinton's leadership begged off the frontal assault. Throughout his presidency, he seemed to do better in playing against Republican stalwarts than in galvanizing his own ranks.[30] He promised to shake things up, but what that shake-up was meant to affirm was another matter. Opposition of this sort is meant to be more preemptive than reconstructive. The clarity of purpose achieved by the great repudiators gives way in such circumstances to leadership that is co-optive, ad hoc, and extremely difficult to pin down. What Clinton drew from his opposition stance was a good measure of independence in crafting and altering his political positions. Preemptive leaders have lots of room to maneuver around received commitments; they are far less beholden to their political allies than are orthodox innovators or late-regime affiliates, far less constrained by standards of doctrinal purity or by the expectation of acting in ways consistent with established party priorities. What sets preemptive leadership apart is just this: It is not designed to establish, uphold, or salvage any political orthodoxy; it is an unabashedly mongrel vision, an aggressive critique of the prevailing political categories and a bold bid to mix them up.

The third way finds its distinctive opportunities in the very schisms within the ranks of the dominant coalition that orthodox innovators are at such pains to assuage. By taking advantage of these schisms, preemptive leaders bid to appropriate much of the field of action carved out by those who built the regime. These presidents threaten to take over the regime's most attractive positions and to leave its defenders holding only its most extreme ones. The political contest is framed by such presidents' purposeful blurring of received political identities and by their opponents' stake in keeping those older identities intact. Whereas the risk to the defenders is that they will lose their hold on the national agenda, the leader seeking to establish a third way risks appearing unscrupulous, cynically manipulative, and wholly lacking in political principles.

Preemptive leaders can be found throughout American history. Woodrow Wilson and Richard Nixon are prime examples. Like Clinton, Wilson and Nixon first reached the presidency in a three-way race that featured a major schism within the dominant party, and each won with about 40 percent of the popular vote. But third-way appeals have been heard from other presidents as well: Zachary Taylor, the military hero of the Mexican-American War elected by the antiwar Whigs; Grover Cleveland, the first Democrat to win the presidency in the aftermath of Civil War Reconstruction; and Dwight Eisenhower, the first Republican to come to power after the New Deal reconstruction. Deep historical antecedents of this stance may be traced to John Tyler and Andrew Johnson—accidental presidents whose position on the national ticket reflected one party's effort to secure majority status by nominating a vice president from a disaffected faction of the other party. (Tyler, a disaffected Democrat, was elected vice president by the Whigs in 1840; Johnson, also a disaffected Democrat, was elected vice president by the Republicans in 1864.) All of these presidents rode to power with a party opposed to the previously established regime, but once in office each was at pains to assert his independence from the dominant ideological factions in both parties.

Hyphenated party labels, hybrid agendas, personal leadership, independent appeals—these are the emblems of the preemptive leadership stance. Taylor's "No Party" brand of Whiggery, Johnson's "War Democrats," Cleveland's "liberal reform Democracy," Wilson's "progressive Democracy," Eisenhower's "Modern" Republicans, the "new Nixon" who spoke for the "silent" or "new" majority, Clinton's "New Democrats"—all exemplify political stances carefully crafted to sidestep established conceptions of the nation's political alternatives and to reach out beyond the president's traditional party base toward some new and largely inchoate combination.

Note further that this preemptive style of opposition has traditionally proven quite effective at the polls. Except for Taylor, who died in the middle of his first term, all of the third-way presidents who were elected to the presidency were reelected to a second term. This record stands in stark contrast to that of the orthodox innovators, and it suggests the seriousness of the political threat that third-way appeals pose to ideologues of all stripes, especially to those still committed to completing the agenda of the most recent reconstruction in a more orthodox manner. At same time, these third-way alternatives have never proven durable. Preemptive leaders, with their "neo" parties and hybrid agendas, have characteristically held only a loose grip on the terms and conditions of national politics, and they have wielded only a temporary influence over its future course. This stance may support a personal success like Eisenhower's or a virtuoso performance like Wilson's, but it is just as likely to foment a constitutional test of wills culminating in a showdown over presidential authority, as it did for Tyler, Johnson, Wilson, Nixon, and Clinton. Historically, no third way has outlasted the president who articulated it. Such leadership efforts have been highly individualized, and the political contests they set up have tended to become radically personalized. Although preemptive presidents may be quite successful in pressing their advantages, their political alternatives have never cut very deep.

Setting Clinton's experience against that of other preemptive presidents recasts understanding of both the typical and extraordinary aspects of his leadership. Although the convulsive character of the Clinton administration stands out among recent presidencies, it fits a recurrent pattern of extraordinary volatility in pursuit of a third way. Preemptive leaders are the wild cards of presidential history. Lacking the repudiative authority to forge a new regime, their independence threatens the regime-based structure of politics itself. In exercising this independence, they taunt those whose values they cannot dismiss outright or blithely disregard; they are in fact out to hijack those values in the name of an amalgamated alternative that is all the more attractive for the fact that it is not all that different. It is the prospect of a wild card disrupting the game without forthrightly affirming anything fundamental that drives all other players to distraction.

Not surprisingly, preemptive politics tends to turn on questions of authenticity. While liberals worried that Clinton was capitulating to Republican priorities, conservatives were at pains to paint him as disingenuous in catering to values they claimed as their own. In fact, the accomplishments of the Clinton years—the deficit-reducing budget, the North American Free Trade Agreement (NAFTA), the crime bill, "ending welfare" as we knew it—all tended to play against type, that is, against the interests expressed (or presumed of) traditional liberal constituencies. The crime bill debate was emblematic: When Clinton offered to put a hundred thousand more cops on the street, Republicans charged a covert liberal conspiracy. They attacked the Clinton plan as a weak-kneed, "hug-a-thug" program wrapped in the veneer of police uniforms. By denying the authenticity of the initiative, they sought to tie the president back to the discredited ideology of his party.

Preemptive leaders are not insensitive to the authenticity issue. In fact, these leaders are prone to grasp for one "signature issue" that will show, in Cleveland's words, that their party still "stands for something." Cleveland and the tariff, Tyler and Texas, Wilson and the League of Nations, Clinton and health care—each of these initiatives pushed the president forward with one clear and attractive commitment that would define his cause and distinguish it from that of his opponents. In the end, however, each of these initiatives was turned against its sponsor, with devastating effect. Instead of isolating the president's opponents and rallying his supporters, the signature issue ended up isolating the president himself. The pattern is suggestive of the underlying resilience of the received political discourse and of the corresponding weakness at the heart of the third way. These leaders do best when they play at the margins of change and leave their core commitments ambiguous. A bid for a clear policy definition of the third way risks exposing the whole problem of definition that lies at its core. Clinton and Cleveland chose for their signature initiatives items that had long been on their party's agenda, and try as they might, neither could dissociate the policy from older, discredited formulas. Clinton drove himself to mystifying complexity in trying to insulate his health care initiative from the conservative repudiation of "big government" and "tax-and-spend" liberalism. Similarly, Cleveland attempted to repackage tariff reduction (an old Jacksonian standard) as a consumer issue essential to business expansion in a new age of capital shortages and government surpluses.[31] The problem, of course, was that these presidents were trying to have it both ways, to nod to traditional coalition priorities while deferring to the new sensibilities of the day. That ambiguity was all their opponents needed to make short work of their efforts at definition. In each case, the signature issue became an occasion for dispelling the aura of "freshness" around the president's cause and relabeling it as the same old thing.

All of this points to the ultimate expression of the authenticity issue: Political agitation over the preemptive leader's character and personal code of conduct. Affiliated leaders may be tarred apostates and even incompetents, but preemptive leaders tend to be judged moral degenerates, congenitally incapable of rising above nihilism and manipulation. Consider in this regard Wilson's reputation among his critics as "the reversible president" who was "constantly changing, moving another way, and turning about."[32] At issue in this characterization were Wilson's stunning shifts on several major public policy issues, his determination, especially after 1914, to find his own way through the Democratic-Progressive-Republican divisions of his day. Theodore Roosevelt, the nominal leader of the Progressives, and Henry Cabot Lodge, the stalwart Senate Republican, engaged in a relentless backstairs campaign of character assassination against Wilson. Taking direct aim at Wilson's legitimacy, they charged that he was a man wholly lacking in core commitments. Roosevelt mercilessly derided Wilson's "adroit, unscrupulous cunning, his pandering to those who love ease . . . his readiness to about-face, his timidity about any manly assertion of our rights, his lack of all conviction and willingness to follow every gust of opinion." Wilson's "soul," Roosevelt said, was "rotten through and through"; he had not "a thought for the welfare of the country; or for our honor; or for anything except his own mean personal advancement."[33] Lodge echoed these diatribes, charging that Wilson was "shifty," "furtive," and "sinister," a man whose "passionate absorption in himself and his own interests and ambitions" overshadowed all other considerations. As Lodge makes clear in his memoirs, Wilson went into the fateful fight over the League of Nations with a reputation for willful deceit, unbridled self-promotion, and false idealism already firmly fixed among his opponents.[34]

The centrality of character issues in preemptive politics helps account for some of the variation we observe in how this leadership stance has played out politically. The presidencies of Taylor and Eisenhower were conspicuous in shutting down the character issue. Both men presented a record of disinterested service to the nation that put character above politics and effectively submerged questions about murky ideological commitments and political objectives. Cleveland addressed the character issue head on. Dogged by charges of personal immorality during his rise to power, he turned the tables on his opponents by charging *them* with corruption and dedicating his administration to a higher morality. "Our stock in trade," he said, must be "absolute cleanliness."[35] When Clinton, like "Tricky Dick" Nixon and "Shifty Tom" Wilson before him, took his stand exclusively on the political attractiveness of his third way, his opponents labeled him "Slick Willy."

Shifty Tom, Tricky Dick, Slick Willy—all of these characterizations are of a type, a political type, not a personality type. They are characteristic of the personalization of politics that occurs when a president is aggressive in preempting established conceptions of the alternatives and trying to substitute a third way. Determined to sustain their contention that Clinton's "New Democratic Party" was really a ploy masking a rear-guard defense of liberalism, Republicans deftly transposed the question of ideology into a question of character. Character flaws offered an explanation for Clinton's repeated forays onto conservative ground; they accounted for his use of the presidency to mask his party's true leanings and to incorporate selectively his opponents' most attractive positions. As Clinton challenged the received definitions of liberal and conservative, of Democrat and Republican, and of Left, Right, and Center, opponents compiled evidence from his personal life to suggest that he really had no standards at all, that he was wholly lacking in principles. By showing Americans a man who never cared much for the truth, who had proven incapable of standing by any commitment, and who had no higher purpose than his own self-indulgence, Clinton's opponents found a way to preserve the truth that they wished to promote—namely, that Democrats remained a desperate party of discredited ideas and debased leadership while the Republicans remained the only legitimate exponents of national solutions.

The extraordinary convulsiveness and character-centeredness of preemptive leadership are revealed most strikingly in the prominent use of impeachment proceedings against third-way threats. Tyler, Johnson, Nixon, and Clinton are not a random set of presidents who happened to have blundered into impeachment crises. Rather, they were all third-way leaders who threatened received conceptions of the political alternatives by taking aim at established orthodoxies. Their shared leadership stance suggests the primacy of political, rather than strictly legal, factors at work in these proceedings. The impulse has been to dislodge the threat to a more orthodox rendition of the governmental agenda by personalizing the political challenge it poses and stigmatizing it as an assault on fundamental values. Just as reconstructive leaders reconstitute the political system on the basis of wholly new commitments, preemptive leaders drive defenders of the system to purge them as threats to the constitutional government itself.

But if Clinton's leadership unfolded in ways true to the preemptive type, it also set itself apart by its extraordinary buoyancy in weathering these storms. Other preemptive leaders were isolated and crushed in showdown confrontations with their adversaries. By contrast, Clinton repeatedly eluded his opponents' efforts to stigmatize and corner him. The "comeback kid" survived a devastating policy defeat on health care as well as a historic and seemingly decisive midterm loss of his party's control of Congress in 1994. He then went on to deftly turn the tables on his opponents in the government shutdown crisis of 1995–1996 and again in the impeachment crisis of 1998. Even in the wake of impeachment, he nearly broke the historic pattern among third-way leaders by coming very close to passing power to his own hand-picked successor, Vice President Al Gore.

In all this, Clinton doubtlessly reaped the benefits of a strong national economy. But he showed as well how nicely the conditions of contemporary government and politics resonate with the preemptive appeal. If the orthodox innovator has been rendered something of an anachronism in this new political environment, the preemptive leader seems right at home. In its basic political structure, preemptive leadership has always been ideologically detached, highly personalized, and aggressively independent. Now, with the rise of a governmental system characterized throughout by a more atomized, entrepreneurial style of politics—one in which the leading actors build personal organizations and construct their own networks of support—the preemptive president is no longer odd man out. Of all the different political ambitions brought to the presidency in recent years, it is this leadership stance that seems to fit most closely the opportunities and constraints emblematic of contemporary political affairs.

CONTINUITY AND CHANGE IN THE POLITICS OF LEADERSHIP

Presidential leadership at the end of the twentieth century was neither all of a piece nor categorically different from what it has been throughout American history. The century's last four presidents adopted very different leadership stances. Each took account of what had immediately preceded him and crafted his bid for leadership authority with an eye to the distinctive situation left to him by his predecessor. Facing different political challenges, each articulated a different premise for national political action, and each set up a different sort of political contest in the process. As different as they were from one another, however, these efforts were far from idiosyncratic. The recent sequence of presidents has, in all its variety, replayed leadership contests that have been part of American politics from the start. The political ambitions and practical effects of these presidents confirmed traditional patterns and, with them, the historical range and political boundaries of the American presidency as an instrument of national leadership.

Though political authority for presidential leadership shifts quite dramatically from one president to the next, basic structures of authority recur and drive similar sequences of political change. Each structure presents a different political configuration of the underlying problem of presidential agency, of trying to reconcile the disruptive order-shattering effects of the exercise of presidential power with an order-affirming purpose. By attending to the priority of authority in the politics of leadership, we can account for some of the most striking and bizarre features of late-century politics. One is the destruction of George H. W. Bush on a political litmus test despite his stunning and brilliant performance as commander in chief. The spectacle of the Clinton wars—of a government in the best of times tearing itself apart over the fate of the third way—is another.

The changes widely observed in the mode of governmental operations at the end of the twentieth century and commonly associated with shifts in the strategies and tactics of our leaders are not without significance for these recurrent patterns; they may be best understood as an overlay upon them. Rather than displacing the more familiar postures or the problems that attend them, these developments seem to be modifying the prospects of each in a particular way. The greater security of institutions and political actors throughout the system seems to encumber the ambitions of reconstructive leaders. At the same time, the expansive new resources made available to the presidency itself in anticipation of a more independent stewardship of national affairs seem to be rendering the struggles of orthodox innovators more anachronistic. The great beneficiary of postmodern conditions may turn out to be the preemptive leaders. The Clinton experience suggests that an office newly enhanced with resources for independent action may make it easier for these traditional wild cards to hold their own and control the most tumultuous game of all.

Or nearly control it. Election Day 2000 yielded nothing quite so definitive. The historic pattern prevailed again, though just barely. Eight years of Republican agitation aimed at stigmatizing the great preemptor as a deviant were not for naught. It set the stage for a return to "normalcy," and in George W. Bush the party found the perfect symbol of restoration. But if Clinton's preemption ultimately went the way of all others before it, it did not do so in a typical manner. Clinton's chosen successor won the popular vote, and although the Bush campaign promised to bring honor, decency, and comity back to Washington, it relied for its postelection victory on a heavy dose of Republican muscle at key sites.

Of all those caught in these crosscurrents, Al Gore may prove the signal historical figure. Eyeing the robust economy, most commentators assumed that the 2000 election was Gore's to lose, and they charged his defeat either to his shortcomings as a candidate or to the mistakes in his campaign. In particular, they took him to task for his determination to stand as "his own man" and detach himself from his intimate association with the Clinton administration. But due regard for the priority of authority in leadership might raise questions about these assumptions and conclusions. Gore may have been the candidate of continuity in good times, but in his bid to follow Clinton, political affiliation was not an unmitigated asset, and in its own way, the effort to go it alone paid homage to the Clinton model. Rather than allege that Gore squandered a clear advantage, commentators might have done well to mark a Gore victory as a wholly new prospect in presidential history. Never has a preemptive leader, not to say an impeached one, been able to pass power to a chosen successor. The Gore campaign was interesting precisely because it tried to go Clinton one better—to preempt the great preemptor—and nearly hit its mark.

4. Leadership by Definition: First-Term Reflections on George W. Bush's Political Stance

This essay, published in Perspectives on Politics *in December 2005, examines the political construction of George W. Bush's leadership stance.[1] The interplay of personal and strategic considerations in the construction of a leadership stance is addressed more directly here than in earlier iterations of the thesis, but historically speaking, the stance itself is unmistakable, and that is what the essay seeks to bring center stage. It examines Bush's rendition of what I have called leadership as "orthodox innovation," identifying the characteristic features of the type and discussing the potential significance of this example's more novel aspects. Special attention is paid to the odd inferences this president drew from the defining events of his tenure and to the way Bush's determination to construct his own reality forced key events to serve the political project that initially brought him to power. Trying to avoid what he perceived as the political mistakes of his father, Bush presented a more stalwart rendition of the type. But rather than eliminating the problems inherent in this stance, his leadership seemed merely to expose their flip side. Whereas the vision of the father appeared too weak for faithful followers, the vision of the son became blinding. In both instances, my suspicion that orthodox innovation has become an increasingly anachronistic premise for leadership in contemporary America appears to be confirmed.*

There are good reasons for caution in evaluating a sitting president. Major initiatives are pending; crucial choices are yet to be made; access is limited; events still hold sway. Arguably, however, certain qualities of leadership are best captured in the moment. One of these is the president's leadership posture, the terms of political engagement he projects to those he intends to move along his chosen course. The principal impression, often the only impression, Americans get of their president is conveyed through this stance. George W. Bush is a president known to evoke intense reactions from friends and foes alike. Perhaps it is because his leadership posture has been so striking, and the reactions to it so visceral, that little thought has been given to its claims and how they figure in a more general assessment of American national politics. This is the stuff that tends to get lost with time, the sort of thing that grandparents try to convey to grandchildren when conjuring their impressions of a president long gone. More often than not, they give up in frustration, saying "Ya' just had to be there."

One reason for the difficulty is that a president's leadership posture is closely related to several other qualities—personal character, governing style, "the times"—that, though ineffable in their own way, serve today as the common parlance of leadership studies. No doubt each has a part to play in determining the political stance a president adopts, and yet a discussion of any one of these factors, or all of them together, will quickly trail off in other directions. The problem is not that we do not have good specifications of these factors or that they do not generate insights of their own into the operations of the American presidency, but that a leadership posture does not readily reduce to them. Thus, when it comes to articulating what we experience most directly in our president, it seems advisable to work the other way around, to consider first what a leadership posture is—its own core attributes—and then circle back to see how related factors contribute to the example currently on display.

A few preliminary reflections may suffice to turn the tables. First, it seems reasonable to assume that a leadership posture is as much a strategic calculation of political advantage in the moment at hand as it is an expression of innate character. Character, as a feature of personality, may place limits on what a given actor can credibly convey on his own behalf, but within those limits, a president's leadership posture is likely to be purposefully constructed with an eye toward leveraging his appeal within the political situation in which he is called upon to act. The stance adopted is a framing device and, as such, far too important an asset to be projected unawares; no astute politician will pass up the opportunity to shape context to a chosen identity and to marginalize alternatives. Much the same can be said about governing style: Though managerial proclivities, organizational sensibilities, and interpersonal skills are likely to factor in the performance of any executive officer, one can imagine a president with impeccable managerial skills whose weak leadership posture succumbs quite quickly to events, and one can imagine a president whose political stance is so compelling as to limit the fallout from managerial blunders of major proportion. As for the role of "the times," a president's answer to the question "What time is it?" would seem to carry as much weight in the construction of his leadership posture as any objective conditions we might discern. To establish a common sense of the times, to say as Lincoln said, "where we are and whither we are tending," is the primal act of leadership and the most politically charged.[2]

All told, then, there does seem to be good reason to think about a president's leadership posture as something distinct. It is less about what is "given" in the situation—a personality and a set of circumstances—than about what is created in the attempt to seize the moment. Calling attention to this points in turn to what seems to be at the crux of the matter: A leadership posture is, first and foremost, an assertion of political authority. It projects a timely warrant for the exercise of power and bids for deference. The claim of timeliness is central to the legitimacy of what is to be done and of the actor who is to do it, and that means that certain contingencies come built in to a leader's political stance. Depending on the terms of the bid and how exactly they interact with ensuing events, a leadership posture may prove an enduring asset, generating resilience over the long haul, or it may become a liability, exposing serious vulnerabilities. For those on the receiving end, it is certain to become a standard of judgment. In looking for the significance of a leadership posture, we should proceed accordingly and examine the way it is constructed to lend meaning to the moment at hand and the way it structures, in turn, the ensuing political contest.

By conveying terms of engagement, a leadership posture will indicate to supporters and opponents alike the political ground to be occupied, the line and manner of the advance, and the larger stakes in play. At the very least, we should expect a president's political stance to be broadly attractive and to provide cover for the interests of powerful allies; in doing both, however, it is also likely to test the patience of allies, alerting them to the adjustments and accommodations they are being called upon to make on their leader's behalf. To the extent that a president's leadership posture provides assurance on substantive priorities, encourages mutual support, and solicits indulgence for tactical maneuvers, it will facilitate the orchestration of a concerted political change; to the extent that it sets expectations too high or delineates deviation too sharply, it is likely to prove the leader's undoing. Calling the president's credentials into question is, of course, what the opposition does instinctively. They will caricature his authority claims, expose his pretensions, find evidence of hypocrisy, advertise the shortfall, and generally try to take advantage of the weaknesses revealed. In all this, however, they labor under the stigma that the president, in his rise to power, has already cast upon them and in full view of his determination to seal his case against them in his exercise of power. The upshot is that, more often than not, opponents will use a president's own authority claims as a foil against which to reposition themselves; that is to say, by observing values that the president's political stance appears in the course of events to submerge or degrade, they will refashion their alternative around whatever it is that seems to be missing.

Leadership postures may be scrutinized accordingly: We can compare and contrast different political stances, we can draw out their particular authority claims and account for them within a strategic context, we can identify strengths and vulnerabilities and see how they manifest themselves in the play of events, and we can look to history to identify typical claims, patterned effects, and variations of potential significance.

This essay assays the leadership posture George W. Bush adopted during his first term and analyzes its authority claims as an intervention in the national political contest. The first part describes the man's political stance and calls attention to its more arresting features, the second considers the various factors that might account for this stance, and the third seeks to situate it in relation to others on a larger historical canvas. In the fourth part, I will reflect on how national politics arrayed itself around the president's leadership stance during his first term and what we saw of the strengths and vulnerabilities of its claims on authority. Finally, so far as history allows us to speak to the systemic political effects characteristic of leadership of this type, I will speculate a bit about the significance of what we see unfolding in the second term.

LEADERSHIP BY DEFINITION

I take my cues in describing this president's leadership posture from the autobiography written for his 2000 campaign, *A Charge to Keep*. In the first lines of the book's foreword, Bush states his precept for political leadership: He vows never to allow himself to be defined by others.[3] The cocky defiance of that opening salvo has long since become familiar. By the same token, one cannot read these lines now without being struck by how well they encapsulate the political stance of this presidency: George W. Bush leads by definition.

I do not mean to ignore the irony that Bush's vow introduced a book that was, in fact, put together by others. Principal responsibility for defining Bush, including the elevated value in this self-presentation of definition per se, lay with ghostwriter and campaign aide Karen Hughes. It is precisely because this genre of writing fuses the personal and the strategic in a collective political project—precisely because campaign biographies self-consciously fashion candidates' life stories to maximize their appeal to others—that *A Charge to Keep* can serve as a useful point of access to the leadership posture Bush assumed.[4] In this instance, it is also a rare point of access. Bush does not say a lot about himself, at least not on the record, nor is he known as an especially profound thinker. In reading further, however, it turns out that there was a lot more to the thinking about Bush's stance than his tart one-liner.

A Charge to Keep is a treatise on the value of definition in leadership. It not only organizes Bush's life story around a series of "defining moments" but also provides instruction on the high costs of losing definition.[5] Chapter by chapter, the reader discovers that definition has been the central preoccupation of this man's political education. In the early pages, for example, Bush recalls watching uneasily "as Bill Clinton's catchphrase—'It's the economy stupid'—became the defining message of the [1992] campaign, even though economists said, and the economy showed, that recovery was underway."[6] Toward the end of the book, that story is repeated: "During the 1988 campaign, my dad was able to define himself. In 1992, Bill Clinton and Ross Perot defined him, and he lost in a long and miserable year."[7] Just a few pages before, the greatness of Ronald Reagan—the man who had defeated his father for the Republican presidential nomination in 1980—is traced to his clear and simple assertion of purpose: "His presidency was a defining one."[8] Chapters earlier, we learn that "failure to define the mission" led to the ruin of Lyndon B. Johnson, and, more important for Bush and his generation, to years of self-doubt and drift in the nation at large.[9]

What is displayed on these pages is an acute sensitivity to the problem of political definition, a view of politics as a struggle for definition, an understanding of leadership as the assertion and control of definitions. This is a man who has pondered the fate of recent leaders and concluded that their success turned on their ability to define themselves and the others around them. This is a man who believes that definitions effectively asserted can create their own reality. The reader of *A Charge to Keep* knows exactly what kind of leader this man intends to be: the kind who lays out terms and upholds them against all comers. Bush's political persona as a man who acts with unflinching resolve on stated purposes follows directly: It was a stance adopted to make him, by definition, a leader.

To be sure, all leaders seek to define themselves one way or another. To set Bush apart as one who has led by definition is to observe something a bit different about him, something that is, to say the very least, an exaggeration of what most others offer. With Bush, definition was not just another attribute of leadership; it was the litmus test of leadership, the signal mark of the genuine article. There was more to it than the sense of a man who was clear about his terms; there was, in addition, the sense of a man who was wholly self-determined. The charge was not just to identify with a party or a set of national priorities; leadership by definition implied a willingness to stand fully committed up front, fully revealed in one's commitments, and ready to act. Some leaders protect options with subtlety; others acknowledge complexity and prescribe sober intelligence. There was no hedge in Bush's stance: "I don't do nuance."[10]

Definition conveys certainty and self-confidence. The posture is that of a man of set mind, one who knows what to do and leads by doing it. Strength is projected through conviction and validated through persistence.[11] Decision making is inner-directed, predictably contained by preformed standards;[12] the "hard work" lies just beyond that, in "getting the job done."[13] As Bush has shown, one who leads by definition need not be indifferent to the rough-and-tumble of the political process or stand above the gritty arts of political maneuver, but enlisting necessary compromises in service to the definition is part of the maneuvering. The president engaged in some serious horse-trading on commitments contained in his education proposal, but that process was itself projected back onto his leadership claims: The education compromise was repeatedly invoked as a marker attesting not only to the president's commitment to a cause long advocated but also to his fabled desire to achieve his goals through bipartisan cooperation. On another front, Bush had to capitulate outright to the creation of a Department of Homeland Security, but no sooner was he forced to relinquish his resistance to the establishment of the new department than he sought to claim credit for it as a symbol of his own commitments. Leadership by definition aims to absorb deviation and create in its place a sense of relentless movement forward toward fulfillment of the goal. Each tactical shift is a necessary regrouping in preparation for the next push down the prescribed path; the posture remains intact so long as others sense that the leader's inner compass is strong enough to safely guide the course. Leadership by definition becomes in this way a driving, multi-front offensive to affirm terms and call forth the corresponding reality.

It is tempting to interpret this as the leadership posture of a hard-line ideologue. There is certainly something of the ideologue in Bush, but that label misses as much as it clarifies,[14] and in so doing, it fails to capture either the challenge or the full potential of his political stance. Consider, for example, the ideological obfuscation of "compassionate conservatism," where a government-friendly social sensitivity, even entitlement, is endorsed alongside a clear reaffirmation of the orthodoxy of the Republican Party of our day. The leadership challenge of definition is not to achieve ideological precision; it is to deploy a political persona strong enough to bring order to timely, if seemingly incongruous, norms, to stabilize the political balance implicit in the program on the strength of the leader's personal convictions. Definition did not make Bush a purist; it made him a stalwart. What it projected was unwavering commitment to stated purposes, a leader completely identified with his cause and thoroughly devoted to its success.

Though a leader who stands fully exposed in his commitments may be tempting fate, the potential appeal of such a stance should be self-evident. So long as what is done affirms the leader's priorities and displays his avowed identity, authority can be claimed on the basis of authenticity, consistency, and dependability. A man guided in this way by his own internal compass cannot be diverted from the tasks at hand; he will not be distracted by momentary lapses or bumps in the road. He is resolute. Leadership by definition offers an escape from faithless cynicism and political disillusionment; it is refreshingly straight up. As Bush told the nation in accepting his nomination in 2004, "Even when we don't agree, at least you know what I believe and where I stand."[15] The authority he claimed transcended the attractiveness of the particular ambitions he articulated and even the practical effects of their implementation, for, as Vice President Dick Cheney never tired of reminding us, it radiated "clear vision and steady determination."[16]

Equally plain, however, are the potential vices of these virtues, the probable downsides of leading by definition. When conviction drives the political process, it places severe limits on open engagement with others in a search for solutions, and when real-world events are approached as so many opportunities to affirm one's priorities, considerations of prudence and plausibility are easily crowded out. As a discipline for leadership, definition will work to narrow options, to lock the leader into his chosen course, to inhibit serious readjustments to unexpected turns, and to heighten susceptibility to authority-indicting events. That is why definitions start to chase events; that is to say, to the extent that it becomes costly to alter commitments in the face of evolving circumstances, commitments will simply get reasserted with a new rationale. Herein lies the irony of a leadership stance that scorns pragmatism and flexibility as leadership traits of intrinsic value: These traits reappear as instrumental values in both claiming credit and in shifting justifications for prescribed actions. All this brings the stance to bear on questions of management, elevating the importance of imposing agreement, projecting consistency, and maintaining control while discounting disconfirming data and discrediting sources of dissent. By purging self-doubt and second-guessing, the posture ultimately leaves the leader to scorn accountability and simply insist on the integrity and essential correctness of decisions made.

Calling attention to the centrality of definition in Bush's leadership posture makes it easier to understand the strong visceral reactions that posture has evoked on all sides. It is not so much that the terms themselves were unattractive: Compassionate conservatism cast a wide net, and Bush's overtures to bipartisan cooperation were reassuring. But definition is a stern taskmaster; its set formula bids others either to fall in behind or get out of the way. That raises some interesting questions. Why not a more reserved, less aggressive posture? Why not maximize instead whatever freedom of action the office of the presidency affords? Why would a president want to lead by definition?

FACTORS IN PLAY

Let me begin with the usual suspects. First, maybe this is just the way it is for leaders today. Bush suggests as much himself when he relates the starkly divergent fates of recent incumbents to their ability to assert and control definitions. The implication is that the challenge of self-definition is becoming sharper for presidents, that it has been heightened in such as way as to trump other values leaders might reasonably want to project or options they would otherwise want to protect. This is a question about our times: Does Bush's leadership stance reflect something of a general nature happening in contemporary American politics; does his example point toward some newly emergent set of circumstances within which all leaders will now have to act?

It is a simple and timeless truth that politicians in a democratic society routinely vie to define one another, that from the moment they put themselves forward, their political identity is subject to challenge by competitors out to deny them authority. But a telling truth of our time is that the mass media and our advanced communication technologies have altered the definition game considerably. The media have magnified the importance of political images to power seekers, for they virtually guarantee that any image projected will be relentlessly, ruthlessly, and nationally scrutinized. The twenty-four/seven news broadcasts thrive on controversy and pretense; their continuous editorial commentary dwells on every quirk of personality and inconsistency in action. Add to this the new capabilities that political rivals have gained through the media—capabilities to spin the daily news with alternative messages, rapid responses, poll-sensitive insinuations, targeted appeals, and incendiary but deniable attacks by surrogates. In this new environment, contenders for power cannot assume anything about their political identities; prior acts and political affiliations no longer suffice in projecting a set of leadership credentials. Definition has become something that must be more carefully cultivated, more assiduously protected, more vigorously asserted, more continuously affirmed. All advantage now would seem to lie with the strategically generated political persona, an identity designed to project as much clarity and determination as possible while still holding up against incessant broadsides.

This explanation for Bush's leadership posture has a ring of truth. In these terms, his political stance may, in fact, be seen as a model for our times. The man's first instinct—never to allow himself to be defined by others—bespeaks a realist's cold commentary on the hyperpoliticized terrain on which American leaders now operate, and his demonstrated penchant for demolishing his opponent's chosen identity while asserting and protecting his own attests to some very timely political skills. Bush did not invent the techniques. Others have selected their audiences to celebrate the message of the day, ignored their critics, covered over their contradictions, strategically updated their explanations, tightly coordinated their rationales, and bludgeoned their challengers. But in showing how a leader can in these ways immunize himself from the risks of media exposure and turn it to his advantage, Bush has set a new standard. The edge gained by knowledge of this sort may be indicative of systemic factors now working to envelop presidential leadership in a world of appearance and political fabrication, but it is no less advantageous for that.

I do not, however, think we can rest content with this explanation. What it demands is mostly tactical talent; exactly how tactics construct a political persona, or what that persona will be, is largely conjecture. Let us assume that Bush has been more declarative and self-contained in his leadership posture and that the opponents he has defeated were more nuanced and open-ended; that does not mean that subtlety has been ruled out. Bush himself observed that Bill Clinton had been very effective in demolishing Bush senior's pretensions while projecting and protecting his own, but Clinton was no stalwart. On the contrary, a few years back we might have thought of the media age as one in which a slick, fuzzy, and emotive image had obviated the need for any conviction at all. There are, in addition, other explanations for Bush's leadership posture that cast serious doubt on its standing as an emblem of "our times" or a model for the future. At a second and more profound level, this president's determination to lead by definition speaks to questions about his political biography, and the calculations behind that political stance reflect factors as unique and intimate as his life story.

Again, I take my cues from the campaign tract. Bush may have found a lot in the experiences of recent presidents that bolstered his vow never to be defined by others, but he is equally clear that the origins of that vow lie elsewhere. It was, in his telling, a lesson learned from his *own* experience, an instinct ingrained in him by the personal battles he has been forced to fight. As the biography tells it, the definition imperative was initially brought home to Bush in his first political contest, a failed race for a Texas congressional seat in which a conservative Democrat (Kent Hance) successfully labeled him a boy of privilege, a scion of the old northeastern establishment, an outsider intruding into Texas politics, a carpetbagger. Ann Richards pursued the same line of personal attack against him in his gubernatorial campaign, dubbing him a lightweight cashing in on inherited privileges. Successfully overcoming those labels in that instance launched Bush's meteoric rise.

What is said candidly in the pages of Bush's autobiography about the origins of his thinking about leadership points to all the other biographical issues elevating definition to central importance in his political advance. It is hardly a stretch to think that Bush and his entourage were alert to the need to counter easy readings of his life's story. Long-standing caricatures had described the man as a shallow and irresponsible fellow, a lost soul without serious interests, driving ambitions, or special talents, a political operative devoid of curiosity about the substance of public policy, a risk taker who entered politics having succeeded at nothing else merely to test his skills at the game. If Bush comes across in the campaign biography as curiously earnest in asserting strength through definition—if his repeated invocation of the value of definition as a leadership trait seems to oversell it—it is, at least in part, because the presumptive alternative stalking his political career portrays him as an empty suit. The appeal to definition was strategically, if not psychologically, a response to this problem, an attempt to fill that void. Such a man advances his authority on the grounds of stated purposes and public displays of unwavering commitment because there is so little ground for a strong assertion of alternative claims. Assertions that otherwise might appear less risky—claims about prior acts of national service, personal history, policy expertise, or superior intellectual capacities— were all, in this case, relatively weak. It is often said that the image of the stalwart works for Bush as a mirror image of his former self, that it allows him to surpass the low expectations derived from his past. What remains implicit is the recognition that if not this definition—if not a stalwart—then nothing.

But I don't think we can stop here either. The unique features of Bush's life story might go a long way in explaining the elevated role of definition in his leadership posture, but we still do not know why a man adopting that posture rose to prominence so quickly at this particular juncture. The missing pieces of the story—the critical pieces in my view—are the larger political stakes at issue in Bush's ascendancy, the imminent prospects that made this brand of leadership ripe for these times. Such an accounting prompts a look beyond the common problems confronted by all recent presidents (the problem of image projection in the media age, for instance) and beyond the personal problems unique to this one individual (the problem of an underperforming past). It asks us to think about "the times" differently, to consider definition as a value that might change from one leader to the next as each reacts to previous leadership efforts and seeks to take account of their political effects. Setting Bush's posture in the sequence of recent leadership efforts—in what I have called "political time"[17]—locates his offer of definition amid stiffening political crosscurrents. It reminds us that his is a political stance crafted amid mounting uncertainties generated by the apostasy of his father, the attractions of Clinton's "third way," the failure of Newt Gingrich's hard line, and the yet-unfulfilled promises of the Reagan Revolution. Asserting definition and binding oneself to terms emerges here as a solution to the larger political problem at hand, the problem of reviving the conservative insurgency in the wake of some serious setbacks, maneuvering it back into the game, and finally securing its hold on power.

In the year 2000, the core constituency for a leader professing to stand foursquare on stated purposes, for a president seemingly prewired to enact a set program and hold steadfast to a governing formula, were frustrated conservatives who longed for fulfillment of the promises of the Reagan Revolution. These people, commonly referred to as "the base," had learned from experience to be suspicious of the Bush family's politics. They hardly needed reminding that "W's" father had renounced Reaganomics in the 1980 primary campaign or that he had betrayed them in 1990 by reneging on the defining commitment of his own presidential campaign, "No New Taxes." W's campaign biography provided the necessary assurances. It cast his political commitments as the homegrown product of Texas conservatism and, thus, as much farther removed than his father's politics from the influence of Connecticut moderation or the penchant of Washington insiders to temporize. Whereas Bush senior was never perceived as fully Texan, Bush junior reveals that he was never quite at home at Andover and Yale; whereas Bush senior never quite got the "vision thing," Bush junior confesses that he never really felt the attraction of political alternatives. What these pages define is a more reliable Bush, one less internally conflicted than the father, a leader who is by instinct at one with his party's prevailing orthodoxy. A Bush defined in this way might be trusted to follow through where his father had questioned, hesitated, and faltered; family loyalties aside, he is a professed true believer whose personal ambitions are fully consonant with the collective work of building a conservative regime, completing the unfinished business of the Reagan insurgency, and consolidating its hold on American government. The title of the campaign biography, *A Charge to Keep,* and the now-famous painting of the horseman with a package traversing difficult terrain that adorns its back cover capture perfectly Bush's chosen role as an agent of the faithful driven to fulfill the mission, ready to do his part, intent on delivering the goods.

But if Bush's appeal to definition countered party disaffection with his father's administration, it was no less pointed or strategically potent in countering the attractions of Clintonism. Leadership by definition broadened Bush's appeal by deftly exploiting the most serious concerns harbored about the character and politics of the Democratic incumbent in the White House. As a challenger running in unprecedented good times, Bush adopted a leadership posture that zeroed in on something, perhaps the only thing, conspicuously absent in Clinton's stewardship.

Implicitly recognizing Clinton's very different claims on authority, Bush inverted Clinton's political persona; he played off it and used its carica- tured form to advance his alternative. Leadership by definition fed on widespread suspicions that Clinton's commitments had no more staying power than the latest poll or focus group, that he was a leader without a compass and wholly lacking in personal integrity, that he was a wild- card, a flashy diversion of uncertain value. Definition offered relief from Clinton's moral confusion, feckless character, and official disgrace. (Had not this president just parsed the meaning of the word "is" for personal advantage?) A stalwart would be incapable of dishonoring the highest office of the land on the whims of the moment. It was this appeal to val- ues missing in Clinton's leadership that made Bush's projection of au- thenticity and resolve so timely, that took his challenge beyond the base to an otherwise happy and contented people.

The strategic potency of definition as a leadership stance worked prospectively for Bush as well as retrospectively. It targeted the difficul- ties Vice President Al Gore faced in upholding the Clinton legacy while convincing people that he was really, in his phrase, "[his] own man."[18] While Gore seemed agitated and compromised by his relationship to Clinton, Bush became the candidate who was "comfortable in his own skin," the one who had found "the inner peace of self-confidence" in his own political identity.[19] In the latest cycle, the drumbeat of charges that John Kerry "flip-flopped" and "waffled" played with the same devastat- ing effect against Bush's stalwart constancy and steely resolve.[20] All told, leadership by definition held in its sights the relative state of the two na- tional parties as instruments of governance. In particular, it identified and relentlessly exploited the central weakness of the Democratic Party in the post-Reagan era. Bush's political stance stigmatized all Demo- crats—Clinton, Gore, Kerry—as politicians unable or unwilling to *define* a clear alternative. Their appeal to nuance, complexity, and prag- matism became, by way of contrast to him, a self-indictment, a revela- tion of the fact that the real identity of their party no longer stood a robust test of political legitimacy. His claim to definition relegated *them* to obfuscation, to crass instrumentalism, to the overly intellectualized hand-wringing of "no easy answers," to leadership of a party without a soul.

Bush's leadership by definition advanced claims to authority that resonated in political time. This was not a triumph of strategy over personality, but the strategic deployment of a personality to establish authority, to impart meaning to a moment in history, and to structure its politics. But what kind of politics did it structure? On inspection, Bush's line of advance was as narrow and demanding as it was clear and full. The operational effect of a fully committed leader is to anticipate great acts of collective fulfillment; indeed, the boundaries of the stance may be marked by the high expectations that it generates for the production of a set product. In the balance of its promises, we find a set of pretensions that are, at least on their face, less forgiving than those of other recent incumbents.

Consider Ronald Reagan. Though Bush bid to lead the party of Reagan back to power, he constructed a very different moment in political time. Reagan was an opposition leader taking a radicalized insurgency to power for the first time. His leadership posture was defined by his forthright repudiation of liberal policy failure. Moreover, Reagan's aggressive stand against the long-dominant liberal regime, coming as it did at a time when events themselves seemed to be indicting the core commitments of that regime, worked at once to discredit received standards of legitimate national government and to elevate new standards, Reagan's own standards, in their place. For this, Reagan was hailed as "The Great Communicator," but like others who assumed similar stances at parallel moments in political time—Jefferson, Jackson, Lincoln, and FDR—Reagan was only loosely bound in practice by the new governing commitments he was calling forth. Between the rhetorical force of their repudiation of the old order and the legitimacy they are lending their still-inchoate alternative, these "reconstructive leaders" are able to sustain their political authority across a wide range of actions and outcomes.[21] Reagan himself found considerable flexibility in responding to problems as they arose, and he exercised that license with impunity.

Bill Clinton was, if anything, even more freewheeling. As the first Democrat to hold power in the post-Reagan era, Clinton took his stand against "stale thinking" of all kinds. His political advantage lay in casting aspersions on political identities as they had become fixed in his day and in exploiting the political attractions of an unabashedly mongrel third way. Like Woodrow ("Shifty Tom") Wilson and Richard ("Tricky Dick") Nixon, Bill ("Slick Willy") Clinton was a 40 percent victor who avoided forthright repudiations of the regime party even while he taunted it with the prospect of installing a hybrid. His "New" Democratic Party—"it's neither conservative nor liberal; it's both and it's different"[22]—was a vehicle all but designed to help him float free. Clinton's stance did not cut as deeply into received commitments of ideology and interest as Reagan's (his successful initiatives on the North American Free Trade Agreement [NAFTA], crime control, budget balancing, and welfare reform seemed far less a departure from received dispensation than a confirmation of it), but it did allow him to range the political spectrum seemingly indifferent to received conceptions of the political alternatives, and like Wilson and Nixon before him, he succeeded brilliantly so long as he avoided the efforts of his opponents to nail him down. To be sure, the elevated value of pragmatism and flexibility in his stance reflected the rather severe constraints imposed on a Democrat by the Republican repudiation of liberalism and its displacement by conservative values; nonetheless, Clinton's ability to maneuver around both the new conservative orthodoxy as well as the old liberal orthodoxy drove his opponents to distraction, and it opened the door to something quite different again.

George W. Bush had neither the repudiative authority of a Ronald Reagan nor the mongrel license of a Bill Clinton. In contrast to both of these, he crafted a political stance that renounced flexibility in the name of commitment. Among all the other things to be said about Bush's leadership posture, perhaps the most important is that his was the stance of a leader affiliated with the regime party, the party that has set the current parameters of American national government. Bush projected that party's self-confidence, its collective pretension to speak for the nation's basic commitments of ideology and interest, its impatient dismissal of alternative specifications, its insistence on the completion of its work. Leadership by definition tapped the transformative ambitions of a robust party establishment, promising to release its energy and to orchestrate the fulfillment of its ambitions.

And yet even as Bush's stance promised to tap this potential, it also laid down certain conditions for the follow-through. His vow never to allow himself to be defined by others did not exclude orthodox Republicans. Since there was no reclaiming the Reagan mantle, no completing the work without overcoming the interim setbacks caused by his father, by Clinton, and by Gingrich, Bush had to craft a leadership posture all his own. That stance would aggressively embellish the party orthodoxy even while it provided firm assurances of his fidelity to it. Whereas Clinton's challenge had been to avoid identification with any orthodoxy at all, the challenge in this case would be to avoid identification with Clintonesque triangulation, and therein lay the great promise of orchestration by a political stalwart.

Consider compassionate conservatism again in this light. It is hardly indifferent to the Reagan orthodoxy: On matters of taxation, defense, regulation, and family values the stand is ironclad. Far from a bid to float free, this was a promise of leadership firmly tied to the base. Just as clearly, however, compassionate conservatism was more than a simple return to orthodoxy. Among other things, Bush has added federally supported education programs, prescription-drug entitlements, faith-based welfare provisions, a stepped-up battle against AIDS, a seemingly progressive initiative to "save" Social Security, and a moderate proposal for immigration reform. Presumably, orthodoxy was to be the foundation upon which this expansive superstructure would be raised. In this, Bush did not offer a different order of things than Reagan had promised;

rather, he has suggested the possibility of a higher ordering of those same values. He set out to show that orthodoxy need not exclude timely new attractions, that it can craft its own solutions to any problem that might arise. This is not "Reagan Lite" (as was said of Clinton) or "Reagan's Revenge" (as was said of Gingrich) but "Reagan Plus." For better or worse, the balance of power in Bush's America would turn on these distinctions, and they were underwritten largely by his credentials as a stalwart. Only a stalwart would be trusted with so delicate a balancing act, the act of securing orthodoxy through innovation.

As with Reagan and Clinton, Bush's leadership posture finds clear echoes in America's past. This one recurs in political time too; in its strategic elements and its construction of national politics, Bush's stance was of a piece with several others. The broader significance of Bush's political leadership is, I think, best assessed by thinking about him in this way, as the latest in a long line of "orthodox innovators" in American presidential history.[23] Coming to power at parallel junctures in the development of prior political regimes, America's orthodox innovators have all tackled the same basic leadership challenge. Fully committed up front, these leaders plunge headlong toward the promised land. They need to deliver the goods to the faithful while putting a fresh face on the faith, to redeem old promises while responding to the demand for something new, to uphold consistency and integrity while changing the game plan for a new day. Accordingly, all efforts at orthodox innovation beg the same basic question: Will the foundations hold?

There is no denying that Bush gave this leadership stance his own special twist. Presidents rise to these occasions by their own lights. I would simply note that of all the leadership projects that recur in presidential history, orthodox innovation is—for reasons internal to the project itself—the one that finds the leader most insistent on setting terms up front and gaining collective agreement on definitions. It is the one that ties the president most closely to mutual consent among the faithful, to preprogrammed understandings, and to set formulas for action. When all is said and done, "orthodox innovation" remains an oxymoron. These leaders are left to reconcile within their own political personas—through their own terms and definitions, if you will—a leadership charge at odds with itself. Between the promise of securing the foundations and the promise of raising an attractive new superstructure, the orthodox innovator risks becoming swamped by charges of betrayal from within his own church and plunging his faithful followers headlong into sectarian warfare.

STRENGTHS AND VULNERABILITIES

Looking back over the course of American political history, it is notable that the most formidable of America's orthodox innovators have been, like George W. Bush, second-generation affiliates. It may be recalled that Bush senior also spoke of compassionate conservatism.[24] But coming directly on the heels of Reagan's reconstructive rhetoric, that slogan sounded like a veiled critique of the new orthodoxy, and it struck many at that time as a failure of vision. It takes a while, perhaps even an interim defeat, before the promise of innovation appears to bolster rather than threaten the cause and the attractions of a second-order synthesis become clear.

The second-generation affiliates have grown up with the new dispensation, and this is reflected in their stance as true believers poised to make the great leap forward on the received faith. Think of James Polk, "Young Hickory," who fused the old Jacksonian orthodoxy to a heady program of Manifest Destiny; of Theodore Roosevelt, the boy who watched Lincoln's funeral procession from his grandfather's balcony and determined to redeem the "bloody shirt" of the Civil War in a "New Nationalism"; of Lyndon Johnson, the youthful New Dealer who referred to FDR as his "daddy" and promised to advance midcentury liberalism to the Great Society. These were all muscle-flexing presidents, impatient to complete the work of their predecessors, to vindicate the vitality and vision of the governing party. Each brought to bear on events at home and abroad the same determination to follow through and get the job done. W's can-do verve and bravado captured the spirit of these faithful sons, leaders who knew exactly where they wanted to lead because they knew precisely where they came from.

Against this comparison set, we may begin to appreciate just what a remarkable exemplar of the type George W. Bush has been. Most arresting in this regard were his responses to the extraordinary events that punctuated his first term. Orthodox innovators begin with a full plate, with bold claims and high expectations, and with a delicate balance among commitments old and new. Their characteristic management style is to insist on tight control from the center, for the only way to hold all their commitments together long enough to deliver sufficiently on each is to closely orchestrate the action from above. Happenstance is surely a source of high anxiety for these presidents, for, as everyone knows, nothing derails intricate plans like unexpected events.

The contested election of 2000 and the terrorist attacks of 9/11 were events of this sort. We call them "defining moments," and for a president not so thoroughly defined up front, they might have been just that. For Bush, however, the matter was more complicated. Neither of these events resonated very well with the promise of completing the work of the past. Each was an unexpected national trauma so far afield from either party's story line as to jolt national politics free of familiar modes of thinking and prewired lines of action. Few leaders are given an opportunity to set aside the baggage of commitments and expectations that they carry into office and define the situation anew; this president was presented with two such opportunities. What is remarkable is that in both instances he refused to allow extraordinary events to interfere with prior commitments and expectations; he simply repaired to the pending agenda, and followed through on old business. Never has a leadership posture so at odds with the contingencies thrust upon it been employed so aggressively in the cause of creating its own reality. Events would not define George W. Bush; he would define them.

Consider the paradoxical character of the play of these two events on Bush's leadership posture: The first seemed to deal him a weak hand, but it exposed latent strengths in his leadership stance; the second seemed to strengthen his hand, but it exposed latent weaknesses. In the first instance—that presented by the contested election—Bush refused the invitation to discard the preformed response and showed thereby where the potency of orthodox innovation really lay. Fulfilling the terms of a set definition turned out to be an unexpectedly effective way of creating something out of nothing. The electorate had not only failed to provide a mandate; it had indicated a marginal preference for Bush's opponent and ushered in a constitutional crisis over the succession. And yet in the face of calls for the creation of a government of national unity, Bush assembled a team committed to his stated program and methodically went about the business of enacting it. More remarkable still, his no-holds-barred offensive failed to provoke his seemingly powerful and testy opposition to an immediate and crushing reaction.

In part Bush was demonstrating just how little the Clinton interregnum had done to define a compelling alternative around which the Democrats could rally the nation and resist. Even more than John Kennedy, whose call to "get the country moving again" was meant to stigmatize the Eisenhower years as a holding action in the larger narrative of liberalism's advance, Bush opened by exposing the hollow core at the heart of the opposition's electoral clout. Challenging the president on policy details, Democrats tacitly accepted the terms of his leadership. They removed school vouchers from the president's education bill but left him the dual champion of performance testing and structural revisions of the tax code.

To those who did complain in those early months that Bush was acting to transform the polity in decisive ways without any political authority to do so, there was a tart reply: "He's doing exactly what he said he would do."[25] The mandate was lodged in the definition. The man had laid out his terms, and he was acting in a way that was consistent and true to them. The full significance of those early months lay in showing that the authority of an orthodox innovator does not rest solely on vote margins, that his is the authority of the nation's only clear political standard. Election returns notwithstanding, Bush had something to stand on, and it is hard to resist something with nothing.

But if repairing to previous commitments proved a source of politi-

cal strength at a time when the president held a relatively weak hand, repairing to previous commitments in the aftermath of 9/11—when the
president found himself suddenly thrust into an unassailable leadership
position—exposed some serious political vulnerabilities. The terrorist
attacks all but transformed the foundations of this president's political
authority, pushing it beyond programmatic and partisan concerns and
lodging it on the firmest ground of all: the constitutional responsibility
of the president to preserve, protect, and defend. This was not only a
rare moment of national unity; it was, to all appearances, a Lincolnian
moment, one in which all Americans were being called upon to "disen-
thrall" themselves, to discard "the dogmas of the quiet past," to "think
anew and act anew."[26] In the days immediately following the attacks, it
was widely proclaimed that "everything had changed," that the people
and their leaders would now have to move in "an entirely different
world."[27] Administration intimates indicated that the president had recalibrated his resolve accordingly, that George W. Bush was ready to act
on a wholly new understanding of what his presidency was all about.[28]

Resolve was, of course, a leadership value that Bush had been carefully cultivating all along. It was the purity of the occasion now calling
for its display that presented the difficulties. The rub came just after the
administration's initial foray into Afghanistan, when the president
equated the war on terror with a turn to Iraq. This, Bush's single most
forceful assertion of leadership by definition, drew heavily on the com-
manding authority bequeathed to him to prevent another attack, and in
so doing, it drew him out on a clear set of refutable propositions. To
make the case, the administration had to press inferences, assert linkages, stretch for evidence, and manipulate key terms. That was risky, and
all the more so considering the source.

All leaders place themselves at risk, especially the great ones. In this
instance, the president was risking the nation's confidence that the attacks had in fact dispelled old conceits and that he himself was acting
with eyes not blinkered by prior assumptions. The alternative possibility—that Bush's understanding of himself as a leader had not changed
after all, that America's approach to this "new world" was being driven

by a president still eager to make good on old assumptions—lingered in the knowledge that regime change in Iraq had long been a central component of the political agenda of Vice President Cheney and key administration advisers in the Defense Department. Skeptics at home and abroad feared that the president was instinctively grasping hold of the pet project of his party's neoconservative wing and using a mandate to crush terrorism to finish up some politically awkward business left behind by his father's administration.

When the invasion failed to support the case built for it, Bush's reputation as a political stalwart came back to haunt him. Moreover, in the ensuing scramble to revise the rationale for the invasion, rivals were reminded of the administration's changing explanations for its commitment to tax cuts and were ready to call attention to a pattern that would put his entire administration in a harsh new light. Charges of dogmatism, arrogance, duplicity, and recklessness in the use of national power ate into what should have been the impregnable authority of the nation's protector. All the administration could do from then on was try to limit the damage that Bush, the political stalwart, had done to Bush, the nation's stalwart.

Was the Iraq imbroglio just a case of bad intelligence? Perhaps. It is notable, however, that orthodox innovators are chronically driven to dubious, high-risk wagers of this sort. We know that Polk manipulated events on the Mexican border to instigate a war of conquest in the greater Southwest; we know that Lyndon Johnson grasped hold of shaky evidence of events in the Gulf of Tonkin to commit the nation to war in Vietnam. What may appear in isolation as a bit of bad luck for Bush fits this larger pattern of overreaching by orthodox innovators, leaders bound by their political commitments, caught up in their own presuppositions, determined to deliver on preformed expectations.

Lincoln, speaking at the moment when he had grasped both a political victory (abolishing slavery) and a military victory (ending the threat of national disintegration), made his famous confession that he had not controlled events but that events had controlled him.[29] Orthodox innovators are, in contrast, loath to let events point the way and simply move with the situation as it develops. Their authority is not so flexible or open-ended; Lincoln's enigmatic resolve—"my policy is to have no policy"—is a luxury they can ill afford.[30] It is telling in this regard that Bush made "preemption" his watchword in the war on terror. For Bush, preemption was a way of getting out ahead of events, defining them, and orchestrating their unfolding. Preemption allowed Bush to stipulate the terms of the war, to redirect its action, to make it a fight of his own choosing. Orthodox innovators are driven by this impulse to try to maximize control up front, and it is precisely that which puts them at greatest risk. By forcing events, they saddle themselves with a challenge of event engineering that can quickly become superhuman in its proportions.

PATTERNS AND PROSPECTS

Orthodox innovators are not often elected twice, so Bush's victory in 2004 calls for some careful reflection on the systemic political effects historically associated with leadership efforts of this type and on how they square—or fail to square—with what has happened so far in the case at hand. All presidents change American politics, but rarely do they change it even roughly in the manner they intend. Orthodox innovators uniformly intend to broaden the appeal of the dominant regime, to secure its hold on governing by demonstrating that theirs is really, in Lyndon Johnson's words, "a party for all Americans." Bush's self-proclaimed role as "a uniter not a divider," his insistence on a polyglot display of speakers at his nominating conventions, his bid to make conservatism more compassionate—all echo that characteristic promise. Historically, however, such efforts have tended to produce quite the opposite. Orthodox innovators characteristically leave behind a political regime overburdened with responsibilities, ideologically distended, and tumbling into disarray. Typically, they take robust governing parties, parties that dominate the national agenda and stand ripe with solutions to the problems of day, and unwittingly spark their sectarian disintegration.

In short order, the stalwart Polk, nationally celebrated in 1844 as "consistent, orthodox and true,"[31] was being denounced as Polk the Mendacious, a devious manipulator of the interests he had promised to serve. Or consider Lyndon Johnson: No sooner did it become clear that he could not deliver on his leadership formula as promised—that he could not deliver the Great Society at home while defending Vietnam—than his presidency collapsed in a tidal wave of recriminations. The typical political effect of orthodox innovators—especially the strongest of them—has been, in a word, schismatic. Even the less personally tarnished Theodore Roosevelt left office with the Progressive and old-guard factions of his party at his and each other's throats.

The reason for this boils down to the fact that the political world seldom conforms to definitions and formulas; no matter how tight, skilled, or hands-on the controls exerted, events can be orchestrated to set terms only for so long. With so many competing commitments so precariously balanced against one another, the orthodox innovator sets in motion a program that sooner or later begins to run at the mercy of events. For these high rollers, everything has to break the right way. Theodore Roosevelt, whose fusion of Progressive reforms and old-guard commitments flourished on what he called the "pulse of prosperity," watched his political synthesis disintegrate in the brief panic of 1907.[32]

When things did finally go awry, these leaders found they had no good response to those among their own followers who, for various reasons of their own, stepped forward to say their leader had mishandled, misinterpreted, or distorted their faith. That is what Johnson called "the Bobby problem"—referring to the rising threat of an internal challenge to his authority from Bobby Kennedy;[33] that is what Polk knew as the Van Buren problem; that is what Theodore Roosevelt experienced as an Aldrich problem and a LaFollette problem; that is what Bush senior faced as a Buchanan problem. For all their muscle flexing and all their programmatic achievements, these presidents are tied to a collective project and are responsible for it; they are ministers to the faithful and have little authority without the full-throated support of the church. In fact, the more orthodox innovators do, the more vigorously they exercise the independent powers of their office and personalize their rendition of the faith, the more vulnerable to these charges of betrayal they are likely to become. That is how some of our greatest orthodox innovators became so quickly isolated; victims of their own grand schemes, they began to appear to others dangerously out of touch with reality and lacking in credibility.

In looking forward to the endgame in the case at hand, it is worth emphasizing that episodes of orthodox innovation characteristically collapse in upon themselves, that historically speaking, squabbling among the faithful over the true meaning of orthodoxy and assaults on the president from within the ranks have been far more effective in breaking up a dominant regime than have direct challenges from the opposition. When these leaders are brought down, it is seldom because the opposition has pressed a frontal assault on established governing commitments or offered a sharp alternative to the dominant agenda; it is almost always because the president's own definitions and formulas— his terms for holding the faithful together and securing their power— have proven too delicate to survive the rough-and-tumble of an unruly world. Orthodoxies are not defeated head on; they are exhausted and enervated by their faithful adherents.

We saw a bit of the characteristic fallout from orthodox innovation during the early months of 2001 when Senator Jim Jeffords of Vermont, a Republican, rejected the president's rendition of his commitments, announced his decision to leave the party, and in the process shook the political foundations of the Bush administration. One suspects that were it not for 9/11, the course of this administration, like those of Polk, Theodore Roosevelt, Lyndon Johnson, and Bush senior, would have been marked by more of the same, a rising tide of sectarian infighting over the true meaning of the faith. With the 9/11 attack, however, the Republicans closed ranks, and what is more remarkable, they stuck together. More than anything else, that is what sealed John Kerry's defeat. There was certainly no lack of material for mounting an internal assault charging that the Bush administration had betrayed fundamentals, distorted the party's true identity, or placed its future at risk. But no one of significance stood up to lead that charge.

Whatever might be said of the weaknesses of the Kerry campaign, it is not the case that he failed to try to leverage Republican discontent. In the first campaign debate, an event that is widely acknowledged to have made the president's reelection a real contest, the challenger sidestepped the kind of personal attacks that might have caused Republicans to rally behind their leader and offered instead a diagnosis of the risks inherent in the president's leadership posture:

> We do have differences. I'm not going to talk about a difference of character. I don't think that's my job or my business. But let me talk about something that the president just sort of finished up with. Maybe someone would call it a character trait, maybe somebody wouldn't. But this issue of certainty. It's one thing to be certain, but you can be certain and be wrong. It's another to be certain and be right, or to be certain and be moving in the right direction, or be certain about a principle and then learn new facts and take those new facts and put them to use in order to change and get your policy right. What I worry about with the president is that he's not acknowledging what's on the ground.[34]

Lighting on the pretense of certainty and its tendency to produce intransigence, Kerry tapped a general unease. The issue, he implied, was not whether the president was a good or likable man, nor was it that he was too conservative; the issue was a dangerously misguided understanding of what makes a leader strong. In that moment at least, Kerry was not trying to outdo the president in a display of stalwart resolve; all the same, he was taking his case directly onto the president's turf. He was holding himself out as the stronger leader for his ability to deal realistically with "what's on the ground," for his willingness to adjust pragmatically, for his wariness of being blinded by things as he wished them to be. The momentum Kerry gained from that critique carried him back from the abyss. For failing to rattle the Republican establishment, however, it left him short of the mark.

If we were to press the perspective of political time for the pivotal figure in all this, the one on whom Bush's reelection really turned, the person who would stand out from all others would be Senator John McCain of Arizona. Bush's McCain problem was legion and uncannily parallel to Johnson's Bobby problem and Polk's Van Buren problem. Like Kennedy and Van Buren, McCain was a leader of national reputation who possessed both the authority and apparent motive to say that his president had gotten it wrong, to deny the leader's authority by calling his administration to account to its own party. Repeatedly, throughout American history, leaders like McCain have found it in their own political interest to subject our orthodox innovators to the American equivalent of a vote of no-confidence and strip their pretensions bare. A personal trashing by the Bush campaign in the 2000 primaries made McCain ripe for that role, and his taunting actions over the course of the first term seemed calibrated to keep the option open. Time and again, from his support for campaign finance reform to his critique of the proposed tax cuts, McCain had challenged the president's interpretation of the faith. Kerry's invitation to McCain to join him on a national unity ticket may have been a bit over the top, but the invitation did make plain McCain's significance, his capacity to determine the future of the Bush administration. When McCain offered hugs to the chief and transformed himself into the Iraq War's most stalwart defender, he removed the greatest threat to Bush's reelection. Whether he advanced his own prospects by disavowing this historic role or simply muddled his political identity by falling into line behind the president remains to be seen.

There was no great swing behind the president's grand synthesis in 2004, but there was no great schism in the ranks either. Since that time, definition-indicting events from New Orleans to Baghdad have besieged the administration, isolated the president politically, and left him clinging to the higher nobility of the principled stand.[35] Though Republican defections on the war policy are, at this writing, still surprisingly few, discontent with the administration's handling of core matters of faith—deficits, entitlements, Social Security, immigration, appointments—has become increasingly pronounced. White House insiders and McCain himself are now speaking a familiar language, blaming the administration for betraying the Reagan Revolution, losing its way, and squandering their once-robust claims to stand as the nation's governing party.[36] In this case, reelection of an orthodox innovator may simply have extended the period of presidential isolation and political disaffection longer than usual.

But let us not sweep the deviation under the rug. At this writing, the most notable departure of this episode of orthodox innovation from the standard patterns remains Bush's success in the 2004 election backed by the support of a seemingly impregnable Republican phalanx. Is there some larger historical meaning to be extracted from this unusual extension of party unity under the pressures of presidential leadership? Let me briefly consider three explanations and their implications.

The most straightforward, commonsense explanation is that Bush's renewed lease on office was a lingering effect of the 9/11 trauma and rally, that for all the fallout from the Iraq invasion, his presidency benefited on balance from the pervasive sense of crisis instilled by the attacks and the general reluctance of the American people to depose their commander in chief in wartime. This was John Kerry's own explanation.[37] With issues of internal and international security at the forefront of events and with troops in the field, the recent campaign was fought on what has traditionally been the sitting president's strongest turf, and for every insinuation that the president had deluded the nation and embraced "the wrong war," there was a reminder of the imminent threat, the ongoing fact of war, and the residual value of a leader who had all along fashioned himself a stalwart. If this explanation is indeed correct, then the president was fortunate that the two most disgruntled national leaders to be found within his party, Colin Powell and John McCain, also prided themselves on being good soldiers. Moreover, with political rumblings suggestive of rising schismatic pressures within Bush's ranks and charges of betrayal in the air, this explanation suggests that the implosive effects more typically associated with an orthodox innovator in the White House were merely forestalled rather than durably altered by these events.

An explanation even more suggestive of a delayed effect looks to prior experience under Republican Party government in particular. There is some reason to think that divisions and resentments within the ranks are simply slower to come to a boil among Republicans than among Democrats. Call this the McKinley explanation. Until November 2004, William McKinley was the only orthodox innovator of either party to be elected twice in unencumbered contests between Democrats and Republicans.[38] (Ulysses S. Grant, another orthodox innovator and another Republican, was also elected twice but with much of his opposition still under force of arms.) It is a commonplace of American politics that the Republican Party and the Democratic Party were put together somewhat differently from the get-go, that the former has always been a bit less dispersed as a coalition of interests and a bit more coherent in its general purposes. Ronald Reagan's Eleventh Commandment—Thou shall not speak ill of a fellow Republican—affirms both faith in this fact and knowledge of its limits. That there are limits—that this greater capacity to forestall implosion in the face of schismatic pressures is only relative—is indicated by the plight of Bush senior in the midst of what would otherwise seem a remarkably advantageous turn of events. Having taken over a party already eight years under the thumb of a Republican president, he found that fighting a tidy little war of his own, a war even more masterfully won than McKinley's, was not enough to hold things together. The success of Bush junior, who took over after eight years of *Democratic* leadership and did everything imaginable in his first term to avoid his father's political fate, might seem a bit less remarkable on this accounting. What appears today like skillful defiance of the implosive political effects of orthodox innovation may be just a matter of the Republicans' relatively slow-ticking clock.

The third explanation cuts the other way. It is that the Republican Party under George W. Bush became something very different from the party of McKinley, that it has become, in fact, an organization unique in American political history. It seems safe to say that America has never seen a party that combined this level of ideological solidarity with political competitiveness in all sections of the country. Moreover, this party was reputed to have developed capacities for central direction, national outreach, interbranch coordination, candidate recruitment, and local surveillance that dwarf those of prior organizations.[39] The emergence of a new kind of party, a party geared specifically for a more continuous adjustment of its ideological and programmatic profile to its president's chosen course, is a development well worth pondering. One of its likely effects would be to limit the appeal of strategies previously open to internal challengers. What was once a reasonable way for fellow partisans to assert their influence within the ranks and call their party back from its leader's missteps may now be perceived, with good reason, as an act of certain political suicide. In retrospect, we may look back to McCain's refusal to step forward in 2004 as signaling a historic foreclosure of this once-potent political option.

Herein lies an unexpected avenue of departure from the characteristic political effects of presidential leadership. Prior to this administration, it appeared that if leadership patterns that have been typical of the American system were to wash out, it would probably be by the development of the modern accouterments of administrative management and by the weakening of political ties among elites as each taps the new resources available for independent political entrepreneurship. In this regard, no one seemed to display the anachronistic character of orthodox innovation in the modern period more vividly than George H. W. Bush, a president who made all the right moves in managing the nation's affairs only to be crushed by fellow partisans on an ideological litmus test. Against this backdrop, the late-breaking appearance of a full-bodied exemplar of orthodox innovation in the figure of George W. Bush has been doubly strange. In trying to avoid his father's fate and make the government safe for orthodox innovation, this president strengthened the ties of party government and built a party organization that would operate more exclusively than ever before as a tool of presidential management. To the extent that new parties like these take hold, they will be, in effect, whatever the president needs them to be, and whatever capacity they once had to hold their leaders to account for the collective project would be correspondingly diminished. If the management tools of the modern presidency were to be permanently strengthened in this way, making it easier for incumbents to impose political conformity to their will from above, the future of American politics might look very different indeed.

This is hardly a sure thing, and we should be especially wary of it in the face of current portents of Republican discontent. Still, in thinking about what this still-unfolding episode might have to tell us about the emergent state of the American polity overall, the surfacing of a new form of party government must be considered the most original and weighty prospect. Were this prospect to develop further, leadership by definition would mark something far more significant than a clever run down a familiar gauntlet. Whether party solidarity behind leadership of this sort is any less anachronistic for a modern superpower is open to debate.

5. The Imperial Presidency Thesis Revisited: George W. Bush at the Point of No Return

When this essay was written, the Republican Party had just lost control of Congress in the 2006 midterm elections, and the victorious Democrats were promising to restore a semblance of constitutional balance to governmental affairs.[1] The comforting old adage "The system works" was back in the air, but in contemplating the likely geopolitical fallout from recent events, that did not strike me as an especially reassuring phrase. Far from appearing aberrant, the excessive zeal of the Bush administration seemed to me to express dynamics deeply ingrained in the workings of our system. To pursue this idea, I returned to a theme that, at first thought, seems to have little to do with the cyclical patterns of political time, the "imperial presidency." As originally presented by the great Progressive historian Arthur Schlesinger, Jr., the imperial presidency thesis captured a relentless secular movement in modern American political development toward unbridled presidentialism. The picture presented in this essay holds in its sights a complicating curiosity: The problem Schlesinger identified has not been at the forefront of American politics for thirty years; why, after fading in the wake of Lyndon B. Johnson and Richard Nixon, did it suddenly surge back with such vengeance under George W. Bush? Several different developmental issues implicit in the idea of an "imperial presidency" are identified in the essay, and the political dynamics behind each are distinguished. The argument traces these different historical currents as they converged on the Bush presidency and points, in this way, to the most volatile of all elements in our latest brush with unbridled presidentialism: the tendency of orthodox innovators to overreach in tapping the robust self-confidence and ideological arrogance of their moment in political time.

It is hard to imagine a more potent indictment of modern American government than that leveled against "the imperial presidency." At issue is the history of American war making, wherein, it is charged, constraints on power that were enshrined as first principles in the U.S. Constitution are eviscerated and autocratic practices that were renounced in the Declaration of Independence become commonplace. The indictment identifies executive aggrandizement and governmental derangement as the twin maladies of American war making and traces the development of these afflictions as it accelerates across the centuries. The developmental frame discounts explanations that relegate these problems to a particular president's personality or character; as the narrative gains momentum, seemingly anomalous practices, such as those of Lyndon Johnson and Richard Nixon, fall into line as late-breaking episodes in a relentlessly unfolding story. We are led in this way to confront what the seminal work on the subject called "the logic of the imperial presidency" as it marches to "the point of no return."[2]

The sense of urgency that was conveyed by this thesis when it first appeared in the 1970s has been rekindled by recent events, and given the current mood, anyone who complicates the story might well be accused of living in a state of denial. On the other hand, it has been more than thirty years since this story line felt so compelling, and that in itself is something of a complication. The logic of history is seldom straightforward, and when the logic is political, the twists and turns can be especially acute. The politics behind the imperial presidency thesis was never very fully articulated; what there is could be summarized in a single sentence: Imperial ambitions breed imperial powers. There is truth in that, but on closer inspection, it appears that truisms will not take us very far.

What, for example, are we to make of the fact that Johnson was driven from office, or the fact that the epitome of the imperial presidency, the Nixon administration, collapsed in disgrace under threat of impeachment? Was this a confirmation of our governmental derangement, or was it, as Nixon's successor insisted, proof certain that "Our Constitution works"?[3] And what of George W. Bush? Has congressional indulgence of his sweeping claims to power in wartime finally pushed American government past "the point of no return," or do recent expressions of judicial skepticism and the Democrats' victory in the 2006 midterm elections signal that another correction is on the way? The questions run even deeper if we reflect back more broadly, for the political advantages to presidents in exercising war powers have not been as clear-cut as we might imagine. Notwithstanding the reputations of Abraham Lincoln and Franklin D. Roosevelt—wartime presidents who died in office—there is little evidence that political capital accumulated by presidents in this way is easily banked. In fact, James Madison is the only one of America's wartime presidents to hand off power electorally to a political ally in arms, and given that Madison is widely known, and often harshly criticized, for his refusal to assert extraordinary executive prerogatives for the conduct of his war, it is hard to say what logic this political distinction affirms. More to the point, many presidents—John Adams, James Polk, Woodrow Wilson, Harry Truman, Lyndon Johnson, Richard Nixon, George H. W. Bush—have found waging war to be politically costly or otherwise ineffective in sustaining their legitimacy. For several of these presidents, including two who saw their war to victory, the postwar political collapse was precipitous.

Suffice it to say, the politics of the matter is a lot murkier than a single sweep across history might lead us to expect. The reason, I will argue, is that the imperial presidency thesis weaves several different issues together into one apparently seamless package. One of these issues is constitutional. It calls our attention to portentous ambiguities in the structure of the government's war powers. A second issue is developmental. It calls our attention to the historical drive toward empowering the presidency and the concomitant evisceration of the constitutional principle of checks and balances. A third issue is more specifically concerned with imperialism. It calls our attention to an episodic impulse to flex the nation's military muscle against others and extend American hegemony. In this essay, I will try to separate these issues out and sort through the different problems they pose. In unpacking them, I do not mean to suggest that they are wholly unrelated to one another; my point, rather, is that they are not all of a piece or readily reducible to one another. On inspection, the political dynamics behind each have been quite different, and thus much depends on their interaction with one another. The presidency of George W. Bush might be best brought into focus accordingly, as a contingent conjunction of different political impulses.

THE WAR POWERS SYNDROME

The president's implied power to make war and its relationship to the extensive war powers specifically reserved to Congress in Article 1, Section 8 of the Constitution is a source of considerable ambiguity and a matter of perennial debate. As some see it, the president's role was to be strictly limited to emergency response and command of troops in the field; as others see it, the president's role was purposefully kept vague and open-ended so as to expand in response to whatever the situation might demand. For some, the ambiguities surrounding the war powers of the president and Congress are a fatal flaw in the Constitution; for others, they are emblematic of the genius of the Framers' design. On one point, however, everyone seems to agree. The constitutional advantages that accrue to the presidency in wartime are enormous. As a practical matter, war invokes the president's most substantive and exclusive constitutional power, the power of commander in chief. It plays to the office's uniquely styled capacities to act with energy, secrecy, and dispatch and greatly enhances the president's leverage against the other branches.

The political dynamic to be drawn from these observations is formal, structural, and stark. Constrained on virtually every other front, presidents would seem to have a built-in constitutional incentive to leverage greater power for themselves from wars and national emergencies. To the extent this is true, a grim developmental chain leading directly to an imperial presidency will unfold apace: The power advantages of the chief executive in wartime will lead to presidential belligerence and military impulsiveness, which, in turn, will gut checks and balances in favor of unbridled presidentialism. This is not a problem that has been seen only in retrospect. The origins of this line of argument go all the way back to the debates over ratification of the Constitution in 1788. Leading opponents of ratification—Patrick Henry in Virginia and Cato, the pseudonymous author of antifederalist essays, in New York—saw the creation of the presidency precisely this way.[4]

The war powers account is simple and direct, but is it compelling? Is presidential power seeking through war the irrepressible engine driving our governmental derangement? Though it is hard to imagine an analysis of the imperial presidency that did not make reference to this syndrome, there is enough noise in both the logic and the history to suspect that there is a lot more going on than the structural mechanics of self-aggrandizement on the part of presidents. Taken by itself, this dynamic simply explains too much.

First, as already suggested, no latter-day president reflecting on the payoff from war making in earlier years is likely to conclude that the political advantages are self-evident. Whatever immediate benefits the Constitution offers to presidents who leverage power from war, it also carries stern warnings of potentially high ultimate costs, and the latter are no less fully manifest historically than the former. If presidents are strategic calculators, there is good reason to suspect that the rationality of warmongering is extraconstitutional. Second, however war-prone the presidency may appear in the basic legal frame, casting the incumbent as a strategic calculator seeking power advantages in an abstract constitutional game suggests a uniformity of behavior and a consistency of interests that we simply do not observe. There is no accounting here for why some presidents resist the war-making impulse, as Dwight Eisenhower did in 1954 when French control of Indochina began to collapse, and by this logic alone, even some wartime presidents put in puzzling performances.[5] Again, why would James Madison push for a war while disavowing extraordinary claims to war powers? Why would Woodrow Wilson hold back on American entry into World War I and then seek to counter militarism and imperialism once and for all in the postwar settlement? Or, to take a more modern example, why would Lyndon Johnson feel compelled to fight a war that he knew from the start was bound to destroy him, and to do so in such a convoluted way as to virtually guarantee that result?[6]

Beyond historical curiosities such as these lies the more basic question: If Cato and Henry were right all along, if Caesar is anointed by the Constitution itself, why were the Framers so quick to dismiss their concerns as the wild imaginings of distempered minds? Why were they so confident that the distribution of powers they had devised would operate in practice to proscribe any such development? Reading into the Constitution the full range of maladies we associate with the imperial presidency is less a logical extrapolation than a political allegation, and as such it traps analysts in endlessly contestable propositions about the essence of the institution and its powers. At some point, constitutional essentialism cannot but give way to other considerations, and first among these, I would suggest, is that the political foundations on which the presidency developed overweening power were popular, collective, and unanticipated by anything in the Constitution itself.

THE PEOPLE'S PRESIDENCY

Attributing the breakdown of checks and balances in favor of unbridled presidentialism to war powers is a stretch because the presidential office has from the get-go been a magnet for political ambitions of all kinds. Whatever the constitutional voice of the presidency might have been, it was immediately caught up in a larger chorus intruding upon it from the outside. One implication of this is that presidential power and its variable exercise have had less to do with the constitutional drive toward individual aggrandizement than with the political problem of orchestrating collective interests and ambitions in the nation at large. Another is that high-sounding constitutional arguments about the legitimate scope of the prerogatives of this office have from the start been thoroughly entangled in the collective political projects afoot in the nation in the moment at hand.

What is crucial here, however, is that for most of American history, the cutting edge of the assault on the constitutional principle of checks and balances—and the most potent engine elevating the presidency in the American system—was not the exercise of war powers but political democratization. Herein lies the great paradox of the Framers' wariness of democracy and of their hope that an independent presidency might operate from on high to correct the political problems they perceived in the post-Revolutionary principle of legislative supremacy. The notion that gentlemen would deliberate more rationally and cautiously if they were placed in different institutions, each of which was secure in its own powers and able to fend off the encroachments of the others, proved to be a nonstarter, and the separated design, far from rendering the legislative branch more responsible in its direction of national affairs, left it irretrievably handicapped in any such effort. As Henry Jones Ford observed more than a century ago, once democracy began to sweep the gentlemen class out of national politics, the American people "lay hold of the presidency as the only organ sufficient for the exercise of their sovereignty." By the time of Andrew Jackson, the presidency had become, in Ford's famous phrase, "the work of the people breaking through the constitutional form."[7]

This second dynamic—presidential empowerment through popular reform—has been far more consistent and robust than the first. Indeed, few things in American political development are more impressive than the ingenuity of reformers in inventing ways to break through the system of checks and balances and enable the presidency to realize their political ambitions. The institutional devices and legitimating ideas they have come up with are now so much a part of the fabric of American government that no appeal back to some pristine form of constitutional relationships for leverage against presidential power is likely to cut very deep.

The most significant of these devices were those put in place earliest, by the Jeffersonians and then the Jacksonians. These insurgencies organized political parties capable of mobilizing interests on a national scale for the purposes of collective empowerment, institutional coordination, and the programmatic release of governmental power. They formulated the claim of a presidential mandate to carry out the will of the electorate. They turned the federal bureaucracy into a repository of patronage for fusing the interests of the executive with those of fellow partisans in Congress and the localities.

These innovations changed the basic operating principles of American government and did so in ways that should significantly alter our thinking about the imperial presidency thesis. One little-noticed fact is that until the First Gulf War in 1990, every war America fought was commenced under a government in which control of the political branches was united by party. To that extent at least, constitutional talk of presidential usurpation of congressional prerogatives seems to miss the point; whatever imperial ambitions may have lurked behind them, these wars were collective efforts supported by an extraconstitutional arrangement of power binding Congress and president together. Just as telling are the travails of Woodrow Wilson, Richard Nixon, and Ronald Reagan—twentieth-century incumbents who pushed the envelope on presidential prerogatives in foreign affairs under conditions of divided party government. The political ferocity with which the latent system of checks and balances kicked back into gear in these instances may not be a ringing endorsement of the constitutional ideal of institutional deliberation, but it is surely a stark reminder of the collective foundations of extraordinary presidential power.

I will return to the problem of divided party government in a moment, for its increased incidence in later years is, it seems to me, deeply implicated in the case for presidential power put forth recently by conservative insurgents in national politics. But the contributions of the Progressive reformers, whose intervening insurgency shaped the office for the first two-thirds of the twentieth century, cannot be overlooked. The Progressives had no more patience with the system of checks and balances than the Jacksonians had, and in detailing the ways in which these impediments to the full expression of popular will protected property and privilege, they echoed many Jacksonian themes.[8] But the Progressives pushed ahead; they capitalized on nineteenth-century alterations of basic constitutional relationships while looking for new ways to nationalize power and deploy it as a reform instrument. First, they weakened the role of local party organizations in presidential selection, creating in effect a presidential party with a national policy agenda. Then they ejected the local parties from the national bureaucracy, in effect recasting the institutional bond between president and Congress around an expandable bureaucracy capable of delivering attractive programs to nationally organized interests. All the while, they loosened the boundaries of governmental power. Exposing the narrow interests served by the original design of the Constitution, they put forward pragmatic theories about an "organic" or "living" Constitution, theories that would establish legitimacy less through reliance on the formal arrangements enshrined in the document itself than through the distillation of national sentiment. Herein lay the basis of their celebration of presidency-centered government as a catchall solution to the problems of modern American government. Incumbents were now duty-bound to assume political leadership of the nation, to test their ability to mobilize national opinion, and to overcome the constitutional obstacles in their path.[9]

Though the Progressives were far more interested in empowering the presidency than in considering the limits of that power, their reliance on public opinion as a boundary condition should not be dismissed out of hand. Woodrow Wilson's example seems doubly poignant in this regard, for the crushing defeat of his effort to rally public opinion after World War I exposed the limits of the Progressive model in a crusade *against* imperial aggression. After five years in which he set a new standard for national policy leadership and another year exercising extraordinary power in an unprecedented war effort, Wilson was broken by an opposition majority freshly installed in Congress and determined to reject his peace treaty as insufficiently protective of the nation's sovereign power and international prerogatives. Characteristically, Wilson turned philosophical in defeat. In a final profession of his faith in the Progressive presidency, he confided to his daughter that he thought "it was best after all that the United States did not join the League of Nations." If he had prevailed, he explained, it would not have been a true expression of national opinion but "only a personal victory," and as such, America would have entered the League of Nations under false pretenses and without the will to make it work.[10]

Fifty years later, a very different sort of reform insurgency developed a far-less-accommodating response to the perils of asserting presidential power in a politically divided polity. In the 1970s, conservatives opposed to the expansive bureaucratic state spawned by the Progressives eyed the makings of a new majority, one that would secure them a competitive political advantage in presidential elections.[11] But any hope of their controlling Congress appeared to be a pipe dream. This meant that if the powers of presidency-centered government were to be tapped on behalf of the conservatives' new national majorities and political ambitions, a few alterations would have to be made in the foundations upon which the Progressives had asserted those powers.

The Nixon presidency anticipated this turn. Richard Nixon was quick to remind his critics of precedents among his Progressive predecessors for everything he sought to do, but he was also acutely aware of the very different circumstances in which he was invoking them: He was acting in a government otherwise controlled by his political enemies; there was no cohesive national sentiment on which to base expansive claims to power; his was a "silent" majority. Faced with these circumstances, Nixon subtly shifted the emphasis in the argument for executive supremacy. He narrowed the relevant domain of public opinion to make the election of the president the only true expression of the national will; at the same time, he expounded upon the exclusivity of the prerogatives granted the presidency under Article 2 of the Constitution to press a case for unilateral action on the people's behalf. This was what led Arthur Schlesinger, Jr., at the time the dean of the Progressive intellectuals and theretofore a leading advocate of presidency-centered government, to rewrite the history of the office and to cast Nixon's administration as the quintessential exemplar of an "imperial presidency" marching to "the point of no return."[12]

Notwithstanding the Progressives' deep complicity in the developments from which they now recoiled, they were genetically programmed to balk at the new game afoot. The Progressives had built the modern presidency on the back of a critique of the Constitution. Their movement had been a revolt *against* formalism. They had set out to expose the original intentions behind the formal design of American government so as to emancipate the nation from them and to ensure that the people would be able to do what they wanted with their government so long as they spoke clearly. The scope of Article 2's "vesting clause," a question that conservative insurgents were soon to exploit in earnest,[13] was something the Progressives were willing to regulate politically and to expand insofar as it accommodated the "common meaning of the common voice."[14] Nixon's appeal to the Constitution was the harbinger of something different. It was not a critique of the sweeping powers the Progressives had insinuated into the presidency; it was a more aggressive, more exclusive, and more personal claim to the exercise of those newfound powers. By adding a formalist twist to the Progressives' handiwork, presidential leadership could be foisted on a people deeply divided in their political sentiments.

The precipitous collapse of the Nixon presidency at the hands of the political enemies he had so feared, and a near repeat under Ronald Reagan during the Iran-Contra scandal, prompted conservative visionaries to consummate this peculiar marriage of formalism with presidentialism in what is now known as the theory of the unitary executive.[15] The unitary theorists have elaborated a view of the Constitution and representative government that purports to rediscover original purposes and to find in the formal endowments of each branch wide berth for presidential self-sufficiency and exclusivity in the exercise of power. Legal theorist John Yoo may be correct in his claim that this theory helps square the Constitution with the way presidential power has evolved over the years, but by the same token, it is notable that this reconciliation minimizes the difference between constitutional intent and monarchical practice.[16] It may not be stretching things to say that the unitary theorists press an interpretation of presidential power that Cato and Patrick Henry saw as grounds for rejection of the Constitution and that the authors of the *Federalist Papers* could have embraced only at great peril to their cause. But at this stage of the game that seems almost beside the point. The fact is that in pushing further beyond the principle of checks and balances and empowering the presidency for their collective political purposes, today's conservatives are merely extending work that previous political insurgencies had already far advanced.[17]

The paradox is twofold: The theory of the unitary executive was prompted by the new realties of divided party government, and divided party government has become the only practical political constraint applicable to a president possessed of these new pretensions to unitary control. This made it all the more worrisome when George W. Bush, the most vigorous proponent of the theory yet, found his party in control of all the branches of government and himself liberated from the condition against which the theory had pushed. In fact, our review thus far indicates a uniquely virulent configuration of developmental dynamics converging on the Bush administration. It was possessed of an insurgent theory of action that justified aggressive assertions of presidential independence and de facto dominance over governmental affairs; it was possessed of all the resources of party government and all the tools and techniques of plebiscitary leadership; and, soon after it came into office, it fell upon the ideal catalytic agent for maximizing presidential claims: an attack on the homeland. Here was a conjunction of circumstances uniquely conducive to no-holds-barred presidentialism, a transit of power and authority from which there might be no turning back.

IMPERIALISM

The story did not end, however, on 11 September 2001. Indeed, as things have shaken out for the Bush administration, neither the constitutional logic of power in wartime nor the developmental logic of presidential supremacy reach to the heart of the matter. The problem is that there is precious little in either dynamic that accounts for the episodic incidence of imperial crusades in American history. The impulse to flex the nation's muscle against others for the purpose of extending American influence and ideals comes to us as an integral part of the imperial presidency thesis, but, present circumstances aside, the imperial impulse in American politics and surges in presidential power do not move in lockstep. Moreover, of the different themes woven into the imperial presidency thesis, the politics of imperial outreach stand out as especially contentious. In other words, the serious difficulties this administration encountered as soon as it redirected the national response to the attacks of 9/11 into an invasion of Iraq have considerable historical resonance. It would be ironic indeed if imperialism turned out to be the Achilles' heel of our national flight to presidentialism, but it would not be inexplicable.

To address the Iraq calamity—the pivot point of this episode—by repairing to idiosyncratic details about the president's personality or individual capacity would, I think, rob the imperial presidency thesis of much of its purchase. What is missing is not detail but a large part of the overall picture and a key source of insight into the operations of the American system as a whole. On inspection, the Iraq invasion fits the profile of another dynamic evident in presidential history. At issue here is neither constitutional essentialism nor developmental trends but a recurrent political syndrome, one that assumed its basic shape very early on, one that still takes hold of the presidency periodically, and one that, more often than not, puts the nation and the incumbent at cross-purposes.

The Constitution ensures that all of America's wars will bear the face of a president, but all wars are not the same.[18] Even if we were to grant that no war waged by a nation-state is entirely free of imperial implications, there was much more than imperial ambition at issue behind the Civil War, American involvement in the two world wars, the Afghan War, and the fight against al Qaeda. By the same token, the United States has fought a series of wars that stand apart from these by virtue of their national ambition, political arrogance, and imperial presumption. I would distinguish this second group as the "muscle-flexing wars";[19] they include the War of 1812, the Mexican-American War, the Spanish-American War, the Vietnam War, and now the war in Iraq. On inspection, these wars share some striking similarities.

Note first that these were all wars of dubious provocation. Notwithstanding the mistaken intelligence that the Bush administration employed to make its case for the turn to Iraq, a pattern of stretching evidence, manipulating circumstances, and overreaching conclusions is unmistakable in each of the muscle-flexing wars. What exactly happened in the Gulf of Tonkin in 1964 or in Havana's harbor in 1898 was less important than the pretext for war that those events provided. Had James Polk not sent federal troops to occupy disputed territory on the Rio Grande, he would not have been able to declare that a state of war existed by virtue of a Mexican attack on "American" soil. London greeted James Madison's war message with surprise; had he waited just a few more days (he had already waited about six years), he would have found out that the British had rescinded the restrictive trade practices that had prompted his war message and justified his plan to seize Canada.

Because of the machinations involved, there has been a tendency to personalize these wars as uniquely presidential—"Mr. Polk's War," "Lyndon Johnson's War." This reinforces the connection between imperial war and the imperial presidency. But on further inspection, one sees that the muscles being flexed in each of these instances were those of a powerful faction within a dominant party. These were supremely political wars, the pet projects of an ideologically charged, upwardly mobile, and strategically situated coterie. The impulse to vent American power idealistically that is so clearly apparent in the neoconservative wing of Bush's Republican coalition is echoed in every episode of this recurrent pattern. Polk was advanced to the presidency by a faction of the Democratic Party—"Young America"—that had grown impatient with the old leadership's cautious approach to the nation's Manifest Destiny. Even if there is overstatement in the conventional wisdom that Madison was held hostage by the "war hawks" in his party for his renomination in 1812, no one suggests that he was insensitive to their growing political clout, their impatience, or their importance to his majority. In 1898, factional enthusiasm for war with Spain simply overran McKinley's initial skepticism, and in Johnson's case, a political determination to keep

Kennedy Cold Warriors in line instigated a self-defeating Vietnam strategy of unqualified commitment backed by incremental action.

One final observation to be made about these muscle-flexing wars is that they are not randomly distributed across presidential history. There is, in fact, one such war for each of the party coalitions that has dominated American government for an extended period of time. The war of 1812 came in the heyday of the Jeffersonian dominance, the Mexican-American War in the heyday of the Jacksonian dominance, the Spanish-American War in the heyday of the Republican dominance, and the Vietnam War in the heyday of the liberal Democratic dominance. This suggests that the imperial impulse is vented most aggressively in America by regime-defining party coalitions at parallel stages in the cycle of their development and disintegration, that the collective conceit driving these crusades bespeaks a moment of singular self-confidence that recurs in political time.

Like the other muscle-flexing wars, the recent incursion into Iraq was propelled by a party possessed of a make-or-break opportunity in government, a party whose political vision faced no coherent challenge and whose dreams of a transformed nation stood on the brink of fulfillment. For the party that is accustomed to power, sure of its mission, and restless with commitments to its various and sundry parts, the president is less an imperious taskmaster than a service provider; he is an instrument for delivering promised goods, taking care of unfinished business, and realizing pent-up ambitions. If the leaders of robust regime-defining parties have been especially prone to embark on imperial adventures, it is not because they have lorded power over everyone else but because they are poorly positioned politically to resist the pent-up enthusiasms of key coalition partners. (On the political costs of resisting partisan enthusiasts intent on realizing their vision, consider the example of John Adams, who scuttled the war plans of his fellow Federalists only to have them turn against him and plot his defeat.)[20] Bringing a long-dominant party to its moment of programmatic fulfillment, these presidents are nothing if not ready and willing to orchestrate the collective leap forward. All political cues prompt leaders in these circumstances to use whatever opportunities are presented to secure the full-throated support of their church; their authority is not that of an independent constitutional officer so much as that of a minister to the faithful.

Of course, the heady factional enthusiasm that makes muscle-flexing wars so irresistible in these circumstances also makes these presidents vulnerable to charges of ideological overreach and debasement of their high constitutional office for programmatic ends. Betting heavily on a political vision raises the stakes of the play of events. Short of a stunning battlefield victory (like the one at New Orleans that salvaged Madison's reputation and pulled the rug out from under his Federalist critics) or a willingness to address problems head on (as Theodore Roosevelt did on the revelation of American atrocities in the Philippines), the political costs extracted by such wars tend to be severe for the president and his party alike. With shaky initial pretexts, such wars tend to be quick to exhaust their political support. Their demands drive disaffection through the president's own ranks and spark political reaction nationwide.

That is why the muscle-flexing impulses of the Bush administration have not operated as just another log on the fire of unbridled presidential supremacy. The fate of the Bush presidency has, in fact, begun to turn on this one dynamic in particular, and its logic appears to be confounding the convergence of all others on presidentialism's final triumph. Whether the fallout will reach further and unravel the Republican Party's grip on the national agenda altogether remains to be seen.

THE SYSTEM WORKS?

This essay began with a truism: Imperial ambitions breed imperial powers. In the past, however, political dynamics in America complicated this story so that there was always something to the opposite claim as well: imperial powers succumbed to imperial ambition. The question for presidential politics in the wake of the 2006 midterm elections is whether this more comforting truth still holds.

In the intermediate aftermath of 9/11, everything was in place to push the claims of presidentialism beyond the point of no return. But for the fact that this portentous moment was overtaken by the dreams of a political faction—but for the fact that a newfound imperative to "preserve, protect, and defend" was pressed into service to clean up some unfinished business on the old party agenda—it might be difficult at present to contemplate any politically effective path back from the brink. This episodic impulse to overreach and rush headlong into the quagmire does not constitute a particularly admirable, efficient, or dependable mechanism for recalibrating constitutional power, nor is it very comforting for those in the rest of the world who look to American hegemony for security and stability. But for a polity that has been playing fast and loose with its constitutional design for 225 years, there may be little left to help balance things out save these contingencies of political time.

A collective sigh of relief could be heard in many quarters after the 2006 midterm elections. Still, it is hard to bracket the Iraq imbroglio and look ahead with renewed confidence in the operations of American government and politics. First, it is not at all clear that the new majority in Congress will succeed in reining in this president's pretensions for the power and independence of his office. Second, even if it does, the power released by this administration has already had an enormous impact, and the fallout is likely to be with us for a long time. Finally, and more to the point, this has not been an aberrant episode. At issue within it is a confluence of persistent constitutional problems, long-term developmental trends, and recurrent political impulses. These implicate the entire history of the office, and their current alignment heightens the stakes at issue in their still-uncertain resolution.

If the old adage "the system works" has not become a wholly empty cliché, it is because we find ourselves today witness to some of its most perverse expressions. The "imperial presidency" is a composite of these. With each of its several elements as deeply ingrained in the operations of our institutions as the others, none seems likely to find a quick fix.

6. Is Transformational Leadership Still Possible? Barack Obama in Historical Perspective

This essay has its origins in the 2008 presidential election campaign, during which I found myself playing host to a far-flung discussion with followers of the political time perspective over whether Barack Obama would prove to be a reconstructive or a preemptive leader. The question prompted close scrutiny of the typology I had developed of historical types of leadership authority, and in particular, of the political dynamics that are captured within and across the four cells of that typology. This is as it should be. The typology is not rigidly deterministic in the sense that every candidate is pegged in one box or another from the get-go; it is, rather, an interactive set of political relationships framing problems and probabilities as they have been manifested historically. Presidents tend to play at the margins of these types. They seek to solve the problems presented by these situations, to test the possibilities and stretch for new resolutions. The possibilities have themselves evolved over the course of American history, with important implications for our political system as a whole. These are the considerations that have guided my own thinking about Obama's leadership as he heads into the midterm elections.[1]

The presidential election of 2008 was fought over the prospects for "change," and the candidate promising the most thoroughgoing change of all won a decisive victory. Barack Obama, the Democratic contender, distinguished himself from other opponents of Republican rule as the agent of "change we can believe in." He agitated for "a new *kind* of politics." He belittled the example of the most recent Democrat in the White House, Bill Clinton, as temporizing, and, taking a larger view of current prospects, he projected himself into one of those rare moments in American history when it becomes possible to alter the nation's "trajectory." Indeed, he spoke of "fundamentally transforming the United States of America."[2]

Presidential campaigns lend themselves to hyperbole. Candidates competing in party primaries need to differentiate themselves from one another, and in the general election, each strives to appear the genuine article. Still, the quest for authenticity can summon up any number of leadership qualities, and on inspection, Obama used the promise of change to conjure something with deep historical resonance. He knew that Hillary Clinton would project the virtues of experience, so he pressed her to reconcile her intimate connections to the politics of the past with her bid to lead an opposition demanding something new. He knew that John McCain would project the military virtues of honor and courage, so he pressed him to reconcile his national appeal as an independent, straight-shooting "maverick" with his partisan credentials as a loyal "foot soldier in the Reagan Revolution."[3] In Obama's hands, the promise of "change" magnified the noise in the leadership stances of his main rivals. Projecting a cleaner and more complete break from the past, it recalled what has traditionally been the most politically potent leadership posture of all.

Obama was hardly subtle in intimating what he had in mind. Launching his campaign in Springfield, Illinois, he cast himself in Abraham Lincoln's mold.[4] Lincoln too had been an unlikely prospect, driven by the compelling power of a transformative vision. Throughout his campaign, Obama reminded the nation that it had been a while since a president had risen to the standard set by the great political leaders in American history. He exuded keen appreciation for the fact that scattered about our past are a few presidents who actually did change the nation's direction, setting it on a new course that would be maintained long beyond their own tenure. It was by just that measure that he rated Bill Clinton as a lesser light.

Obama was especially attuned to the primacy of circumstance in determining these prospects. He dismissed the notion that his leadership was sui generis, that he was "a singular figure," a phenom who defied all historical references. Like McCain, he invoked the example of Ronald Reagan, but whereas McCain appealed to Reagan as the preeminent authority on proper governing principles, Obama evoked Reagan to elevate the importance of context and opportunity over party, program, and personality: "[Reagan] put us on a fundamentally different path because the country was ready for it."[5] Identifying Reagan as the nearest historical exemplar of transformational leadership, Obama underscored the parallels of circumstance in Reagan's rise to power and his own; he identified 2008 as a similar turning point and cast himself as an iconic figure poised to transform the nation once again. It was his studied effort to convey the sense of this time as one of *those* times that made his campaign appear so pregnant with possibility: "This is our moment . . . our time to turn the page on the policies of the past . . . our time to offer a new direction for this country that we love."[6]

Anticipating decisive change in his rise to power, Obama invited equally categorical evaluations of his performance in office. Last January, the election of Scott Brown as senator from Massachusetts was deemed a fatal blow to Obama's bid to change the trajectory of government and politics.[7] Then, in March, passage of comprehensive health care legislation was heralded as evidence that Obama would stand with Franklin D. Roosevelt as the catalyst of a new era.[8] Today, with pollsters forecasting major losses for the president's party in the midterm elections, speculation has turned toward the default option—trimming in the Clinton style. Trying to make sense of change when its scale and scope is being contested day by day, in the moment, is risky, to say the least. It is not just that every new assessment is vulnerable to the next turn of events; it is that a shorthand reference to icons—to Reagan, FDR, or Lincoln—is no substitute for careful reflection on what transformational leadership in the American presidency has actually entailed.

The more productive way to consider these prospects is to take a closer look at the past. If we resist the temptation simply to hoist Obama on his own petard, we might use the historical references in his leadership posture to bring the current juncture more fully into focus. It may be that the promise of transformational leadership has been hollowed out by modern campaign hyperbole, that it is now just a matter of electoral positioning for momentary advantage. But there has been more to it than that in the past. Obama's assessment of transformational moments in American politics is worth taking seriously because it was roughly correct. Our stake in evaluating his performance goes far beyond score keeping, for much about political possibilities in contemporary America turns on how we read the strengths and weaknesses of the parallels he drew.

So just how closely did Obama's rise to power track the rise of other transformational presidencies? How did leadership of this sort play itself out in earlier periods? Given what was involved in prior episodes, how likely is it that we are in the midst of a repeat performance? And given the vast changes that have taken place in American government and politics more generally, what are the chances going forward that *any* president will be able to do what the transformational leaders of the past did? We may never be able to game the future perfectly, but we are not completely at the mercy of events. There are historical standards to scrutinize, patterns and crosscurrents to identify, alternatives to consider, and contemporary implications to probe.

It is easy to conflate issues in an assessment of this sort, so it might be useful at the outset to flag some of the more obvious miscues. By inquiring into prospects for an Obama transformation, we are not asking whether or not he will be reelected. Clinton was reelected, and as Obama observed, there was no Clinton transformation. Nor are we asking whether Obama will get a lot done. All presidents get a lot done, and Obama has already done more than most. The transformational presidents in American history did particular things, not necessarily more things. It should be underscored as well that we are not asking here whether Obama is an admirable leader or a good president. The general impression is that transformational leadership is good leadership; it is certainly associated with great presidents. But there are presidents in our history who did the right thing at a critical moment whom we would not describe as transformational, and there are those whom we would describe as transformational who took actions we might well condemn. The notion that anything short of a political transformation represents a failure of leadership is a common conceit, but reflection reveals it as also a rather dangerous one. It is one thing to wish every president great success; it is quite another to expect each of them to transform America.

The issue, as it is posed historically, is a specific one. American government and politics are transformed when new interests secure a firm grip on power, when institutional relationships are rearranged to support them, when governmental priorities are durably recast, and when a corresponding set of legitimating ideas becomes the new common sense. Thomas Jefferson, Andrew Jackson, Abraham Lincoln, Franklin Roosevelt, and Ronald Reagan all, in varying degrees, brought about changes of that kind. In earlier chapters, I have called these the "reconstructive" presidencies. Transformational leaders reconstruct American government and politics; they set it operating on (to use the Obama locution) "a new foundation."[9] Other presidents have done very important things, but they did not do *that*. At issue is whether Obama will alter the playing field of national politics, durably, substantially, and on his own terms, whether he is likely to shift the axis of commitment and conflict so that American government itself is understood differently.

But even when looking for evidence of something fairly specific, what we see at this early date admits of a variety of interpretations. The inquiry here will proceed accordingly. The title of this essay asks whether leadership of this sort is still possible. Casting the question that way opens the investigation to a range of responses, some bearing directly on Obama's prospects and others on the prospects for contemporary presidents generally. These responses engage the relevant history in different ways, and since each can be supported with reference to Obama's performance thus far, none can be dismissed out of hand. The best course at this juncture is to sort them out and interrogate them one by one. We will assess their relative plausibility by clarifying the ground for each.

Two of the responses to be considered assume that the model of reconstructive politics to be drawn from the past remains a reliable guide to present and future transformations. That is to say, both assume that reconstructive leadership in the classic mode is still possible and simply inquire into the likelihood that Obama will pull it off. The responses differ, depending on just how exacting the application of historical standards is, that is, on just how closely the Obama presidency must track the patterns displayed in prior reconstructive episodes to reach a similar result. Two other responses test the reliability of the classic model itself. They explore a possible mismatch between the iconic leadership role Obama conjured for himself and the "ruthless pragmatism"[10] reflected in his actions. The questions here are whether, and to what extent, Obama's conception of political transformation is the same as that projected by reconstructive leaders in earlier periods of American history; whether, and to what extent, an alternative understanding of change has been sown in the basic operations of modern American government; and whether, and to what extent, a model of transformative leadership that has been drawn forward periodically from the early nineteenth century still has legs.

Response 1: Transformational leadership is still possible, and Obama might yet pull it off.

When Obama elevated the example of Reagan over the example of Clinton, he was thinking in political time. Opportunities for reconstructive leadership are rare, but, as Obama observed, they have recurred over long stretches of history in circumstances roughly similar to those propelling him to power. Like Obama, reconstructive presidents have all been opposition leaders. They have all, like Obama, sought to displace a dispensation in political affairs that had held sway over the nation for decades. More to the point, events liberated them to press the vulnerabilities of those long-established orthodoxies far beyond the middling critiques previously ventured by that regime's opponents. In the years running up to our reconstructive presidencies, the priorities of the old order appeared to exhaust themselves and to leave the government wildly overextended in its commitments. Affiliates of the established regime were seemingly unable either to stand by their commitments or to generate credible solutions to the new problems of the day. In most cases, reconstruction was presaged by a calamitous event implicating the regime's basic conception of legitimate national government.

When an old regime begins to flounder in its own commitments and its affiliates are thrown on the defensive, the opposition leader is liberated to repudiate it outright, to hold it responsible for present calamities, to declare it bankrupt. Bolstered by a groundswell of popular discontent, the new president is thrust into power with expansive warrants for independent action and an encompassing mandate for reform. Many elements of the classic scenario for political reconstruction came together late in 2008, and Obama has been reminding us of that fact ever since. The standard rhetorical tropes of reconstructive politics echo through Obama's early months in office, and not just when he takes to the hustings to rally his troops. Emblematic is the opening statement of the 2009 Economic Report of the President, where Obama railed against "a legacy of misplaced priorities" and took aim at systemic failures: "[The current economic] crisis is neither the result of a normal turn of the business cycle nor an accident of history. We arrived at this point as a result of an era of profound irresponsibility that engulfed both private and public institutions from some of our largest companies' executive suites to the seats of power in Washington. D.C."[11]

Of the many arguments that have been ventured since January 2009 against the proposition that Obama is a reconstructive president or transformational leader, the weakest is the notion that he has been reluctant to engage in forthright repudiation of his inheritance. There are, of course, many points of contention that Obama has sidestepped in his first two years, but no president, no matter how virulent his critique of the received order, has taken on every issue under contention from the get-go or has tried to change everything at once. It may be that so many major issues are presented simultaneously in a modern presidency that it has become harder for the public to calibrate the balance of repudiation and accommodation, but it is certainly the case that no president since Reagan has invoked the authority to repudiate more often or has been more doggedly determined to set a new course. Now, at midterm, Obama is depending on voters to recall and to reject "the folks who drove the economy, drove the nation . . . into the ditch."[12]

The companion concern is that Obama is too enamored of the idea of overcoming divisions—too committed to the notion of "one America"—to push effectively for a transformative break with the past. The paradox is that the election of the first African American president, an event of enormous cultural significance, may have made it more difficult to exploit the reconstructive opportunity at hand: Obama may be constrained by virtue of his unique historical status to pull his punches in order to avoid appearing too angry or vindictive. But if Obama really is "a singular figure" after all, if the code of conduct in office is different for him than for any other leader, one would be hard-pressed to make the case with reference to the public posture of past reconstructive presidents. It is not just that he has repeatedly cast himself against an "era of profound irresponsibility"; it is that *all* reconstructive leaders connect this authority to repudiate to a unifying purpose. Beginning with Jefferson ("We are all Republicans; we are all Federalists"),[13] the reconstructive presidents in American history consistently claim that they have discovered the true basis of national unity and that they are acting to restore it. They characteristically connect forthright repudiation of their immediate inheritance to a ringing reaffirmation of values emblematic of the American polity that seem to have been lost or squandered in the indulgences of the old order. They characteristically reach across the aisle for support in the cause of restoring consensus. They characteristically set out with reform programs that invite cooperation in meeting the current crisis. The projection of a unifying vision—independent and above the fray—has always proven an invaluable resource for presidents engaged in reconstructive politics. Combining repudiation with outreach, Obama has been true to form.

The intensity of the opposition Obama has generated, and the complaints now being evoked by his relentless reminders of the misguided policies of the recent past, should suffice to caution against the notion that he has been too timid. But is stiff resistance itself dispositive? Obama has been fiercely challenged in Washington, and the concerns of the public at large have been evident in polls and in electoral contests. But reconstruction is never a cakewalk; it is a wrenching affair, full of risk. Transformative presidencies are forged through an extended series of unsettling political contests; the obstacles are always severe, and the struggles to overcome them usually extend over the course of two full terms. Jackson was defied and defeated outright throughout his first term, on issues as routine as political appointments and as central to his cause as reform of the National Bank. No one could confidently predict a successful transformation after the first year or two of the Lincoln presidency or after the first year or two of the Reagan presidency. The midterm election of 1934, when FDR's party gained seats, was an anomaly even among our reconstructive leaders. These presidents have survived significant midterm losses and have still been able to forge a new foundation for government and politics in the end.

If history is a guide, the critical tests for an Obama reconstruction will come after the 2010 midterm elections and in reaction to mounting resistance. The test is whether the president will be able to maintain his repudiative authority, whether he will deploy it to stigmatize those who continue to resist as extremists and to follow through with more systemic changes. Historically, this has meant moving decisively against institutions and interests upon which the old politics rested. Court battles, bank wars, civil war—these have been the telltale signs of reconstructive politics, and they take time to reach a decisive phase. Reconstruction does not depend on winning every contest. It depends on systematically weakening, perhaps even destroying outright, the infrastructure of the old order, on clearing the political and institutional ground upon which something fundamentally new can take hold. On the positive side, the telltale test of reconstructive leadership is party building. Reconstructive leadership is not about discarding the old party of government in favor of the old party of opposition. It is about bringing new groups to power, about rearranging political alliances, about securing an alternative unanticipated by the prior lines of political conflict. Reconstructive leaders establish a new majority that can be depended upon to support the president's new commitments and priorities.

Party building and institutional reconstruction reconstitute the system. Historically, this is what has made presidential leadership in America politically transformative. No one should expect a clear resolution of these prospects a mere two years into a term, nor should one suppose that there is nothing in sight that might propel reconstructive politics toward these more decisive tests. A standoff with the Supreme Court under Chief Justice John Roberts has already been intimated. Immigration reform is a pressing issue, and it could present party-building opportunities. Relentless resistance has drawn out the stalwart defenders of the old regime, and time and again, nay-saying of this sort has served to stiffen the resolve of the reconstructive leader to undertake more decisive actions. Repudiation and affirmation are the key tools; managed effectively, they create new and durable standards of legitimate national government. When order-shattering initiatives are aimed at order-affirming ends, when they are directed against an old regime that has been shorn of all credibility, the president stands apart from all prior conceptions of the alternatives and establishes standards of his own.

Response 2: The reconstructive model of transformational leadership may work for some future president, but it was never likely to work for Obama.

I have laid out what seems to me to be the best case for keeping an open mind about a prospective Obama transformation. But is it an especially strong case? And if not, what exactly are its weaknesses? Is it just too early to dismiss the possibility of an Obama reconstruction, or was that possibility implausible from the start?

The first place to look for weaknesses is in the specifics, in certain more subtle and as yet unexamined aspects of the Obama case that fail to comport with what we know of reconstructive leadership as it has played out in the past. An accounting of this sort does not question the contemporary relevance of the historical exemplars of transformational leadership; on the contrary, by drawing us more deeply into prior episodes of reconstructive politics and demanding something more than just a rough approximation of the historical patterns, it places even greater weight on the reliability of the old model for an assessment of Obama's prospects. Once we take account of elements that are usually found in presidencies of this type but were absent or oddly configured in Obama's rise to power, once we reckon with the significance of those elements in accounting for past successes, the conclusion seems plain: We may see transformational leadership again sometime in the future, but it was never very likely that Obama would rise to that standard.

A closer look at the patterns of presidential leadership in political time brings this alternative assessment of Obama's leadership into focus. It is clear on inspection that political regimes in American history have had considerable staying power, that each has survived several rounds of opposition leadership before succumbing to something categorically new. It is hardly a surprise that each successive round of opposition leadership is a bit more strident in its assaults on the established regime and a bit more forthright in its quest to displace it. Obama is the second opposition leader to come to power since the Reagan Revolution, and if his assault on the conservative regime has been more forceful and direct than Bill Clinton's, it is because the passage of time always brings the limitations and adverse consequences of received prescriptions more clearly into view. Something similar might be said of Woodrow Wilson and Richard Nixon. Wilson's critique of the Republican regime of the post–Civil War era was more direct and strident than Grover Cleveland's; Nixon's critique of the liberal regime of the post–New Deal era was more direct and strident than Dwight D. Eisenhower's. Moreover, Wilson and Nixon each anticipated the new coalition that would later serve to anchor a new regime. Neither, however, consummated a political reconstruction himself. In fact, no second-round opposition leader has successfully reconstructed American government and politics. Obama can hardly be faulted for anticipating the possibility—all opposition leaders are out to test the reconstructive possibilities—but on a strict accounting of political time, he is probably pressing the case prematurely.

Leadership is not clockwork, but if we pursue the patterns of political time a bit further, it is possible to point to something quite specific that was out of sync in Obama's bid for a political transformation. Close scrutiny of the predecessor's leadership is vital in this perspective for determining what comes next, and what is conspicuous in examining this particular sequence is the absence of an affiliated president who came to power candidly acknowledging deep-seated problems within the older order and directing his leadership to resolving them. Notwithstanding the debacles of Iraq and Katrina, George W. Bush is an odd fit for that historic role. He may have left the conservative regime overextended in its commitments and exposed in its priorities, but until the very final weeks of his second term, he remained a supremely self-confident booster of those commitments and priorities. This left open the argument that the problems rumbling out of his presidency stemmed from his particular rendition of the old orthodoxy, or from his mistakes in implementing it, not from the orthodoxy itself. It meant that Republicans could rebound by marginalizing Bush, just as Democrats rebounded for a time after 1968 by marginalizing Lyndon B. Johnson.

In contrast, every reconstruction in the past has been immediately preceded by the election of an affiliated president who would spend his entire term trying to rehabilitate and repair an old order already in deep trouble: John Adams, John Quincy Adams, James Buchanan, Herbert Hoover, Jimmy Carter. None of these presidents was a resolute advocate of regime priorities in the mold of George W. Bush; on the contrary, each was something of an insider critic, a leader alert to the crisis of legitimacy brewing in the land and intent on saving the old order from itself. More than anything else, it was the long and hapless struggles of these leaders to grapple with their own compatriots' complicity in the crisis at hand that sealed the case that the old regime was indeed beyond repair. It was their sustained stewardship of a predicament to be laid at their own doorstep that finally broke the back of the regime party and scattered its support. As bad as things got late in 2008, there was no extended display of the inability of conservatives to respond to the crisis and solve their own problems, no clear demonstration that the nation was suffering from something more than "Bush fatigue."

There is no need to stretch for a pertinent counterfactual. John Mc-Cain, the self-styled "maverick" of the Republican Party, was about as clear an example as American history affords of the insider critic who offers to rehabilitate and repair a regime in deep trouble. McCain's message in 2008 was that the Republican Party had lost its way, that the Bush administration had made mistakes, that McCain's leadership was needed to put conservatism back on track. McCain's 2008 campaign was the perfect setup for a classic political disjunction. A McCain victory, coming on the heels of a financial crisis and a more extended economic meltdown, would have ushered in a direct and extended test of the conservatives' capacities to respond to manifest problems in their fundamental commitments without destroying themselves in the process. As it happened, the vulnerabilities of the conservative regime were not allowed to ripen in this way, and the Obama reconstruction came to hinge on the hope that Bush's second-term travails would serve as an adequate surrogate. Skipping the disjunctive phase has, however, made it all too easy for supporters of the conservative regime to rally in a defense of old orthodoxies—as Wilson rallied the Republicans and Nixon rallied the liberals.

The equivocal political effect (so far) of the financial collapse of the fall of 2008 is especially telling in this regard. As suggested above, the financial crisis indicted some of the founding principles of the conservative regime—its commitment to government deregulation and its faith in self-correcting markets. In doing so, it significantly strengthened the prima facie case against it, and Obama seized the rhetoric of repudiation to press an expansive case for change. The problem with acting on this rhetoric, however, was that Obama also assumed the immediate burdens of crisis management. The timing could not have been more awkward. The collapse did not force conservatives into a long-drawn-out confrontation with their own principles under the maverick leadership of McCain. Instead, it allowed conservatives to reunite by disavowing Bush's mistakes and reasserting their principles against Obama's improvisations. Moreover, the Obama administration was, as a practical matter, engaged from the get-go in stabilizing the system it was repudiating rhetorically. Candidate Obama had joined the deliberations on the bank bailout in the final days of the Bush administration, and he had lent them support. From that moment, the traditional boast of the reconstruction leader—the claim that he could address the crisis with "clean hands"—was compromised. Bold demonstrations of Obama's "new kind of politics" took a back seat to taxpayer support for corporations deemed "too big to fail." The absence of a fully played-out disjunctive phase made it harder for Obama to act on his political premise that the financial collapse was the epistemic crisis of the old order, and the actions he took to meet the emergency raised serious questions about his reconstructive credentials.

Pushing the historical record further, it appears that skipping a disjunctive phase and moving directly to reconstruction is problematic for other reason as well. Time and again, the disjunctive phase has proven a critical period of ripening for mass-based social movements insisting on fundamental change. The abolition movement was an independent force pushing Lincoln and the Republicans toward reconstructive politics; the labor movement was an independent force pushing FDR and the Democrats; the conservative movement was an independent force pushing Reagan and the Republicans. By deepening the crisis of legitimacy generated under disjunctive politics, these movements helped expose the vulnerabilities of the old order to the nation at large. Moreover, because they had an organizational standing independent of the candidates that drew on their support, they could pressure those candidates to do more once they gained office.

Obama acknowledged the point himself. In accepting his nomination at the Democratic National Convention, he reminded his audience that "change comes because the American people demand it—because they rise up and insist on new ideas and new leadership."[14] To the extent that Obama's election was movement based, however, it was not well anchored. It drew its initial support from an antiwar movement, but by Election Day, changes on the ground in Iraq and the late-breaking financial crisis had stolen much of that energy. In the end, the "movement" was organized largely around the candidate himself. It was built on his personal charisma, and by and large, he was left pretty much to his own devices in sketching his vision of "a new kind of politics." One might imagine a real social movement ripening under a President McCain as he struggled to get conservatives to respond to the financial crisis and economic contraction, but as it happened, the Obama movement developed little independent leverage over anyone. Instead of being pushed to do more, Obama has been left to court the uncommitted, the independents, and the swing voters from doubtful states. To the extent that Obama's leadership has catalyzed the formation of an independent movement pressing insiders for fundamental change, it is, paradoxically, the Tea Party, a movement organized and directed against him.

And this suggests one final implication of a truncated disjunctive episode. Short of a crisis of legitimacy sufficient to break the back of the old regime's party base, overtures for unity in the cause of a national redirection are likely to fall flat, and prospects for presidential party building are likely to be severely limited. All the reconstructive leaders in our past have been able to pick up substantial support from factions of the old regime coalition that had become disillusioned by the course of events or had lost the rationale for their prior allegiance.[15] This opportunity is critical for refashioning political coalitions, altering the terms of debate, and charting a course that supersedes the old conflicts. Notwithstanding Obama's overtures to the likes of Arlen Specter and Olympia Snowe, no president has been able to reconstruct American government and politics in the face of a rebounding phalanx of stalwarts bent on perpetuating the old formulas and continuing the old debates. On this score, even Wilson and Nixon had more to work with than Obama.

Response 3: The reconstructive model of transformational leadership is irrelevant. It has, in effect, been superseded by more purely progressive models of reform.

Models of political change drawn from the past identify Obama as a second-round opposition leader testing the line between another momentary preemption of the old order and a more decisive reconstruction of it. They also show that while many of the elements traditionally associated with reconstructive breakthroughs were present in his rise to power, some important ones were not. Past examples of second-round opposition leaders who failed to cross this line are not hard to find, so, on balance, it seems that political transformation in this case remains a long shot.

If we leave it at that, however, we may find that we are correct about the prospects for political change under Obama but wrong about the larger implications of his presidency for thinking about leadership in political time. History never repeats itself exactly, so a strict, mechanical application of a model of change drawn from the past is likely to miss as much as it picks up. Exclusive reference to the current alignment of familiar historical elements leads to two conclusions: first, that a political reconstruction of American government and politics is probably premature; second, that another opposition leader, in the line of Clinton and Obama, might be better positioned to deliver on this promise later on down the road. But is that latter expectation warranted? Have no new factors come into play over the years, no alternative understandings of change that might complicate and attenuate the traditional rhythms of political time?

Thinking about the Obama administration along these lines puts prior reconstructive episodes in a very different light. Indeed, it suggests that though American progressives may still refer ritualistically to prior episodes of transformational leadership, they have, in effect, gone a long way toward abandoning the old reconstructive formula. This assessment considers an underlying mismatch between the ideational tenets of American progressivism and the reconstructive style of leadership. It calls attention to the Left's commitment to programmatic development, social experimentation, interest management, and pragmatic adaptation, to a general disposition toward political affairs that is ill-suited to a starkly repudiative posture in politics or a strong dismantling impulse in leadership. It eyes, at the very heart of progressivism, a philosophical skepticism about durable reconstructions of power, a studied resistance to the whole idea of anchoring government and politics in firm "foundations." It highlights the progressives' alternative conception of political transformation—one in which change is open-ended, ongoing, and evolutionary. Against this backdrop, the Obama administration stands out as the strongest signal yet of a historic displacement of an old model of political renewal by a new one.

Evidence of this mismatch has emerged gradually. FDR (on the Left) and Reagan (on the Right) both drew the traditional reconstructive posture in leadership forward through the twentieth century. But the nineteenth-century origins of the model are unmistakable. The earliest examples, Jefferson and Jackson, are still the clearest and the cleanest. FDR repeatedly invoked Jackson as his inspiration, but by the Jackson standard, the New Deal transformation turned out to be a complicated and qualified affair. FDR railed against "economic royalists" as loudly as Old Hickory had, but actually destroying their institutional support, as Jackson did, was out of the question for Roosevelt. The New Deal could not dispense with the institutions its enemies controlled; in large measure, it depended on their healthy operation.

Clearly, FDR was trying to reconfigure a larger array of interests and powers in the now-interdependent industrial economy. But there is more to it than that. Far more than Jackson, Roosevelt was interested in the transformative potential of programmatic action.[16] When Jefferson and Jackson repudiated the established order of things and set about re-arranging political and institutional relationships, they were, in the main, looking for ways to return American government to its original foundations and save it from what they perceived to be a rising tide of deviant and corrupting influences. This determination to secure the foundations against drift led them to make categorical demands for a change of direction; it prompted them to build parties that would recommit the nation to the decentralization of power and to the enforcement of constitutional limits on federal action. The first reconstructive leader to suggest that the Constitution, as originally drafted, might not have all the answers to the problems of the day, that it might admit of different interpretations and require some embellishment, was Abraham Lincoln. Subordinating the Constitution to the guiding principles of the Declaration of Independence, Lincoln introduced into American politics a new conception of political change, one that was far more open-ended in its programmatic entailments than anything that had been articulated before. Little wonder that conservatives ever since have been demanding a return to "the Constitution as it was."

By the time of the New Deal reconstruction, the more progressive understanding of political change hinted at by Lincoln was firmly ensconced on the American Left. The general thrust of reform was now decidedly positive and forward-looking. The movement was outward against limits, and the alternative envisioned was less firmly anchored in the texts of the Founding. FDR still professed to be guided by the "ancient truths" of the American tradition in charting a new way forward, but the guidelines, as he understood them, were not much of a constraint. He proceeded true to what he thought was the spirit of the Constitution, all the while expressing his antagonism toward those sticklers for stricture who would return the nation to "the horse and buggy days." When Roosevelt appealed to fundamental values, it was, more often than not, to elaborate upon them—to propose, for example, that an Economic Bill of Rights be appended to the original. To be sure, the actions Roosevelt took on behalf of party building and institutional reconstruction were categorical and firmly planted in the classic style of reconstructive politics. Nor should one underestimate the Court battle and the Executive Reorganization initiative as instruments for clearing and securing the ground on which his alternative took hold. But in all these initiatives, and most especially in the party purge, Roosevelt was forced in the end to continue dealing with those he was trying to bend to his will. All told, he did less to topple interests in power than to add to them.

Progressivism rode to prominence on the heels of two reconstructive presidencies. It developed through and between the crises of the Civil War era and the Great Depression. But as a fight for social justice, progressivism harbored a sensibility all its own; social outreach through public policy making was a portentous new element in the politics of transformation. Social Security reform established a beachhead for the future expansion of a welfare state; the National Labor Relations Act brought organized labor into negotiations with industry; the Agricultural Adjustment Act tied the farm economy to a national plan; the Tennessee Valley Authority developed an entire region that had been left behind in national economic development. The progressivism of the New Deal bequeathed to its contemporary heirs an ever-larger stake in an ever-broader range of interests and concerns. It fostered pluralism, elevated the importance of interest management, and institutionalized ameliorative forms of action. That could not but complicate reconstructive action in the old mold.

Ultimately, the progressive commitment to interest service and programmatic action cautions against freewheeling assaults on established power, even for leaders otherwise well-positioned to deliver them. To the extent that it defines leadership positively, as socially effective innovations in public policy, the emphasis will be on practical problem solving. A premium will be paid for bringing all interested parties to the table and negotiating to find common ground. And so long as change is an ongoing and open-ended proposition, it may suffice to establish new beachheads in public policy and allow them to expand incrementally as needed. The progressive leader may forcefully renounce the politics of the past, but he or she is likely to do so in the cause of acting more constructively and responsibly, railing against systemic failures while nevertheless projecting an abiding faith in expertise and cooperative problem solving.

In lashing out against an "era of profound irresponsibility," Obama has drawn forward a pure form of this modern, progressive ideal. The central premise implicit in virtually everything his administration has done is that good policy will transform American politics. So far at least, he has expressed far more interest in moving his policy priorities forward than in building a new party,[17] far more interest in deploying institutional resources for policy development than in institutional reconstruction. His "new kind of politics" privileges the pragmatic, rational, problem-solving ethos. He exudes the progressive spirit of postpartisan engagement, of openness to new information, of realism in dealing with friend and foe alike, of steadiness in pursuit of policy solutions to big national challenges, of faith in expertise.[18] Full "engagement" is the keynote of his leadership. As sustained, intense, and productive as the efforts along these lines have been, they suggest neither the early stages of a classical reconstruction nor the temporizing actions of a lesser light; they suggest that Obama is operating with a different model of political transformation altogether.[19]

If the health care initiative is emblematic of Obama's leadership, it is because the initiative reflects this view of leadership as tackling big national problems and finding practical solutions that enlist all the key players in the cause of doing something new. By the same token, no policy breakthrough so historic in its social sweep was ever achieved with so little disruption to the position of established interests and with so much accommodation to the preexisting arrangements of power. Accommodating all the major players *in* the current system for a major reform *of* the system proved to be a mind-boggling challenge; that is what made the arrangement ultimately arrived at so incredibly complicated. But this is just the sort of challenge that Obama excels at. Somehow he was able to weave a major reform through the thicket of interests that controlled things as he found them.

Action like that might be responsive to the nation's problems and provide new services to a lot of people who did not have them before, but does action like that transform American politics? Of all the questions that might be raised about the Obama presidency thus far, the one most laden with historic significance is whether, and to what extent, progressive policy making is effective as an *alternative* route to political transformation. The early signs are not very encouraging. Policy making on the big issues is, as we have seen, a very complicated business; it is multifaceted, difficult to understand, and even with success, it is likely to disappoint. It is such a huge consumer of political energy that any model of political transformation that elevates policy accomplishment above all else is likely to exhaust itself rather quickly. The health care victory was impressive in its own way, but in *these* ways it appears to be no substitute for the historical practice of reconstructive leadership.

Dedication to solving the nation's problems is an admirable trait in a political leader, but it sets up a daunting standard of success. The reconstructive leaders of our past did not so much solve the problems that brought them to power as move the nation past those problems in pursuit of other political possibilities. When push came to shove, it was the disruptive potential of presidential office to upend the interests and institutions that supported the politics of the past that opened the ground necessary for a "new foundation" to take hold. Policy innovations unaccompanied by a more decisive reconfiguration of power or a new coalitional alignment seem more likely to perpetuate than to transcend or displace the politics of the past.

And this seems especially true today. For better or worse, the great rhetorical divide in American politics over the past thirty years has been less over which policies to pursue than over the "policy-mindedness" of contemporary politics itself.[20] The Reagan Revolution was categorical in its critique of progressive interventions, and progressivism's opponents are all the more so today. As Glenn Beck has put it, "progressivism is a cancer and it is eating our Constitution."[21] Far from offering a new formula for transcending old debates, leadership in the progressive mold seems just more fuel for the fire.

Response 4: The reconstructive model of political transformation is still operative but only for the American Right.

Though Lincoln and FDR introduced new and complicating elements into the politics of reconstruction, Reagan repaired to the clarity and simplicity of the original posture. He rejected in principle the open-ended, pragmatic approach to change. He enlisted the Constitution's Framers as libertarians to renounce federal aggrandizement and the tyranny of the welfare state. He stigmatized the realists' faith in a "living" Constitution as a disastrous corruption of standards; his substitutes were originalism and idealism. Casting the nation's policy-making elite as meddlesome interlopers intruding on social and economic freedom, he called into question the problem-solving ethos itself. FDR may have invoked the example of Andrew Jackson more often, but Reagan more fully captured the categorical character of its redemptive vision.

The aura of insurgency that accompanied Obama's rise to power was magnified against this backdrop. His distillation of the progressive spirit appeared radical only by comparison to the prevailing conservative orthodoxy. I have raised some questions about the reconstructive potential of Obama's brief for progressivism pure and unaided, but we have yet to consider the other way in which his leadership might play to a transformative effect. With the Republican Party prodded on by the Tea Party movement, the prospect cannot be ruled out that Obama's presidency will serve to propel the conservative movement forward toward a final, more decisive rout of the progressive alternative. A passing thunder on the Left might be just the thing to catalyze a second and more thoroughgoing reconstruction from the Right.

Nothing in our history suggests that reconstruction must come from an ideological position polar opposite to that which animated the one immediately prior. Jackson drove a second, more thoroughgoing reconstruction in the spirit of Jefferson's, and FDR's deepened the progressivism implicit in Lincoln's. The Reagan reconstruction is especially suggestive of this potential, for of all the reconstructive episodes in American presidential history, his proved to be the least thoroughgoing. To be sure, Reagan did many of the things that we associate with reconstructive politics. He consolidated a new Republican coalition, strengthened the party organization, and recast its ideological appeal. He moved decisively against core constituencies of the liberal regime—organized labor and welfare recipients most prominently—and he installed a durable set of new priorities in the federal government. But Reagan did not actually dismantle any liberal program of significance, nor did he dislodge any institution vital to the support of progressive government.

This reconstruction proved to be shallower even than Roosevelt's. It was more rhetorical and political than institutional and governmental. Beneath the rhetoric was no small dose of pragmatic action.

This itself had a durable effect. With so much of the infrastructure of liberalism and progressivism still in place, movement conservatives have never been at a loss for targets to mobilize against. Though the nation's agenda has been bound for decades by conservatives' priorities, they have never completely relinquished their reconstructive posture, and the Obama administration has given them plenty with which to revive its latent potential. Their reconstructive rhetoric continues to resonate with a clarity and simplicity no longer matched on the American Left. The flip side of progressivism's current limitations as a vehicle for political transformation is the persistent drumbeat for its categorical rejection on the Right.

But if movement conservatives are still on the offensive, seemingly unhampered by the latter-day complications of the progressive mindset, is their reconstructive posture really the more potent one? Can reconstructive politics on the Right move beyond a rhetorical assault on the legitimacy of progressive government toward something more institutionally decisive? In the near term at least, there is good reason for skepticism. For one thing, whatever Obama's limitations as a transformational leader, his circumstances are hardly dire, and he is unlikely to let anyone forget the national calamity that gestated on the conservatives' watch. Pointing back to the still-considerable freedom to maneuver that attends Obama's authority as an opposition leader brings this inquiry full circle. By sharpening its ideological stance, the Right risks marginalizing itself and reinvigorating the president's appeal to more consensual norms.

A second, more fundamental, reason for skepticism has to do with the conservatives' reconstructive vision. The reconstructive stance in conservative rhetoric is sharpened both by its categorical rejection of progressivism as a corruption of the original Constitution and by its appeal back to a limited government that maximizes individual liberty. But there is nothing, either in history or in modern social reality, to suggest that such an alternative could actually be implemented. When policy making in America was more strictly limited, liberty was maximized only for some. The prerogatives of masters over slaves, employers over employees, and husbands over wives meant, in effect, that for most Americans, government was far more oppressive in earlier times, when it was small and relatively passive, than today, when it is big and relatively active. By the same token, though the state built by the progressives extends far beyond anything contemplated by the Framers, so too does the range of interests that are now free to make demands on it. A small government that maximizes liberty may have great rhetorical appeal in America, but it is a purely theoretical proposition without precedent in an advanced democracy teeming with contending interests and enmeshed in global commerce. It is not clear how a more thoroughgoing pursuit of the conservative project could, as a practical matter, reconcile and manage the demands now routinely placed on the American state.

A final and closely related reason for skepticism is that modern democracy has gone far toward eliminating alternative ways of governing. Absent formal social exclusions, contemporary conservatives have no choice but to propose policy solutions of their own to all the same problems, and those policies are now subject to the same performance standards as their opponents' policies. As George H. W. Bush discovered after making his "No New Taxes" pledge and as George W. Bush acknowledged in expanding the Medicare entitlement, a categorical critique of big government only goes so far. To the extent that government is a practical affair, to the extent that the demands for government continue to grow apace, to the extent that government has itself become one gigantic policy-generating machine, to the extent that the standard is "whatever works," there is a progressive bias built into the system itself. Especially telling in this regard is that contemporary conservatives have done more to duplicate the policy-generating machinery of progressivism than to displace it. They have set up their own think tanks, cultivated their own cadres of experts, and developed their own media outlets. This has prepared them to parry and defeat the Left's substantive preferences with policy proposals of their own, but so long as government is a matter of policy and performance, everything about it is more contingent, open-ended, and changeable.

But if prospects for a more thoroughgoing reconstruction from the Right are not especially bright, neither are they wholly implausible. Consider the mechanisms now at hand to pursue it. First, and most familiar, is a legislative mechanism: "Starve the beast." So long as the federal government remains awash in a sea of debt and resistance to new taxes remains high, it will be easier for conservatives to find legislative allies than it has been for progressives. This is the flip side of the coalition-building difficulties Obama has faced both in breaking the unity of the opposition and in overcoming the dissonance within his own ranks. Although conservatives have done little to shrink the size of government, a long-term strategy of block, delay, and neglect with regard to progressive priorities can itself have systemic effects.[22] Second, and of increasing importance, is the judicial mechanism. The rise of a younger and more decidedly conservative majority on the Supreme Court is a new element in play. Originalism may be little more than a theoretical proposition, but currently it is the only coherent theory of the Constitution strongly represented on the Court. If sympathetic judges take more direct aim at the "living Constitution," if they roll back loose interpretations of, say, the commerce clause, much of the legal ground on which the progressive state was built will be destabilized.

But the most interesting of the new reconstructive mechanisms developed by the Right is executive. Rounding out the arsenal of new instruments developed over the years by conservatives to change the foundations of American government and politics is the "unitary theory" of the executive. All reconstructive movements have relied on presidential power to break the back of the old regime and chart a new course, but hitherto they have also offered up other institutions that would match their indulgence of greater power in the presidency with new instruments for enforcing collective responsibility, collaborative decision making, and cooperative management. The progressives were especially creative in this regard. They elevated the authority of professionalism, science, expertise, and public opinion; they introduced the values of pluralism, information sharing, and publicity into the policy-making process itself; and they surrounded the presidency with independent agencies and offices geared for cooperative management. The Obama administration has exemplified the progressive approach to executive aggrandizement, pulling power away from committee chairs in Congress by transferring the agenda-setting role to an expert medical board (in the case of health care) and a bipartisan debt commission (in the case of reordering budget priorities). The unitary theory of the executive is an instrument of a different sort.[23] It harkens back to the Constitution to argue that executive power is all vested in the president alone, and on that ground, it joins the legitimating claims of originalism to the practical assertion of exclusive and unilateral presidential control over the vast powers and resources of the modern executive establishment. Not only is this a potent formula for circumventing the values and institutions upon which the progressives relied for maintaining collective responsibility, but it is also a potent new tool for redirecting the substantive commitments and priorities of the government itself.

Win or lose, presidents change things, and that gives us all a stake in the outcome of their efforts. The perspective of political time offers a window into current prospects for the polity, and in the case of a president whose leadership came wrapped in promises of political transformation, it is an especially telling one. We know what that sort of leadership has looked like in the past, we know what it has entailed, and we know how valuable it has been to the periodic revitalization of American government and politics. The history of presidential leadership does not foretell the future, but it does help to focus our attention on the systemic stakes in play, to specify the live possibilities, and to draw out their respective implications.

The first two years of the Obama presidency have brought four different scenarios into view. The first, in which Obama stiffens his reconstructive posture in the face of intensifying push back and presses ahead toward a decisive transformation, remains on the table, but just barely. It was given credence by events during the very last weeks of the Bush administration, and it remained even then a long shot. The stars were only partially aligned for such an outcome; too many of the familiar elements were missing or only weakly present to instill confidence in an outcome of that sort.

Throughout the presidential campaign, a second scenario seemed the more plausible. In this scenario, Obama is a second-round opposition leader pressing the critique of the old regime and probing for reconstructive possibilities but still finding the material for such a transformation limited. It is true that Obama, unlike most other preemptive leaders, actually secured passage of his signature reform policy, health care reform. But rather than securing the legitimacy of his alternative standard of rule, health care reform seems to have rallied opposition to it and revived the old lines of political cleavage, and that seems more consistent with the preemptive pattern.

Obama's experience has highlighted the significance to reconstructive politics of social mobilization independent of campaign organizations and interest groups, and at present, a broad-based social movement mobilized on behalf of progressive priorities remains a dim prospect. Indeed, the more we see of the Obama presidency, the more reason we have to wonder whether a political reconstruction is ever again likely to come from the American Left. Progressives built a government more readily disposed to the responsible management of social interests, and that appears to be the nub of the paradox of Obama's leadership. Notwithstanding his high ambitions, his presidency marks a trend toward the abandonment of the classic model of transformational leadership. His leadership bespeaks a pure form of progressivism in which wrenching, ground-clearing change appears increasingly irrelevant, if not downright irresponsible. It points to an alternative vision of transformation, one more fully attuned to the complexities of modern democracy and more accommodating to incremental problem solving. For better or worse, it also directs presidents to exhaust their transformational ambitions on a few big policy initiatives.

Does this attenuation of the classic model extend to transformative ambitions on the Right? My guess is that it does. Progressivism has proven hard for conservatives to dislodge in any decisive fashion because it is as much a way of governing as a set of substantive commitments. The progressive bias in governmental affairs runs deep; policy is king and performance is the standard of rule. These values seem now to be sown into the basic operations of American government and politics. Still, there are new instruments for reconstruction gestating in the conservatives' toolkit that give me pause.

Notes

PREFACE TO THE SECOND EDITION

1. Stephen Skowronek, *The Politics Presidents Make: Leadership from John Adams to George Bush* (Cambridge, MA: Belknap Press of Harvard University Press, 1993).
2. Barack Obama, campaign rally (Columbia, MO, 30 October 2008).
3. Skowronek, *The Politics Presidents Make*, 407.

CHAPTER ONE.
THE PRESIDENCY IN AMERICAN POLITICAL
DEVELOPMENT: A THIRD LOOK

1. Stephen Skowronek, "The Presidency in American Political Development: A Third Look," *Presidential Studies Quarterly* 32 (December 2002): 743–752.
2. Henry Jones Ford, *The Rise and Growth of American Politics: A Sketch of Constitutional Development* (1898; repr., New York: Da Capo, 1967), 56, 279.
3. *Report of the President's Committee on Administrative Management with Studies of Administrative Management in the Federal Government*. Submitted to the president and to Congress in accordance with Public Law 739, 74th Congress, 2nd sess. (Washington, DC: Government Printing Office, 1937); see also Richard Polenberg, *Reorganizing Roosevelt's Government: The Controversy over Executive Reorganization, 1936–1939* (Cambridge, MA: Harvard University Press, 1966).
4. Richard Neustadt, *Presidential Power: The Politics of Leadership* (New York: John Wiley and Sons, 1960).
5. Arthur Schlesinger, Jr., *The Imperial Presidency* (Boston: Houghton Mifflin, 1973).
6. Theodore Lowi, *The Personal President: Power Invested, Promise Unfulfilled* (Ithaca, NY: Cornell University Press, 1985).
7. Terry Eastland, *Energy in the Executive: The Case for a Strong Presidency* (New York: Free Press, 1992); Harvey C. Mansfield, Jr., *Taming the Prince: The Ambivalence of Modern Executive Power* (New York: Free Press, 1989).
8. The Iran-Contra episode refers to a scandal in which operatives in the Reagan White House sold arms to Iran in violation of President's Reagan's

stated policy and used the proceeds to fund the Nicaraguan Contras in violation of an explicit congressional ban.

9. In this regard the most interesting thing about the Iran-Contra affair may be that it did not derail insurgent conservatives. On the contrary, they took it as an opportunity to discredit their political and institutional detractors and push forward their own understanding of the Constitution. *Report of the Congressional Committees Investigating the Iran-Contra Affair: The Minority Report,* 100th Congress, 1st sess., S. Rep. 100-216, 13 November 1987, Washington, DC, 430–633.

10. Bruce Bartlett, *Imposter: How George W. Bush Bankrupted America and Betrayed the Reagan Legacy* (New York: Doubleday, 2006); Richard Viguerie, *Conservatives Betrayed: How George W. Bush and Other Big Government Republicans Hijacked the Conservative Cause* (Los Angeles: Bonus Books, 2006); Jeffrey Goldberg, "Party Unfaithful: The Republican Implosion," *New Yorker,* 4 June 2007, 40–46.

11. Sidney Milkis, *The President and the Parties: The Transformation of the American Party System since the New Deal* (New York: Oxford University Press, 1993).

12. Phillip Abbott, *The Exemplary President: Franklin D. Roosevelt and the American Political Tradition* (Amherst: University of Massachusetts Press, 1990); William E. Leuchetberg, *In the Shadow of FDR: From Harry Truman to George W. Bush,* 3rd ed. (Ithaca, NY: Cornell University Press, 2001).

13. *Report of the President's Committee,* 1.

14. Stephen Hess, *Organizing the Presidency* (Washington, DC: Brookings Institution, 1976), 53–56.

15. James David Barber, *The Presidential Character: Predicting Performance in the White House* (Englewood Cliffs, NJ: Prentice-Hall, 1972); Thomas Cronin, "An Imperiled Presidency?" *Society* 16, no. 1 (1978): 57–64; Terry M. Moe, "The Politicized Presidency," in *The New Direction in American Politics,* ed. John E. Chubb and Paul E. Peterson (Washington, DC: Brookings Institution, 1985).

16. Lowi, *The Personal President;* Moe, "The Politicized Presidency."

17. William G. Howell, *Power without Persuasion: The Politics of Direct Presidential Action* (Princeton, NJ: Princeton University Press, 2003); Steven G. Calabresi, "The Vesting Clauses as Power Grants," *Northwestern University Law Review* 88 (Summer 1994): 1377–1405.

18. Abraham Lincoln, "Speech at Peoria, Illinois (October 16, 1854)," in *Collected Works of Abraham Lincoln,* ed. Roy P. Basler, 9 vols. (New Brunswick, NJ: Rutgers University Press, 1953–1955), 2:276.

19. Franklin D. Roosevelt, "Inaugural Address" (Washington, DC, 4 March 1933), in *The Public Papers and Addresses of Franklin Roosevelt,* ed. Samuel Rosenman, 13 vols. (New York: Random House, 1938–1950), 2:14–15.

20. Ronald Reagan, "Remarks Accepting the Republican Nomination in 1984" (Dallas, Texas, 23 August 1984), in *Public Papers of the Presidents of the United States: Ronald Reagan,* 15 vols. (Washington, DC: Government Printing Office, 1984), 2:1180.

21. Lowi, *The Personal President,* xi.

22. Fred I. Greenstein, "The Need for an Early Appraisal of the Reagan Presidency," in *The Reagan Presidency: An Early Assessment,* ed. Fred I. Greenstein (Baltimore: The Johns Hopkins University Press, 1983), 3. A more fully developed statement of the modern-presidency perspective can be found in Fred I. Greenstein, "Continuity and Change in the Modern Presidency," in *The New American Political System,* ed. Anthony King (Washington, DC: American Enterprise Institute, 1979), 45–86.

23. Terry Moe, "Presidents, Institutions, and Theory," in *Researching the Presidency,* ed. George C. Edwards III, John H. Kessel, and Bert A. Rockman (Pittsburgh: University of Pittsburgh Press, 1993); Terry Moe and William Howell, "The Presidential Power of Unilateral Action," *Journal of Law, Economics, and Organization* 15, no. 1 (1999): 132–179; Howell, *Power without Persuasion;* Kenneth R. Mayer, *With a Stroke of a Pen: Executive Orders and Presidential Power* (Princeton, NJ: Princeton University Press, 2001).

24. Ryan J. Barilleaux, *The Post-Modern Presidency: The Office after Ronald Reagan* (New York: Praeger, 1988); Richard Rose, *The Postmodern President* (Chatham, NJ: Chatham House, 1988).

25. Samuel Kernell, *Going Public: New Strategies of Presidential Leadership* (Washington, DC: Congressional Quarterly Press, 1997).

26. Abraham Lincoln, "A House Divided" (Springfield, IL, 16 June 1858), in Basler, *Collected Works of Abraham Lincoln,* 2:461.

27. Carter made various statements to this effect. See Jimmy Carter, "Playboy Interview: Jimmy Carter," by Robert Scheer, *Playboy Magazine,* November 1978, 64; *The Presidential Campaign 1976,* vol. 1, part 1, *Jimmy Carter* (Washington, DC: Government Printing Office, 1978), 292; Betty Glad, *Jimmy Carter: In Search of the Great White House* (New York: Norton, 1980), 321.

28. Ronald Reagan, first inaugural address (Washington, DC, 20 January 1981), available at http://www.reaganfoundation.org/reagan/speeches/first.asp.

29. The regime-based structure of American political history is widely recognized but is seldom related directly to dynamics of presidential leadership. The explanation most commonly offered in the literature is the theory of critical elections. See V. O. Key, "A Theory of Critical Elections," *Journal of Politics* 17 (1955): 3–18; Walter Dean Burnham, *Critical Elections and the Mainsprings of American Politics* (New York: Norton, 1970).

30. Woodrow Wilson, *Constitutional Government in the United States* (New

York: Columbia University Press, 1908), 57. For his earlier view, see Woodrow Wilson, *Congressional Government: A Study in American Politics* (1885; repr., Boston: Houghton Mifflin, 1956).

31. Ford, *The Rise and Growth of American Politics,* 293.

32. Neustadt, *Presidential Power,* 33.

33. Terry M. Moe and Michael Caldwell, "The Institutional Foundations of Democratic Government: A Comparison of Presidential and Parliamentary Systems," *Journal of Institutional and Theoretical Economics* 150, no. 1 (1994): 176; Terry M. Moe and Scott A. Wilson, "Presidents and the Politics of Structure," *Law and Contemporary Problems* 57 (Spring 1994): 1–44; Terry Moe, "Presidential Power and the Power of Theory," in *The Evolution of Political Knowledge: Theory and Inquiry in American Politics,* ed. Edward Mansfield and Richard Sisson (Columbus: Ohio State University Press, 2004).

34. Jeffrey Tulis, *The Rhetorical Presidency* (Princeton, NJ: Princeton University Press, 1987).

35. Alexander Hamilton feared the disruptive political impact of presidential succession, observing that it would create "a disgraceful and ruinous mutability in the administration of the government." He argued for minimizing the disruption and stabilizing the regime by avoiding term limits and allowing incumbents to stand for reelection as many times as they desired. Alexander Hamilton, "Federalist 72," in *The Federalist,* ed. Jacob E. Cooke (Middletown, CT: Wesleyan University Press, 1961).

CHAPTER TWO. PRESIDENTIAL LEADERSHIP IN POLITICAL TIME

1. Stephen Skowronek, "Presidential Leadership in Political Time," in *The Presidency and the Political System,* ed. Michael Nelson (Washington, DC: Congressional Quarterly Press, 1984). Copyright © CQ Press, 2005, a division of Congressional Quarterly Inc.

2. Woodrow Wilson, *Constitutional Government in the United States* (New York: Columbia University Press, 1908), 70.

3. Thomas A. Bailey, *Presidential Greatness: The Image and the Man from George Washington to the Present* (New York: Appleton-Century-Crofts, 1966), 23–34. Bailey critically discusses the ratings by professional historians. See also the more recent work of Sidney Milkis and Mark Landy, *Presidential Greatness* (Lawrence: University Press of Kansas, 2000).

4. Robert Remini, *Andrew Jackson and the Course of American Freedom, 1822–1832* (New York: Harper and Row, 1981), 2:12–38, 74–142.

5. Quoted in Frank Freidel, *FDR and the South* (Baton Rouge: Louisiana State University Press, 1965), 42.

6. Remini, *Andrew Jackson and the Course of American Freedom,* 2:152–202, 248–256.

7. The famous veto of the Maysville Road bill, for example, was notable for its limited implications. The veto challenged federal support for an *intrastate* project and the bill was specifically selected as an example because the road to be funded was located in Henry Clay's Kentucky. On Jackson's objectives in civil service reform, see Albert Somit, "Andrew Jackson as an Administrative Reformer," *Tennessee Historical Quarterly* 13 (September 1954): 204–223; Eric McKinley Erikson, "The Federal Civil Service under President Jackson," *Mississippi Valley Historical Review* 13 (March 1927): 517–540. Also significant in this regard is Richard G. Miller, "The Tariff of 1832: The Issue That Failed," *Filson Club History Quarterly* 49, no. 3 (July 1975): 221–230.

8. The analysis in this and the following paragraphs draws on the following works: Remini, *Andrew Jackson and the Course of American Freedom;* Robert Remini, *Andrew Jackson and the Bank War: A Study in the Growth of Presidential Power* (New York: Norton, 1967); Marquis James, *Andrew Jackson: Portrait of a President* (New York: Grosset and Dunlap, 1937), 283–303, 350–385; and Arthur Schlesinger, Jr., *The Age of Jackson* (Boston: Little, Brown, 1945), 74–131.

9. Charles Sellers, Jr., "Who Were the Southern Whigs?" *American Historical Review* 49 (January 1954): 335–346.

10. Harry Scheiber, "The Pet Banks in Jacksonian Politics and Finance, 1833–1841," *Journal of Economic History* 23 (June 1963): 196–214; Frank Otto Gatell, "Spoils of the Bank War: Political Bias in the Selection of Pet Banks," *American Historical Review* 70 (October 1964): 35–58; Frank Otto Gatell, "Secretary Taney and the Baltimore Pets: A Study in Banking and Politics," *Business History Review* 39 (Summer 1965): 205–227.

11. Quoted in James MacGregor Burns, *Roosevelt: The Lion and the Fox* (New York: Harcourt, Brace and World, 1956), 208.

12. The analysis in this and the following paragraphs draws on Burns, *Roosevelt;* Freidel, *FDR and the South.*

13. Burns, *Roosevelt,* 223–241.

14. Freidel, *FDR and the South,* 99.

15. Richard Polenberg, *Reorganizing Roosevelt's Government: The Controversy over Executive Reorganization, 1936–1939* (Cambridge, MA: Harvard University Press, 1966).

16. The analysis in this and the following paragraphs draws on the following works: Charles Sellers, *James K. Polk: Continentalist, 1843–1846* (Princeton, NJ: Princeton University Press, 1966); John Schroeder, *Mr. Polk's War: American Op-*

position and Dissent, 1846–1848 (Madison: University of Wisconsin Press, 1973); Norman A. Graebner, "James Polk," in *America's Ten Greatest Presidents,* ed. Morton Borden (Chicago: Rand McNally, 1961); Charles McCoy, *Polk and the Presidency* (Austin: University of Texas Press, 1960).

17. Sellers, *James K. Polk,* 50.

18. Ibid., 113–114, 123.

19. Ibid., 282–283.

20. Ibid., 162–164; Joseph G. Raybeck, "Martin Van Buren's Break with James K. Polk: The Record," *New York History* 36 (January 1955): 51–62; Norman A. Graebner, "James K. Polk: A Study in Federal Patronage," *Mississippi Valley Historical Review* 38 (March 1952): 613–632.

21. James K. Polk, "Special Message" (8 August 1846), available at John T. Woolley and Gerhard Peters, *The American Presidency Project* (Santa Barbara: University of California [hosted], Gerhard Peters [database]), http://www.presidency.ucsb.edu/ws/?pid=67941.

22. Sellers, *James K. Polk,* 483.

23. Frederick J. Blue, *The Free Soilers: Third Party Politics, 1848–54* (Urbana: University of Illinois Press, 1973), 16–80; John Mayfield, *Rehearsal for Republicanism: Free Soil and the Politics of Antislavery* (Port Washington, NY: Kennikat Press, 1980), 80–125.

24. McCoy, *Polk and the Presidency,* 197–198, 203–204.

25. Arthur M. Schlesinger, Jr., *A Thousand Days: John F. Kennedy in the White House* (Boston: Houghton Mifflin, 1965), 675–676.

26. Carroll Kilpatrick, "The Kennedy Style and Congress," *Virginia Quarterly Review* 39 (Winter 1963): 1–11; Henry Fairlie, *The Kennedy Promise: The Politics of Expectation* (New York: Doubleday, 1973), esp. 235–263.

27. Freidel, *FDR and the South,* 71–102.

28. Herbert S. Parmet, *The Democrats: The Years after FDR* (New York: Oxford University Press, 1976), 80–82.

29. The analysis in this and the following paragraphs draws on material presented in the following works: Carl M. Brauer, *John F. Kennedy and the Second Reconstruction* (New York: Columbia University Press, 1977); Schlesinger, *A Thousand Days;* Parmet, *The Democrats,* 193–247; Bruce Miroff, *Pragmatic Illusions: The Presidential Politics of John F. Kennedy* (New York: David McKay, 1976), 223–270; Fairlie, *The Kennedy Promise,* 235–263.

30. Brauer, *John F. Kennedy and the Second Reconstruction,* 30–38; Schlesinger, *A Thousand Days,* 47–52.

31. Brauer, *John F. Kennedy and the Second Reconstruction,* 61–88; Schlesinger, *A Thousand Days,* 30–31.

32. Parmet, *The Democrats*, 211; Brauer, *John F. Kennedy and the Second Reconstruction*, 128–130.

33. Holman Hamilton, *Prologue to Conflict: The Crisis and Compromise of 1850* (Lexington: University of Kentucky Press, 1964), esp. 156–164.

34. Roy F. Nichols, *The Democratic Machine, 1850–1854* (New York: AMS Press, 1967).

35. Parmet, *The Democrats*, 220–228.

36. The analysis in this and the following paragraphs draws on Roy F. Nichols, *Franklin Pierce: Young Hickory of Granite Hills* (Philadelphia: University of Pennsylvania Press, 1969); Nichols, *The Democratic Machine*, 147–226.

37. Nichols, *Franklin Pierce*, 292–293, 308–310; Nichols, *The Democratic Machine*, 224.

38. Roy F. Nichols, "The Kansas-Nebraska Act: A Century of Historiography," *Mississippi Valley Historical Review* 43 (September 1956): 187–212; Nichols, *Franklin Pierce*, 292–324, 333–338.

39. Nichols, *Franklin Pierce*, 360–365, 425–434.

40. Jack Knott and Aaron Wildavsky, "Skepticism and Dogma in the White House: Jimmy Carter's Theory of Governing," *Wilson Quarterly* 1 (Winter 1977): 49–68; James Fallows, "The Passionless Presidency: The Trouble with Jimmy Carter's Administration," *Atlantic Monthly*, May 1979, 33–58, and June 1979, 75–81.

41. The analysis in this and the following paragraphs draws on the following works: Robert Shogun, *Promises to Keep: Carter's First Hundred Days* (New York: Thomas Y. Crowell, 1977); Haynes Johnson, *In the Absence of Power: Governing America* (New York: Viking, 1980); Robert Shogun, *None of the Above: Why Presidents Fail and What Can Be Done about It* (New York: New American Library, 1982), 177–250; Alan Wolfe, *America's Impasse: The Rise and Fall of the Politics of Growth* (New York: Pantheon, 1981), 200–229; also the essays collected in Thomas Ferguson and Joel Rogers, eds., *Hidden Election: Politics and Economics in the 1980 Presidential Campaign* (New York: Pantheon, 1981), especially Gerald Epstein, "Domestic Stagflation and Monetary Policy," 141–195.

42. Shogun, *None of the Above*, 220.

43. Johnson, *In the Absence of Power*, 233–245.

44. "Transcript of the President's Address to the Country on Energy Problems," *New York Times*, 16 July 1979.

CHAPTER THREE. THE POLITICS
OF LEADERSHIP AT THE END OF
THE TWENTIETH CENTURY

1. Stephen Skowronek, "The Setting: Continuity and Change in the Politics of Leadership," in *Elections 2000*, ed. Michael Nelson (Washington, DC: Congressional Quarterly Press, 2000). Copyright © CQ Press, 2001, a division of Congressional Quarterly Inc.

2. Stephen Skowronek, "Notes on the Presidency in the Political Order," in *Studies in American Political Development* (New Haven, CT: Yale University Press, 1986).

3. Bruce Miroff, "The Presidency and the Public: Leadership as Spectacle," in *The Presidency and the Political System*, ed. Michael Nelson (Washington, DC: Congressional Quarterly Press, 1998). Also see Elizabeth Drew, *White House Showdown: The Struggle between the Gingrich Congress and the Clinton White House* (New York: Simon and Schuster, 1996).

4. See, for example, Theodore Lowi, *The Personal President: Power Invested, Promise Unfulfilled* (Ithaca, NY: Cornell University Press, 1985); Richard Rose, *The Post-Modern Presidency* (Chatham, NJ: Chatham House, 1988); Samuel Kernell, *Going Public: New Strategies of Presidential Leadership* (Washington, DC: Congressional Quarterly Press, 1986); Benjamin Ginsberg and Martin Shefter, *Politics by Other Means: Politicians, Prosecutors, and the Press from Watergate to Whitewater* (New York: Norton, 1999).

5. Bob Woodward located Clinton in a contemporary pattern of investigation-wracked administrations: *Shadow: Five Presidents and the Legacy of Watergate* (New York: Simon and Schuster, 1999).

6. Kernell, *Going Public*, 25–38.

7. See in particular Rose, *The Post-Modern Presidency;* Lowi, *The Personal President.*

8. *The Presidential Campaign 1976*, vol. 1, *Jimmy Carter* (Washington, DC: Government Printing Office, 1978–1979), part 1:244.

9. Ibid., 174, 203, 298.

10. See, for example, Emmet John Hughes, "The Presidency vs. Jimmy Carter," *Fortune*, 4 December 1978, 50–64; Sidney Weintraub, "Carter's Hoover Syndrome," *New Leader*, 24 March 1980, 5–6; James L. Sundquist, "The Crisis of Competence in Our National Government," *Political Science Quarterly* 95 (Summer 1980): 182–208.

11. Jimmy Carter, "Energy and National Goals, July 15, 1979," in *Public Papers of the Presidents of the United States: Jimmy Carter*, 8 vols. (Washington, DC: Government Printing Office, 1977–1981), 6:1235–1239.

12. Jimmy Carter, "Remarks Accepting the Presidential Nomination at the 1980 Democratic National Convention in New York" (14 August 1980), available at John T. Woolley and Gerhard Peters, *The American Presidency Project* (Santa Barbara: University of California [hosted], Gerhard Peters [database]), http://www.presidency.ucsb.edu/ws/?pid=44909.

13. Ronald Reagan, "Speech Accepting the Republican Nomination," *New York Times*, 18 July 1980.

14. Ronald Reagan, "Inaugural Address, 20 January 1981," in *Public Papers of the Presidents of the United States: Ronald Reagan*, 15 vols. (Washington, DC: Government Printing Office, 1982), 1:1.

15. Abraham Lincoln, "Speech at Peoria, Illinois (16 October 1854)," in *Collected Works of Abraham Lincoln*, ed. Roy P. Basler, 9 vols. (New Brunswick, NJ: Rutgers University Press, 1953–1955), 2:276.

16. Franklin D. Roosevelt, "Inaugural Address" (Washington, DC, 4 March 1933), in *The Public Papers and Addresses of Franklin Roosevelt*, ed. Samuel Rosenman, 13 vols. (New York: Random House, 1938–1950), 2:14–15.

17. Ronald Reagan, "Remarks Accepting the Republican Nomination in 1984" (Dallas, TX, 23 August 1984), in *Public Papers of the Presidents of the United States: Ronald Reagan*, 15 vols. (Washington, DC: Government Printing Office, 1984), 2:1180.

18. Ronald Reagan, farewell address to the Nation (Oval Office of the White House, Washington, DC, 11 January 1989), available at http://www.reaganfoundation.org/reagan/speeches/farewell.asp.

19. Daniel Galvin, "Presidential Party Building in the United States, 1953–2001" (Ph.D. diss., Yale University, 2007), 595–680.

20. Jacob S. Hacker, "Privatizing Risk without Privatizing the Welfare State: The Hidden Politics of Social Policy Retrenchment in the United States," *American Political Science Review* 98 (May 2004): 243–260.

21. George H. W. Bush, speech to the Republican National Committee (Washington, DC, 18 January 1989), Federal News Service.

22. Walter Dean Burnham, "The Politics of Repudiation in 1992: Edging toward Upheaval," *American Prospect* (Winter 1993): 22–23.

23. George H. W. Bush, "Acceptance Speech before the Republican National Convention," *New York Times*, 19 August 1988.

24. A. M. Rosenthal, "Mr. Bush Steps Aside," *New York Times*, 13 October 1992.

25. The seven presidents who voluntarily withdrew from second-term bids were James K. Polk, James Buchanan, Rutherford B. Hayes, Theodore Roosevelt, Calvin Coolidge, Harry S. Truman, and Lyndon B. Johnson.

26. Vernon Van Dyke, *Ideology and Political Culture* (Chatham, NJ: Chatham House, 1995), 274–283.

27. For example, Robin Toner, "Arkansas' Clinton Enters the '92 Race for President," *New York Times,* 4 October 1991.

28. William Jefferson Clinton, State of the Union address (Washington, DC, 23 January 1996), available at http://clinton4.nara.gov/WH/New/other/sotu.html.

29. William Jefferson Clinton, second inaugural address (Washington, DC, 20 January 1997), available at *The Avalon Project at Yale Law School,* http://www.yale.edu/lawweb/avalon/presiden/inaug/clinton2.htm.

30. Even on his health care initiative, Clinton felt compelled to try to accommodate the altered standards of legitimacy set by the Reagan Revolution. On this point, see Theda Skocpol, *Boomerang: Clinton's Health Security Effort and the Turn against Government in U.S. Politics* (New York: Norton, 1996).

31. "Our progress toward a wise conclusion [of the tariff issue] will not be improved by dwelling upon theories of protection and free trade. This savors too much of bandying epithets. It is a condition which confronts us, not a theory." Grover Cleveland, third annual message (Washington, DC, 6 December 1887), in *Messages and Papers of the Presidents,* ed. James Richardson, 8 vols. (New York: Bureau of National Literature, 1897), 8:590. Cleveland's third annual message was the first time a president devoted his entire annual address to a single issue.

32. "Our Reversible President," *Collier's Weekly,* 18 April 1914.

33. Theodore Roosevelt, *The Letters of Theodore Roosevelt,* ed. Elting Morrison, 8 vols. (Cambridge, MA: Harvard University Press, 1954), 8:1031, 1199.

34. Henry Cabot Lodge, *The Senate and the League of Nations* (New York: Scribners, 1925), 79–80, 212–213, 216–226.

35. Quoted in Geoffrey Blodgett, "The Political Leadership of Grover Cleveland," *South Atlantic Quarterly* 82 (Summer 1983): 290–291; see also Pearl Louise Robertson, *Grover Cleveland as a Political Leader* (Chicago: University of Chicago Libraries, 1939).

CHAPTER FOUR. LEADERSHIP BY
DEFINITION: FIRST-TERM REFLECTIONS
ON GEORGE W. BUSH'S POLITICAL STANCE

1. Stephen Skowronek, "Leadership by Definition: First Term Reflections on George W. Bush's Political Stance," *Perspectives on Politics* 3, no. 4 (December 2005): 817–831.

2. Abraham Lincoln, "A House Divided" (Springfield, IL, 16 June 1858), in *Collected Works of Abraham Lincoln,* ed. Roy P. Basler, 8 vols. (New Brunswick, NJ: Rutgers University Press, 1953–1955), 2:461.

3. George W. Bush, *A Charge to Keep* (New York: William Morrow, 1999), ix.

4. In calling attention to the Bush campaign biography as a portent of his leadership posture in office, I am broaching the much-discussed collapse in recent years of the distinction between campaigning and governing. See, for example, Norman Ornstein and Thomas Mann, eds., *The Permanent Campaign and Its Future* (Washington, DC: American Enterprise Institute Press, 2000). I am not saying that campaign tracts are always so revealing, though it might be interesting to see whether they have over time become better indicators of postures assumed in government. In the next section, I suggest why in this case the biography became such a good guide to the president's political posture in office.

5. Bush, *A Charge to Keep*, 1.

6. Ibid., 4.

7. Ibid., 184.

8. Ibid., 177.

9. Ibid., 55.

10. Jeff Greenfield, Candy Crowley, Mike Chinoy, Kyra Phillips, and Leon Harris, "Bush Vows to Defend Taiwan if Necessary," *CNN's Live Today*, 25 April 2001, available at http://transcripts.cnn.com/TRANSCRIPTS/0104/25lt.01.html; Joe Klein, "Why the 'War President' Is under Fire: Bush's Anti-Terror Policies Are Dangerously Simple," *Time*, 23 February 2004, available at http://www.time.com/time/magazine/article/0,9171,993453,00.html.

11. A different but insightful assessment of conviction as a foundation for leadership is found in Patricia Sykes, *Presidents and Prime Ministers: Conviction Politics in the Anglo American Tradition* (Lawrence: University Press of Kansas, 2000).

12. There are, however, striking moments in which Bush insists on explaining the labored thought processes that went into a decision. One example of this in the campaign biography is his extended discussion of the different decisions he made as governor in death-penalty cases. Another, perhaps not unrelated, example from his presidency is his treatment of his decision on stem-cell research. Before setting out his terms and conditions, the president went out of his way to elaborate publicly on the wide range of opinions he had sought out and the difficulty of sorting through them. In both cases, the revelation was of a leader who is determined to remain true to himself in the face of a difficult issue. As Henry Clay said of James Monroe's disquisition laying out his studied opposition to federal support for internal improvements, the president did not invite discussion but simply revealed the ruminations of his own mind. See George W. Bush, "President Discusses Stem Cell Research" (Crawford, TX, 9 August 2001), available at http://whitehouse.gov/news/releases/2001/08/20010809-2.html.

13. The phrase "getting the job done" was used throughout the first term and was picked up by observers during the 2004 campaign. See Nedra Pickler and Scott Lindlaw, "I'm Getting the Job Done," *Chicago Sun Times,* 14 August 2004.

14. David Brooks, "How to Reinvent the GOP," *New York Times,* 29 August 2004.

15. George W. Bush, "President's Remarks at the 2004 Republican National Convention" (New York City, 2 September 2004), available at http://www.white-house.gov/news/releases/2004/09/20040902-2.html.

16. See, for example, Mark Niquette, "Cheney Follows Campaign Trail to Northern Ohio," *Columbus Dispatch,* 4 July 2004; Richard Cheney, remarks by Vice President Dick Cheney at event for congressional candidate Geoff Davis (Marriott Cincinnati Airport Hotel, Hebron, KY, 29 June 2004), Federal News Service; Jon Craig and Marc Sandalow, "Democrats' Dilemma—What to Say about the War," *San Francisco Chronicle,* 22 May 2004; Richard Cheney, remarks by Vice President Dick Cheney at Victory 2004 event (Pfister Hotel, Milwaukee, WI, 30 April 2004), Federal News Service; Jon Craig, "Cheney Raises Spirits," *Columbus Dispatch,* 27 March 2004.

17. Stephen Skowronek, *The Politics Presidents Make: Leadership from John Adams to George Bush* (Cambridge, MA: Belknap Press of Harvard University Press, 1993).

18. Albert Gore, "U.S. Vice President Al Gore Delivers Acceptance Speech at Democratic National Convention" (Los Angeles, 17 August 2000), available at http://www.cnn.com/ELECTION/2000/conventions/democratic/transcripts/gore.html; see also Mike Allen, "Style Counts, Strategists Say: In Campaign's Final Week, Demeanors of Bush, Gore, as Important as Stands on Issues," *Washington Post,* 1 November 2000; Jodi Enda, "Gore Still Defends Clinton, While He Stresses Difference," *Pittsburgh Post-Gazette,* 26 August 2000; David Barstow, "In a Place Called Clinton, Gore Finds His Own Groove," *New York Times,* 21 August 2000; David Shribman, "'I Stand Here . . . as My Own Man': A Clear Sense of the Challenge: A Nominee of Many Phases Lays Out His Own Agenda," *Boston Globe,* 18 August 2000.

19. See, for example, Mickey Edwards, "There's a Comfort Factor with Bush," *Boston Herald,* 27 March 2001; Cokie Roberts and Steven V. Roberts, "Bush and His Staff Enjoy a Summer Full of Sunshine," *Daily News,* 21 July 2000.

20. See, for example, David M. Halbfinger, "Kerry Says Flip-Flop Image 'Doesn't Reflect the Truth,'" *New York Times,* 30 September 2004.

21. Skowronek, *The Politics Presidents Make.*

22. See, for example, Robin Toner, "Arkansas's Clinton Enters the '92 Race for President," *New York Times,* 4 October 1991.

23. Skowronek, *The Politics Presidents Make.*

24. See, for example, Jeffery H. Birnbaum, "Campaign '88: Bush's Speeches Are Moving Closer to the Middle in a Bid to Broaden the Base of Support among Voters," *Wall Street Journal,* 11 October 1988; John W. Mashek, "George Bush: After 7 Years of Loyalty, He Must Sell Himself to Voters, Articulate His Own Positions," *St. Louis Post-Dispatch,* 12 February 1988; Jerry Roberts, "'She's Getting Tough': Bush Tells GOP Some Wife Jokes," *San Francisco Chronicle,* 19 January 1989; Gerald F. Seib and Joe Davidson, "Campaign '88—The Issues: Presidential Battle Spawns Strange Vocabulary—New Shorthand for Proposed Social Programs," *Wall Street Journal,* 20 September 1988; Joseph D. Rice, "Bush Visit to Columbus Expected to Raise $1 Million for Ohio GOP," *Plain Dealer,* 8 February 1990.

25. William Bennett, for example, said on CNN's *Crossfire* on 29 March 2001, "In fact, Bush is doing exactly what he said he would do in the campaign. Nobody should be surprised" (available at http://transcripts.cnn.com/transcripts/0103/29/cf.00.html). Even former president Bill Clinton said in May 2001, "The messages were always there, no one was reading between the lines. He's doing exactly what he said he was going to do" (quoted in Richard L. Berke, "Clinton Has Praise and Rebukes for Bush, Friends Say," *New York Times,* 4 May 2001). Ari Fleischer, White House press secretary, said on 30 April 2001, "The President is doing exactly what he promised and said he would do on the campaign, and he is moving forward with the development of the missile defense system that he'll outline tomorrow" (available at http://www.whitehouse.gov/news/briefings/20010430.html). And on 9 February 2001, regarding Bush's defense plan that "displeased" the military establishment, Fleisher said, "The President said help is on the way, and help is on the way. And the help will be delivered in the manner exactly as the President said during the campaign" (available at http://www.whitehouse.gov/news/briefings/20010209.html). See also: "I couldn't believe such garbage against the man, a man who is doing what he said he was going to do, not just politics as usual. He is an honest man and a good man, and he is a man for the people." Joe Reed, "Editorial: Anti-Bush Bias," *San Antonio Express-News,* 5 June 2001. And: "I couldn't be happier with President Bush. He is doing exactly what he said he would do. He is working to lower the onerous tax burden, he has brought rationality and moderation to the process of cleaning up the environment, and he is working to ensure that our energy needs will be met." Wayne Hatton, "Editorial: One Satisfied Voter," *Oregonian,* 2 June 2001.

26. Abraham Lincoln, "Annual Message to Congress" (Washington, DC, 1 December 1862), in Basler, *Collected Works of Abraham Lincoln,* 5:537.

27. See, for example, Anthony Lewis, "Abroad at Home: A Different World," *New York Times,* 12 September 2001.

28. For example, Bush family friend Brent Scowcroft described George W. Bush in the aftermath of the attacks as "a president who has seized on this crisis and sees this as his mission. . . . He's been transformed." Judy Keen, "Same President, Different Man in Oval Office," *USA Today,* 29 October 2001; see also Simon Beattie, "Sept. 11 Attacks: The Making of President Bush," *Evening Post,* 20 March 2002; Dana Milbank, "For Bush, a Sense of History—and Fate; Response to Iraq Reflects Self-Beliefs," *Washington Post,* 9 March 2003; Howard Fineman, "Bush and God: A Higher Calling," *Newsweek,* 10 March 2003.

29. Abraham Lincoln, "To Albert Hodges" (4 April 1864), in Basler, *Collected Works of Abraham Lincoln,* 7:282.

30. David Donald, *Lincoln* (New York: Simon and Schuster, 1995), 332.

31. Eugene Irving McCormick, *James K. Polk: A Political Biography* (Berkeley and Los Angeles: University of California Press, 1922), 261.

32. As cited in Skowronek, *The Politics Presidents Make,* 250.

33. Jeff Shesol, *Mutual Contempt: Lyndon Johnson, Robert Kennedy, and the Feud that Defined a Decade* (New York: Norton, 1997).

34. John Kerry, debate transcript, "The First Bush-Kerry Presidential Debate," 30 September 2004, Commission on Presidential Debates, available at http://www.debates.org/pages/trans2004a.html.

35. Kevin Freking, "Bush Says He'll Stand by His Principles Like Lincoln Did in Wartime," *Associated Press Online,* 23 April 2007, available at http://www.newsmax.com/archives/ic/2007/4/24/74619.html.

36. Bruce Bartlett, *Imposter: How George W. Bush Bankrupted America and Betrayed the Reagan Legacy* (New York: Doubleday, 2006); Richard Viguerie, *Conservatives Betrayed: How George W. Bush and Other Big Government Republicans Hijacked the Conservative Cause* (Los Angeles: Bonus Books, 2006). McCain characterized the Bush administration and the Republican Party more generally in these terms: "We Republicans have lost our way. We came to Washington to change government, and government changed us: the spending, the ethics, the massive programs such as the Medicare prescription drug program, our failure to address their priorities as opposed to our own." McCain, quoted in Dana Milbank, "McCain to Form Committee to Explore White House Bid among Democrats, Biden Affirms Plans to Run; Feingold Won't Seek Nomination," *Washington Post,* 13 November 2006; Jeffrey Goldberg, "Party Unfaithful: The Republican Implosion," *New Yorker,* 4 June 2007, 40–46.

37. John Kerry, interview, *Meet the Press,* 30 January 2005.

38. This historical distinction may be implicated in the fact that former Bush strategist Karl Rove liked to invoke McKinley as a model of Republican success. See, for example, Todd S. Purdum and David D. Kirkpatrick, "Campaign Strategist Is in Position to Consolidate Republican Majority," *New York Times,* 5 No-

vember 2004; Delia M. Rios, "Presidents and Precedents: History Guides Bush through His Challenges," *Seattle Times,* 19 January 2003; Donald Green and Eric Schickler, "Winning a Battle, Not a War," *New York Times,* 12 November 2002; E. J. Dionne, "Harder Than McKinley," *Washington Post,* 2 April 2002.

39. See, for example, "The Emerging Democratic Minority," *Economist,* 8 January 2005, available at http://www.economist.com/world/na/displaystory. cfm?story_id=E1_PVQVTNR; Tom Hamburger and Peter Wallsten, "GOP Sees a Future in Black Churches," *Los Angeles Times,* 1 February 2005; Harold F. Bass, "George W. Bush, Presidential Party Leadership Extraordinaire?" *Forum* 2, no. 4 (2004), http://www.bepress.com/forum/vol2/iss4/art6/; Ronald Brownstein, "Bush Names Campaign Manager as GOP Chairman," *Los Angeles Times,* 16 November 2004.

CHAPTER FIVE. THE IMPERIAL PRESIDENCY THESIS REVISITED: GEORGE W. BUSH AT THE POINT OF NO RETURN

1. Stephen Skowronek, "The Imperial Presidency Thesis Revisited: George W. Bush at the Point of No Return" (paper presented at "A New Imperial Presidency?" Centre d'Études et de Recherches Internationales, Sciences Po, Paris, 11–12 January 2007).

2. Arthur Schlesinger, Jr., *The Imperial Presidency* (Boston: Houghton Mifflin, 1973), 217.

3. Gerald Ford, "Remarks on Taking the Oath of Office" (White House, East Room, Washington, DC, 9 August 1974), available at John Woolley and Gerhard Peters, *The American Presidency Project* (Santa Barbara: University of California [hosted], Gerhard Peters [database]), http://www.presidency.ucsb.edu/ws/ ?pid=4409.

4. Andrew Rudalevige, *The New Imperial Presidency: Reinventing Presidential Power after Watergate* (Ann Arbor: University of Michigan Press, 2006), 22–23.

5. See John Burke and Fred Greenstein, *How Presidents Test Reality: Decisions on Vietnam, 1954 and 1965* (New York: Russell Sage, 1986).

6. Michael Beschloss, *Reaching for Glory: Lyndon Johnson's Secret White House Tapes, 1964–1965* (New York: Simon and Schuster, 2001), 166–196.

7. Henry Jones Ford, *The Rise and Growth of American Politics: A Sketch of Constitutional Development* (1898; repr., New York: Da Capo, 1967), 279, 293.

8. See J. Allen Smith, *The Spirit of American Government: A Study of the Constitution; Its Origin, Influence, and Relation to Democracy* (1907; repr., Cam-

bridge, MA: Harvard University Press, 1965); see also Charles A. Beard, *An Economic Interpretation of the Constitution of the United States* (New York: Macmillan, 1913).

9. See Woodrow Wilson, *Constitutional Government in the United States* (New York: Columbia University Press, 1908). See also Richard E. Neustadt, *Presidential Power: The Politics of Leadership* (New York: John Wiley and Sons, 1960).

10. Edith Reid, *Woodrow Wilson: The Caricature, the Myth, and the Man* (New York: Oxford University Press, 1934), 236.

11. Kevin Phillips, *The Emerging Republican Majority* (New Rochelle, NY: Arlington House, 1969).

12. Schlesinger, *The Imperial Presidency*, 187–198.

13. See Steven G. Calabresi, "The Vesting Clauses as Power Grants," *Northwestern University Law Review* 88 (Summer 1994): 1377–1405; see also Michael A. Froomkin, "The Imperial Presidency's New Vestments," *Northwestern University Law Review* 88 (Summer 1994): 1346–1376.

14. Woodrow Wilson, "Abraham Lincoln: A Man of the People," in *The Papers of Woodrow Wilson,* ed. Arthur Link, vol. 19 (1909; repr., Princeton, NJ: Princeton University Press, 1993), 42.

15. *Report of the Congressional Committees Investigating the Iran-Contra Affair: The Minority Report,* 100th Congress, 1st sess., S. Rep. 100-216, 13 November 1987, Washington, DC, 430–633; Terry Eastland, *Energy in the Executive: The Case for a Strong Presidency* (New York: Free Press, 1992); Steven G. Calabresi and Kevin Rhodes, "The Structural Constitution: Unitary Executive, Plural Judiciary," *Harvard Law Review* 105, no. 6 (1992): 1153–1216.

16. See John Yoo, *The Powers of War and Peace: The Constitution and Foreign Affairs after 9/11* (Chicago: University of Chicago Press, 2005).

17. Jeremy Bailey, "The Unitary Executive and Democratic Theory" (unpublished manuscript). I am grateful to Professor Bailey for sharing his ongoing work on these themes and for comments on this present paper.

18. Alexander Hamilton, "Federalist 6," in *The Federalist,* ed. Jacob E. Cooke (Middletown, CT: Wesleyan University Press, 1961).

19. Stephen Skowronek, *The Politics Presidents Make: Leadership from John Adams to Bill Clinton* (Cambridge, MA: Belknap Press of Harvard University, 1997).

20. John Ferling, *Adams vs. Jefferson: The Tumultuous Election of 1800* (New York: Oxford University Press, 2004), 126–134, 140–145.

CHAPTER SIX.
IS TRANSFORMATIONAL LEADERSHIP
STILL POSSIBLE? BARACK OBAMA IN
HISTORICAL PERSPECTIVE

1. An earlier version of this essay was presented at the Redpath Lectures on the American Presidency, 2 October 2010, Chicago, Illinois. I want to thank Bruce Miroff, Elizabeth Sanders, Dan Galvin, Steven Engel, Sidney Milkis, and Karen Orren for their comments and criticisms.

2. Barack Obama, "change we can believe in": nomination acceptance speech, Democratic National Convention (Denver, CO, 28 August 2008); "a new *kind* of politics": video message announcing the formation of exploratory committee (16 January 2007); "fundamentally transforming the United States of America": campaign rally (Columbia, MO, 30 October 2008).

3. John McCain, South Carolina primary victory speech (Columbia, SC, 19 January 2008).

4. Barack Obama, announcement of presidential candidacy (Springfield, IL, 10 February 2007).

5. Barack Obama, interview with the *Reno Gazette-Journal* editorial board (Reno, NV, 14 January 2008).

6. Barack Obama, primary election night rally (St. Paul, MN, 3 June 2008).

7. Paul Kane and Karl Vick, "Republican Brown Beats Coakley in Special Senate Election in Massachusetts," *Washington Post*, 20 January 2010.

8. "Jonathan Alter: Health Care Puts Obama in FDR's League," Interviews, *Truthdig*, 26 May 2010, http://www.truthdig.com/report/item/alter_health_care_puts_obama_in_fdrs_league_20100526/#.

9. Barack Obama, speech at Georgetown University (Washington, DC, 14 April 2009).

10. Alexandra Starr, "Case Study," *New York Times Magazine*, 19 September 2008, 1.

11. Barack Obama, "President's Message," in Office of Management and Budget, *A New Era of Responsibility: Renewing America's Promise* (Washington, DC: Government Printing Office, 2009), 1.

12. "Obama Rolls Out Mid-Term Metaphor, *New York Times*, 18 August 2010.

13. Thomas Jefferson, "First Inaugural Address" (Washington, DC, Wednesday, 4 March 1801), in *The Political Writings of Thomas Jefferson*, ed. Edward Dumbauld (New York: Bobbs Merrill, 1955), 46.

14. Barack Obama, "Speech Accepting Nomination, Democratic National Convention" (Denver, CO, 28 August 2008).

15. I am grateful to Bruce Miroff for this point.

16. Sidney Milkis, *The President and the Parties: The Transformation of the American Party System since the New Deal* (New York: Oxford University Press, 1993).

17. Daniel Galvin, "Barack Obama's 'Organizing for America' and the Dynamics of Presidential Party Building," *Vox Pop Newletter* 28, no. 3 (Spring 2010): 1–3.

18. Frank Rich, review of *The Promise: President Obama, Year One*, by Jonathan Alter, *New York Review of Books*, 19 August 2010.

19. Franklin Foer and Noam Scheiber, "Nudge-Ocracy: Barack Obama's New Theory of the State." *New Republic*, 6 May 2009, 22–25.

20. Hugh Heclo, "Sixties Civics," in *The Great Society and the High Tide of Liberalism*, ed. Sidney Milkis and Jerome Mileur (Amherst: University of Massachusetts Press, 2005), 60.

21. Glenn Beck, address to the Conservative Political Action Conference (Washington, DC, 20 February 2010).

22. On this point generally, see Jacob Hacker, "Privatizing Risk with Privatizing the Welfare State: The Hidden Politics of Social Policy Retrenchment in the United States," *American Political Science Review* 98, no. 2 (2004): 243–258.

23. Stephen Skowronek, "Conservative Insurgency and Presidential Power: A Developmental Perspective on the Unitary Executive," *Harvard Law Review* 122, no. 8 (2009): 2070; Peter Shane, *Madison's Nightmare: How Executive Power Threatens American Democracy* (Chicago: University of Chicago Press, 2009). I do not mean to suggest that recent Democratic presidents, Clinton or Obama, have disavowed unilateral action or failed to make use of the unitary theory. I expect that presidents will make use of whatever tools and justifications fit their interests in action. My point is that the progressive movement developed and deployed a theory of presidential action that was far less formalistic and far more committed to reaching common judgment and ensuring collective responsibility. The new theory of presidential power propounded by movement conservatives combines formalism with presidentialism in a startling new way.

Index